An Infamous Mistress

An Infamous Mistress

The Life, Loves and Family of the
Celebrated Grace Dalrymple Elliott

Joanne Major

&

Sarah Murden

PEN & SWORD
HISTORY

First published in Great Britain in 2016 by
PEN & SWORD HISTORY
an imprint of
Pen & Sword Books Ltd
47 Church Street
Barnsley
South Yorkshire
S70 2AS

Copyright © Joanne Major and Sarah Murden, 2016

ISBN 978-1-47384-483-4

The right of Joanne Major and Sarah Murden to be identified as the authors of
this work has been asserted by them in accordance with the Copyright,
Designs and Patents Act 1988.

A CIP catalogue record for this book is available from the British Library.

Typeset by Concept, Huddersfield HD4 5JL.
Printed and bound in England by CPI Group (UK) Ltd, Croydon CR0 4YY.

Pen & Sword Books Ltd incorporates the imprints of Pen & Sword Archaeology, Atlas,
Aviation, Battleground, Discovery, Family History, History, Maritime, Military, Naval,
Politics, Railways, Select, Social History, Transport, True Crime, and Claymore Press,
Frontline Books, Leo Cooper, Praetorian Press, Remember When, Seaforth Publishing
and Wharncliffe.

For a complete list of Pen & Sword titles please contact
PEN & SWORD BOOKS LIMITED
47 Church Street, Barnsley, South Yorkshire, S70 2AS, England
E-mail: enquiries@pen-and-sword.co.uk
Website: www.pen-and-sword.co.uk

Contents

List of Plates

Portrait of Grace Dalrymple Elliott by Thomas Gainsborough.

South view of St Pancras Church.

Parish Register entry for the marriage between Dr John Eliot and Grace Dalrymple.

Mrs Elliott and Lord Valentia from the 'Histories of the *tête-à-tête* annexed' in *Town and Country Magazine*, 1774.

'The Indiscretions of noble blood cured medicinally', from *Matrimonial Magazine*, February 1775.

Portrait of George, Prince of Wales (later George IV) by Thomas Gainsborough, c.1781.

Portrait of George James, 4th Earl and later 1st Marquess of Cholmondeley, by Sir Joshua Reynolds, 1780.

Grace Dalrymple, Perdita and the 'Bird of Paradise' from *Rambler's Magazine*, January 1783.

Portrait of Georgiana Seymour by Sir Joshua Reynolds, c.1784.

Parish Register entry for the baptism of Grace's daughter Georgiana.

The Aerostatick Stage Balloon, December 1783.

Miss Dawson and the 4th Earl of Peterborough from the 'Histories of the *tête-à-tête* annexed' in *Town and Country Magazine*, 1777.

'A Bath of the Moderns', March 1782.

Lady Anne Foley and the 5th Earl of Peterborough from the 'Histories of the *tête-à-tête* annexed' in *Town and Country Magazine*, 1785.

'The Battle of Bunker Hill, 17 June 1775' by John Trumbull, 1786.

'Colonel Mordaunt's Cock Match at Lucknow.'

Louis Philippe Joseph, Duc d'Orléans, engraving by John Raphael Smith after Sir Joshua Reynolds, 1786.

'A View of Paris from the Pont Neuf' by Jean-Baptiste Raguenet, 1763.

Acknowledgements

We would firstly like to thank family and friends, in particular Joanne's children Luke and Aeron, who have all patiently tolerated us researching, writing and becoming totally absorbed in Grace's world.

A special thanks must go to Kate Bohdanowicz, without whom this book may never have seen the light of day; to Pen & Sword for taking a chance with us; and to our lovely copy-editor Pamela Covey who patiently tolerated our love of certain items of punctuation about which we will say no more!

Thanks also to the author Hallie Rubenhold for all her encouragement, support and for being our mentor (for more on Lady Worsley see her excellent biography, reissued as *The Scandalous Lady W*). We would also like to thank the Marquess of Cholmondeley for all his very kind help and for allowing Joanne, with the help of David Yaxley, archivist at Houghton Hall, to delve into documents pertaining to Grace, and the staff at Houghton who dealt with our numerous emails and telephone calls. Thanks go to Pete Huggins, Pete Jones and Peter Trenchard for taking such excellent photographs; to the Kinloch family for allowing us to use the photographs of Jessy Lawrence Brown and John Kinloch; and to the Earl of Jersey and the Trustees of Radier Manor.

During our research we have contacted numerous archives and libraries throughout the UK, France and the USA and we would need another book to thank them all individually. We would, however, like to give a special thanks to the University of Nottingham Manuscripts and Special Collections who battled with technology to ensure that we were able to access a useable copy of a document previously unread due to its poor condition, which unlocked previously unknown information. Also the Royal Archives for their assistance in providing documents relating to Grace's connection with the Prince Regent.

Joanne Major and Sarah Murden, 2016

Introduction

Grace Dalrymple Elliott was infamous as a celebrated courtesan and her reputation as such remains to this very day, with people repeatedly trying to answer questions that remain about her life. For although she left behind her own journal recounting her adventures during the French Revolution, published posthumously by her granddaughter, so much of her life remained in the shadows, unknown and misremembered, with even accredited sources mistaking such basic facts as her mother's maiden name and the real names of both Grace and her sister.

Interest in her continues because she is one of history's 'strong women'; she survived, on her own merits and through her own actions, despite being cast out by Georgian society and present during the Reign of Terror in France, her *Journal of My Life* remaining one of the few first-hand female perspectives of life in the midst of the French Revolution. Today, her story resonates with women the world over and the life she led, the events she witnessed and the people she knew make for a totally fascinating story. Blessed with stunning looks and exceptionally tall for the era, Grace became notorious when she was publicly divorced by her husband, propelling her into life as a courtesan and a fixture in the eighteenth-century gossip columns.

Her lovers included a duke, an earl and a prince (indeed both the earl and the prince were reputed to be the father of her child). Grace's life was not merely about scandal though; there is much more to her story, and to tell it in the context of a woman at the heart of a large extended family, with their examples before her, makes one view her actions in a way not previously perceived. It has long been thought that, as a young girl about to be married, she had no one to turn to for advice, certainly no maternal presence. In fact she had two maternal aunts present in London at the time, both knowledgeable women, fully versed in the ways of their own society and of the world in general: does it still then follow that she was pushed into an unsuitable marriage with no female counsel? These same two aunts had both realized their own positions in society by being mistresses to great men, so what counsel did they give to their niece before and after her own divorce and subsequent career as a demirep?

Little has hitherto been known about either her early life or her old age at the beginning of the nineteenth century, and the documents providing details of these periods of her life have lain undiscovered in dusty files at a variety of archive offices until now. Also largely unknown have been any details of her extended family and parentage, even two of her siblings being neglected. Her paternal family has been noted, although her father has remained a somewhat shady character and his family's claim to be related to the Earls of Stair largely misunderstood, but nothing has been told of her maternal family and it is they who are central to her story, for Grace was just one woman in a strong, matriarchal Scottish family. Better still, her wider family also lived intensely interesting lives and each member has their own story to tell, independent of Grace, although hers is the narrative that binds them all together. Her own actions and decisions become clearer when one understands her family.

The lives of Grace and her family encompass travel across the globe, leaving their Scottish roots behind to journey across the seas to India, the United States, Canada and Europe, covering varied and wide-ranging topics including the abolition of slavery, military action, the French Revolution, aristocracy, illegitimacy and social climbing. Of course, as might be expected, a large portion of the action takes place in London society drawing rooms and ballrooms, with a few scandals along the way. As befits a well-connected family, many famous and well-known faces from the Georgian period tumble in and out of their story; the actress and courtesan Mary Darby Robinson ('Perdita'), Lord Byron, Beau Brummell and the Prince Regent himself, to name but a few.

We make no apologies for including the lives of Grace's maternal and fraternal relatives in full here: their own stories need to be told, even if it means we deviate from Grace herself on occasion, for in knowing them we get to know and become conversant with Grace's own private world. However, Grace herself is the central theme and we always return to her. For those already familiar with Grace's story, we hope that the inclusion of so much new information that sheds light on her decisions and actions in a way not previously discussed and introduces hitherto unknown brothers, aunts, an uncle, several cousins and grandparents into her story will justify revisiting her. For those who have yet to discover Grace, we can now tell her story more completely than it has ever been told before.

With so much that is new to Grace's story and so many new characters to introduce to it, there was plenty of information we just didn't have room to include. Our online blog provides more detail on that and on the many fascinating people whose stories touched upon and merged with those we are about to tell. As genealogists we just couldn't let go when faced with an interesting tale and, while these people and their own histories might not be relevant to the story of Grace and her family except where the two briefly collided, we could not help but be interested in them. Our information has been painstakingly pieced together over a number of years from a wide variety of sources including family wills, newspapers, magazines and diaries of the period, parish register entries, marriage bonds, legal documents and personal letters.

We have undertaken all our own research personally rather than employing anyone to search on our behalf and we found that by questioning the smallest references, we have uncovered things that someone else might not have noticed or pursued further. That has also been part of the enjoyment, as well as the frustration, throughout this lengthy journey.

Our discoveries during the course of our research have excited and delighted us so much and we have been longing to share our knowledge of Grace with those who we know will be as enchanted as ourselves with her story. We very much hope you will enjoy the following narrative.

Dalrymple of Waterside

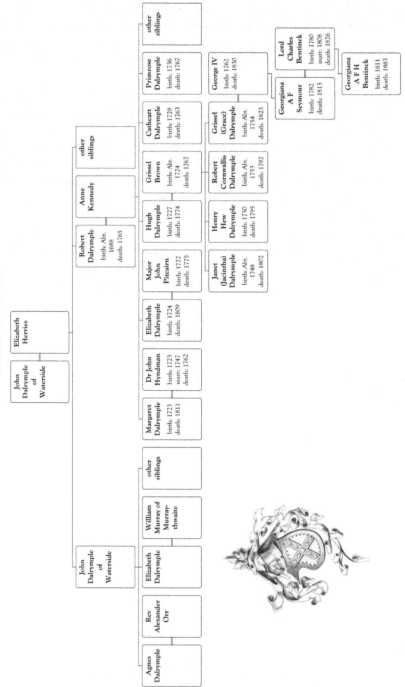

John Dalrymple of Waterside — Elizabeth Herries

John Dalrymple of Waterside

Agnes Dalrymple — Rev Alexander Orr

Elizabeth Dalrymple — William Murray of Murray-thwaite

other siblings

Robert Dalrymple
birth: Abt. 1688
death: 1765
— Anne Kennedy

other siblings

Margaret Dalrymple
birth: 1723
death: 1811
— Dr John Hyndman
birth: 1723
marr: 1747
death: 1762

Elizabeth Dalrymple
birth: 1724
death: 1809
— Major John Pitcairn
birth: 1722
death: 1775

Hugh Dalrymple
birth: 1727
death: 1774
— Grissel Brown
birth: Abt. 1724
death: 1767

Cathcart Dalrymple
birth: 1729
death: 1763

Primrose Dalrymple
birth: 1736
death: 1767

other siblings

Janet (Jacintha) Dalrymple
birth: Abt. 1748
death: 1802

Henry Hew Dalrymple
birth: 1750
death: 1795

Robert Cornwallis Dalrymple
birth: Abt. 1753
death: 1792

Grissel (Grace) Dalrymple
birth: Abt. 1754
death: 1823
— George IV
birth: 1762
death: 1830

Georgiana A F Seymour
birth: 1782
death: 1813
— Lord Charles Bentinck
birth: 1780
marr: 1808
death: 1826

Georgiana A F H Bentinck
birth: 1811
death: 1883

Brown of Blackburn

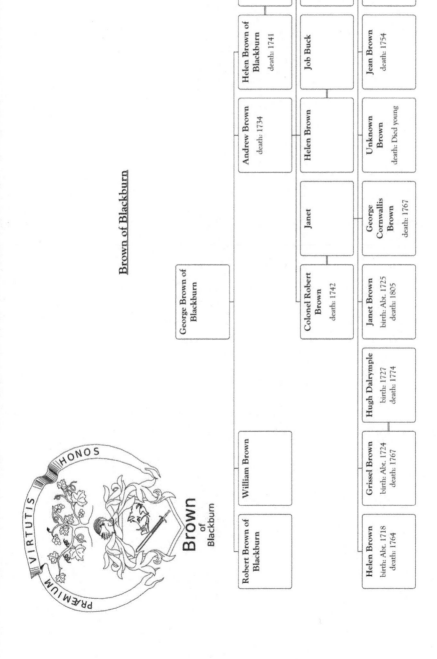

Drawing of the Brown of Blackburn crest © Sam Major

Janet (Jacintha) Dalrymple, her husbands and children

Janet (Jacintha) Dalrymple birth: Abt. 1748 death: 1802	**Thomas Hesketh** birth: 1748 marr: 1770 death: 1782

Thomas Winckley birth: Abt. 1731 marr: 1785 death: 1794	**Major James Barrington** birth: 1747 marr: 1799 death: 1815

Harriet Anne Hesketh birth: 1771 death: 1848

Thomas Hesketh birth: 1773. death: Died young

Dorothea Hesketh birth: 1774 death: 1837

Jacinthia Catherine Hesketh birth: 1775 death: 1801

Thomas Dalrymple Hesketh birth: 1777 death: 1842

Anne Charlotte Hesketh birth: 1778 death: 1837

Lucy Hesketh birth: 1782 death: 1836

Margaret Winckley birth: 1786 death: 1786

Frances Winckley birth: 1787 death: 1873

Sir John Eliot of Peebles

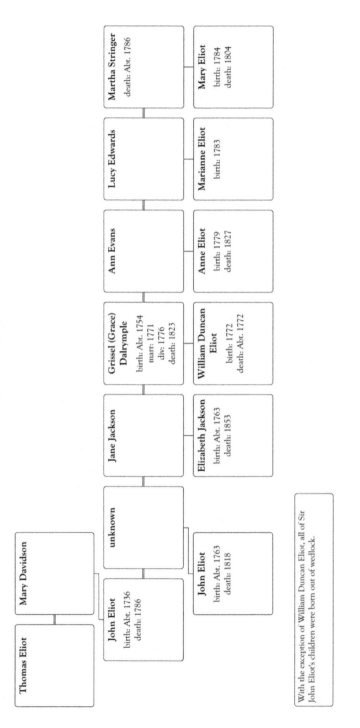

Thomas Eliot

Mary Davidson

John Eliot
birth: Abt. 1736
death: 1786

unknown

Jane Jackson

**Grissel (Grace)
Dalrymple**
birth: Abt. 1754
marr: 1771
div: 1776
death: 1823

Ann Evans

Lucy Edwards

Martha Stringer
death: Abt. 1786

John Eliot
birth: Abt. 1763
death: 1818

Elizabeth Jackson
birth: Abt. 1763
death: 1853

**William Duncan
Eliot**
birth: 1772
death: Abt. 1772

Anne Eliot
birth: 1779
death: 1827

Marianne Eliot
birth: 1783

Mary Eliot
birth: 1784
death: 1804

With the exception of William Duncan Eliot, all of Sir
John Eliot's children were born out of wedlock.

Chapter One

Scottish Roots

Around 1754, in Edinburgh, Grissel Dalrymple was born. This child would leave both her Scottish roots and first name behind her, to become infamous as the 'celebrated Grace Dalrymple Elliott'.

Her father was Hugh Dalrymple, formerly a lieutenant in the British army but, at the time of Grace's birth, an advocate in the legal profession. Hugh's wife, also named Grissel, was a beauty, a few years older than her husband and from a family with a strong military heritage. Their three older children were Janet, who adopted the name Jacintha, Henry Hew and Robert Cornwallis Dalrymple. Thus was Grace's background before it was rudely torn apart when her parents separated shortly after her birth.

Hugh Dalrymple was born on 12 July 1727 in Edinburgh to Robert Dalrymple, Writer to the Signet, and his wife Anne Kennedy, and was their eldest surviving son. He chose to join the British army, declining initially to follow in the legal footsteps of his father, and this was probably how he met his future wife as Grissel, the daughter of a deceased army colonel, would no doubt have looked favourably upon a handsome young officer. The *Town and Country Magazine*, writing in 1774, made the claim that Hugh was 'bred to the army'. Hugh could possibly have been legally a minor when his marriage to Grissel took place, and it may have been conducted amidst subterfuge and secrecy.[1]

Janet, the eldest child, made her arrival into the world in the late 1740s and must have done so with almost indecent haste after the marriage. Her name was chosen in honour of Grissel's mother but, just as her sister changed her name to Grace (an Anglicized version of Grissel), so Janet chose to be known, as an adult at least, by the more stylish name of Jacintha, possibly a derivative of Jessy which was used as a pet name for Janet in the family. To their Scottish family though, the two girls were simply Janet and Grissel.

The eldest son, Henry Hew, was born on 26 March 1750, baptized H[e]ugh for his father but, like his sisters, as an adult he was known by the slightly different name of Henry Hew Dalrymple. To avoid confusion both with his change of name in later life and with his father, we will refer to him as Henry Hew for the purposes of this book, as we will also refer to his sisters by the names by which they are known to history and not the ones used by their family. Young Henry Hew was baptized two days after his birth at the Canongate in Edinburgh:[2]

> 1750 – Mr Heugh Dalrymple late Lieutenant & Grissel Brown his Lady, had a son born 26 March bap. 28 March n[amed] Heugh. Wit[nesses] Mr Robert Dalrymple Writer to the Signet & Mr Hyndman Min[iste]r at Collington.[3]

This is a very informative baptism entry: not only does it place the young couple firmly in Edinburgh, it also confirms, in the absence of other records, the marriage of Hugh and Grissel and her maiden name of Brown. Furthermore, it tells us that by March 1750 Hugh had both attained the rank of lieutenant in the army and resigned his commission (because, according to the 1774 *Town and Country Magazine*, he had not met with 'the preferment he expected' and a lieutenant was a junior officer). Since the Jacobite uprising of 1745 the British army had been actively recruiting soldiers from Scotland and Hugh was one such recruit, subsequently overlooked for promotion. The two witnesses to the baptism were Hugh's father Robert and Dr John Hyndman, a Scottish churchman and husband to Hugh's sister Margaret, which implies that the young married couple were living with, or at least relying on, the Dalrymples rather than the remaining relatives of Grissel.[4]

There are several branches of the Dalrymple family in Scotland and Grace Dalrymple's father was a scion of the branch that hailed from Waterside, Dumfriesshire in the Lowlands. The Dalrymples of Waterside shared their coat of arms with those of the most senior branch of the Dalrymple family, the Earls of Stair, with the Waterside arms having a *bordure engrailed gules* or red border to it, denoting their descent from a fourth son of the family.

Grace's family always claimed to be kin to the Earls of Stair and the assumption has been that the connection was a lot closer than it actually was, for by the eighteenth century the true link between the two families may have been all but forgotten. In fact, the line of both Dalrymple families goes back to a Malcolm de Dalrymple who split his lands between his two sons, John and Roland. Of these two sons the eldest, John, had several sons and the eldest of these, William, acquired the lands of Stair-Montgomery in the year 1450, took his father's arms and was the ancestor of the Earls of Stair. The succeeding sons also took their father's arms, but with borders denoting their place as second, third, fourth son and so on.[5]

The fourth son was James Dalrymple and he was the ancestor of the Waterside branch. However, some 300 years later the sense of kin still existed between the various branches of the family and even though they were a

Lowland family, the Scottish clan system should not be ignored and no doubt played a large part in connecting them. Grace herself, once embarked upon her career as a courtesan, proudly used the Dalrymple arms with their notorious 'nine of diamonds' design, placing herself firmly within the aristocratic echelons of society.[6]

Grace's grandfather, Robert Dalrymple, was the second son of John Dalrymple and his wife Elizabeth Herries, and was born c.1688. Both his father and his elder brother, who was also named John, were in turn laird of Waterside and John also acted as chamberlain to the Dukes of Queensberry, as did John's son William, and the 4th Duke, known as 'Old Q', was to prove a friend to Grace Dalrymple in her later life. Grace's grandfather Robert, as a younger son, turned to the law and qualified as Writer to the Signet, essentially a solicitor but historically denoting those who were authorized in Scotland to supervise the usage of the king's signet or seal. From 1735 to 1754 Robert Dalrymple was the owner of a fine seventeenth-century mansion known as Dreghorn Castle in the parish of Colinton, Edinburgh.

Hugh Dalrymple had nine siblings, two of whom died in infancy. His two surviving younger brothers were Cathcart, who became a merchant trading in tobacco between Virginia in the United States and Glasgow in Scotland, and the wonderfully-named Primrose (or Primerose; it is actually a Scottish surname and possibly denotes that a Primrose was his godparent or relative) who became a lieutenant in the Royal Navy, serving on HMS *Coventry*. Both of these brothers died young: Cathcart after his business eventually failed, leaving behind a young family to manage as best as they could, while Primrose had a steady naval career before dying in London in 1767 at the age of just 30 and in his will leaving everything he owned to the woman he had loved and intended to marry.

The sibling who was to become most relevant to Hugh's family and children was his sister Elizabeth. She married John Pitcairn, who rose to become a major in the Marine division of the British army, and the Pitcairns would later become almost a second family to at least two of Hugh and Grissel's children, Jacintha and Henry Hew Dalrymple.

Back in Edinburgh, around 1753 a second son was born to Hugh and Grissel and named Robert Cornwallis Dalrymple; Robert after both grandfathers and Cornwallis in honour of Grissel's younger brother, George Cornwallis Brown (it was likely he was asked to be godfather to his nephew), and it was around the time of this second son's birth that Hugh began to practise as a lawyer or advocate in Edinburgh. After failing in the army, he had turned instead to his father's profession.

Then, around the latter half of 1754, Grace Dalrymple herself was born.[7]

That Hugh and Grissel were most definitely resident in Edinburgh in late 1754, a little time after Grace's birth, is proved by a marriage entry for an Archibald Colquhoun on 17 November, who described himself as a 'servant to Mr Hugh Dalrymple, advocate in S.W.p.' (S.W.p. is the south-west kirk or church parish of Edinburgh served by Greyfriars Kirk).[8]

It is worth noting that in two sources Hugh and Grissel are reputed to have had three daughters. In a pencilled notation in the book *Some Old Families* in the library of the Society of Genealogists in London which records Hugh Dalrymple's father is the information that 'Hugh had at least 3 daughters and 1 son'.[9] Furthermore, the preface to Grace's *Journal of My Life during the French Revolution*, which was published posthumously (but with information supplied by Grace's granddaughter and a friend), states that Grace was the youngest of three daughters. Perhaps the pencilled notation in *Some Old Families* is using information taken from the preface to Grace's journal but even so, one would assume the information given in the preface, supplied as it was by a descendant and within living memory of Grace, to be reasonably accurate.

However, if the third daughter did exist, she has so far remained hidden and was never mentioned in any family wills or documentation. It seems likely that one of the sons had been incorrectly recorded at some point, as both sources agree on there being four children in all.

Primrose Dalrymple's intended bride, Susan Orr, was also his first cousin once removed. When Primrose died she turned instead to another of their relations, William Murray, whose mother was first cousin to Hugh.[10] The Dalrymple and Murray families were close to one another and a letter survives that was written by William's brother, John Murray, upon his return to Britain from South Carolina to his kinsman and friend, Hugh Dalrymple.[11]

The letter was dated 31 March 1754, the reputed year of Grace's birth, and John Murray was writing from London where he had just arrived following a journey to America. While Hugh's address was not given, it is clear from the contents that Hugh was not in London himself, so again the assumption must be that he was then in Scotland. John talked little of his travels, instead saying he would 'deferr till we meet any account of the New World & its natural production wh[ich] differ widely from these of the country's on our side of the globe'. He talked instead of the London theatre and ends the letter with a comment on Hugh's brother-in-law, George Cornwallis Brown. Both Murray brothers lived for periods in South Carolina, travelling back and forth between there and Scotland.

Hugh Dalrymple had not long been practising as a legal advocate when he found himself on the wrong side of the courtroom, accused of assaulting another man, one Hugh Lawson, a bailie from Dumfries, with a horsewhip. The case was heard in the Justiciary Court on 6 May 1756. Hugh's defence was that Lawson had called him a fool, 'whereupon he having a whip in his hand waved it gently ... with no design of hurting him.'[12] Judgement was passed on 9 May, finding in favour of Hugh Lawson, and Hugh Dalrymple was fined 100 Scottish merks and ordered to pay a further 1,000 merks in expenses, a not inconsiderable sum. Was this then the reason for Hugh leaving Scotland, to avoid paying this fine?

Tradition has always had him leaving before his daughter Grace was born, the cause of his departure being the discovery of him indulging in an extramarital affair, Grissel then returning alone to her father's house to give birth to her youngest child and Hugh not having any further contact with his children until after his wife's death. However, Grissel had no father to turn to at this time as he had died over a decade earlier; instead we have the evidence that Hugh was still present in Scotland in 1756, some eighteen months after his youngest child had been born.

The *Town and Country Magazine* claimed that Hugh had 'become enamoured with a lady of fortune' while travelling the Dumfries circuit as an advocate. The 'lady of fortune' being married, the affair was carried on by his entry to her bedchamber at night via a rope ladder which the lady helpfully dangled beneath her window each evening and his exit via the same method next morning. This continued for some months before Hugh was discovered leaving the house by a neighbour, the couple having dallied too long one morning. Was this lady the wife of Hugh Lawson and the cause of the argument between the two men? The magazine claims that subsequent to this discovery, Hugh Dalrymple and the lady of fortune 'judged proper immediately to decamp for England'.

The story of Grissel returning to her father's house at the time of the birth of her youngest daughter comes from the preface to Grace's journal and, as this information came from Grace's granddaughter and from a close friend, we can be reasonably certain that Grace did indeed spend her formative years living among her Brown relatives in Scotland without her father being present, but which relatives?

Chapter Two

The Browns of Blackburn House

Grace's maternal forebears had owned Blackburn House and its surrounding acres near to Cockburnspath in the Scottish Lowlands, with successive owners being known as the Laird of Blackburn but, by the early 1700s, it had passed tantalizingly just out of their reach.

Andrew Brown, a merchant in the Scottish capital city of Edinburgh, died in the year 1734. His testament dative names his children: two daughters, Anne and Helen (Helen was married to Job Buck, a shipmaster from Dunbar), and a son and heir, Robert Brown, 'Captain of ye Honourable Collonell Stephen Cornwallis Regiment of foot'.[13] Although he was never to know her, Robert Brown was the grandfather of Grace Dalrymple, and therefore Andrew her great-grandfather.

The Browns were an ancient Berwickshire family of minor nobility, living in 'the Merse' or marshlands of that county in the lowlands of Scotland. The term 'the Merse' was historically used in place of the county name of Berwickshire so when a scion of this family, George Cornwallis Brown, at his wedding in 1760 named his home parish as 'Cockburnspath, county Merse' he was using the local dialect of the area. From at least the mid-1600s the family home was Blackburn House.

Andrew was a younger son and it was therefore his brother, another Robert Brown, who succeeded to the family estate of Blackburn, becoming Laird of Blackburn.[14] In 1672 this elder Robert Brown registered his coat of arms with the Court of the Lord Lyon, the heraldic authority for Scotland. The arms feature a dagger and a boar's head on a sable background, with a helmet showing the nobility of the bearer, and the motto *Præmium virtutis honor* ('Honour is the reward of virtue').[15]

These arms and motto, together with the family name, feature on a pair of duelling pistols from the 1690s. They are now very rare due to their highly ingenious mechanical features, and they must have been an expensive purchase.[16] The pistols were made by Andrew (Andreas Rheinhold) Dolep, one of the finest and most important London gunsmiths of the late seventeenth century, who counted King Charles II and Prince George of Denmark among his clients. The pistols' original owner, given the date of the 1690s, was probably Captain James Brown, son of Robert Brown, Laird of Blackburn, and therefore cousin to Grace's grandfather Robert. Captain James was an officer in Strathnaver's Regiment of Foot; he died in 1718.

At the time the pistols were commissioned, Scotland was in a state of turmoil. The Scottish Covenanters (adherents to the Presbyterian religion) had ruled Scottish politics during the period 1638 to 1651 but, by the end of the English Civil War, Oliver Cromwell's forces had completely defeated them and Scotland was occupied by his New Model Army. Upon the Restoration, Charles II maintained the stance on the covenanters and they were forced to gather in secret to avoid persecution. However, many of the Scottish nobility still adhered to the Presbyterian faith, including the Laird of Blackburn who was steadfast to the covenanting principles. For this he was fined £600 in 1662 and a further £1,200 in August 1680 for his absence from the muster of the king's troops who marched against the covenanters at Bothwell. George Turnbull, a covenanter and minister at Alloa and Tyningham, left behind a diary that recorded his journey from England back into Scotland in 1688 and on Saturday, 26 May he 'came to Scotland and stayed at Blackburns in the merce till moonday [Monday]'. [17]

Possibly the fines he suffered as a covenanter were the ruin of Robert Brown and his family for, after his death, the estate of Blackburn was taken not by either of his two brothers or their male heirs but by Mark Ker, the husband of his sister Helen. Maybe it was deemed best to keep the estate in the family by whatever means possible and Helen Ker, née Brown, was henceforth known by the courtesy title of Lady Blackburn. A laird was not a lord but rather denoted that the bearer of the name was 'landed gentry', a title one step above the English esquire, and Helen, as the wife of the new laird and sister of the last, adopted the title of lady, there being no feminine equivalent of laird.

In the meantime, denied his ancestral estate which, in default of other male heirs would have descended to him, Andrew's only son Robert had married. His wife was Janet, possibly a Davidson.[18] Robert had joined the army as an ensign in November 1712, the most junior rank of officer, and a commission to ensign at this time would seem to place his birth date in the 1690s.

Robert and Janet Brown were to have at least seven children: Helen, born c.1718; Grissel, c.1724; Janet, c.1725; George Cornwallis, Robinaiana, Jean and a second son whose name stays, so far, unknown.[19] Throughout this period Robert was serving with the 34th Regiment of Foot and they spent much time in Ireland, with the officers' families living with them if they chose to do so, increasing the possibility that the older Brown children, at least, were born there.[20]

In March 1727 the 34th were sent as reinforcements to relieve the Siege of Gibraltar (the Spaniards had surrounded the British fort there) and following the successful conclusion of that, to garrison the island of Gibraltar for a year and a half before being ordered directly from Gibraltar to Jamaica. This last posting was an unmitigated disaster: the regiment was sent, with others, to quell reported riots on the island, only to arrive and find the reports unfounded and instead they were beset by disease and illness. The regiment's colonel, Robert Hayes, did not survive the posting and Lieutenant Colonel Stephen Cornwallis took command. Robert Brown also benefited from the many vacancies left by the deaths of his comrades and received a commission to the rank of captain of a company in the 34th which was signed, at Hampton Court Palace, by King George II on 25 June 1731.

In 1734, the year in which Captain Robert Brown's father Andrew died, the regiment was back home and quartered for some time in Scotland where he was reunited with his wife and children. By the end of the next year they were stationed at Marlborough in Wiltshire before moving on to Dublin.

Mark Ker, the new Laird of Blackburn, died before 1737, his wife Helen surviving him, and to her he left the annual rents of the estate for her lifetime but the ownership of the estate he left to his young namesake nephew in default of any child of his own. In the summer of 1737 Robert Brown, albeit described as 'Major Broun' when he was still a mere captain, had travelled back from Ireland and was in Cockburnspath in the company of Sir James Hall of Dunglass, another Berwickshire landowner.

Sir James Hall wrote to Alexander Hume-Campbell, the 2nd Earl of Marchmont, on 8 August 1737 from Dunglass:

> Yesterday the Act was read at Colb[randspeth]. No preaching at Old[hamstocks]. The minister read it before the first psalms. The elders that were gathering the offering threw doun the box and went away whenever the minister took the Act in his hand. I'm afrayed we shall hear of some disturbances. My familie with Major Broun's daughter went there but came late to the reading of the Act. The Major and I stayed at home; went out to take a walk and we were kept half ane hour under a beach to save us from a very havie rain.
>
> Just now at breakfast my Tiby is fain out with Mis Broun who is pritty but squints teriblie. A Scots hagges was not to be born. Ye'r ane wish, Patato, dear joy ... The Major has inclosed ane which I hope ye'l see to get done for him. It seems to be necessary his stay here for some time. His ant [aunt] is makeing a new will and I believe will live him at least 20 or 22,000 merks to help purchase the estate of Blackburn besides her

executive which will be considerable. Let me know if ye can do the Major's business.

The Act in question was the Act of Parliament for bringing to justice the murderers of Captain John Porteous, and 'Miss Broun, pretty but with a squint', must be Robert's daughter Helen.[21] The pertinent part is the fact that Robert Brown's aunt was making a new will and confirmation that the estate of Blackburn was indeed, in 1737, out of the hands of the Brown family. Robert's letter to the Earl of Marchmont has also survived, written on the same day and also sent from Dunglass:

I beg you will do me the faver to writ to my Lord Cornwallis to write to his brother, my Collonell, to git me live [leave] to stay in Scotland untill the winter session is over. I have verie presing business, it being five and tunte or therte thousand merks difference to me if I should be obliged to go. If your Lordship can git me the Duke of Devenshirs' live it will do as well, he being Lord Leutenant of Irland. If the regement war not on Dubling deute [Dublin duty] I would find no deficulty in gitting live and I belive with a verie littel intrest to my Collonell and telling him the nesesety he will make no deficulty. I am now about purchising the lands of Blakburn and if I git them your Lordship has allways a shur vot [sure vote] more for your famille. I wish it may be in my pour [power] to show my gratetud to your Lordship for the honor you did me, recomending me to my Lord Stars [Lord Stair] at London in the twinte siven which was of great us [use] to me in giting this company. I beg your Lordship will excus this fridom but nescesaty has no law which I hope will plead for my boldnes.[22]

It is not known if Robert's request for leave was complied with, nor whether he was allowed to remain in Berwickshire until his aunt Helen had made her new will but, with or without his presence, Helen Ker née Brown did indeed make a 'Settlement of her affairs' dated 15 September 1737 and lodged in the Commissar of Lauder court books.

The document begins:

Be it known by these presents me Helen Brown Lady Blackburn widow of Mr Mark Ker of Blackburn for the love favour and affection I have and bear to George Cornwallis Brown son to Captain Robert Brown my nephew son of the deceast Andrew Brown Merchant in Edinburgh my brother german and to his other children and to Helen Brown my niece daughter to the said Andrew Brown spouse to Captain Job Buck shipmaster.

In this document Helen made an attempt to order her affairs so that, on her death, the estate might pass back to her family. She left nothing to her nephew Robert, son of her brother Andrew, but instead, after a monetary bequest of £100 to her eldest great-niece Helen Brown which was payable when she reached her 21st birthday, her will directed that any and all wealth she left be allowed to accumulate until it was of sufficient value for Blackburn to be bought for her eldest great-nephew, George Cornwallis Brown.[23] If Blackburn couldn't be purchased, either by the fund being insufficient or the owner refusing to sell, then George and his younger brother were each to receive £200, Helen as the eldest daughter a further £100 to add to the inheritance she had already received and the other girls were all to get £100 each. Any remaining money was to be divided equally between George and his brother.

The document contained the following reference to Robert: 'And I doe hereby exclude the said Capt Robert Brown from any share or concern either of liferent or other ways.'

Without knowing more of the character and personality of Captain Robert Brown it is impossible to second-guess the reasoning behind his aunt's actions. Was he excluded with his full consent, for the long-term benefit of his two sons, a long period of time being needed for the money to accumulate to an amount sufficient to buy Blackburn? Was he a wastrel, a gamester, who would squander the estate and its assets and Helen deliberately bypassed him? Did Helen have guardianship of the children in Scotland while their father was elsewhere with the army and was reluctant to relinquish control of them back to their father in the event of her death, instead appointing tutors and curators (guardians) for them in her will and exerting her authority from beyond the grave?

She appears, from this document in which she nominates guardians for her great-nephews and nieces when both their parents were still living, to have considered herself the matriarch of the family. However, Lady Blackburn, in making this settlement and directing how she wanted her money to be used to benefit her great-nephews and nieces, neglected to include one important detail. She didn't stipulate any timescales.

In 1738 command of the 34th Regiment had been given over to Lord James Cavendish, a brother of the 3rd Duke of Devonshire, and by the autumn of 1739 the regiment was home from Ireland and stationed in Salisbury where Robert's daughter Helen was married to John Dundas, an officer from the same regiment as her father.

As befitted a daughter of an army officer, she married a man who, after their marriage, steadily rose through the ranks to become major of a regiment of foot. Her husband, John Dundas, was a younger son of William Dundas of Blair Castle in Perthshire, Scotland.

The Dundas family had suffered misfortune in backing the Jacobite cause as John's father had supported the Old Chevalier in the 1715 uprisings, for which he was forced to sell his estate of Airth, and John's sister Anne married John Blaw of Castlehill, a known Jacobite.[24] Perhaps to counter the taint of Jacobite sympathies, both John and his brother Charles joined the English army, while two other brothers, James and Ralph, served in the Dutch army.

John Dundas had joined the 34th Regiment of Foot as an ensign on 29 July 1731, the same regiment in which Robert Brown, Helen's father, had recently been promoted to captain of a company. Indeed, John Dundas may well have been a junior officer in Captain Robert Brown's regimental company.

By 18 September 1739 Captain Robert Brown's company was stationed at Salisbury and just over two months later on 28 November Lieutenant John Dundas and Helen Brown applied for a marriage licence there, the bride's parish given as Salisbury St Thomas.[25] Historically, Salisbury has long been associated with the army and it is a distinct possibility that Robert Brown had his entire family in tow with him. The marriage took place two days later on 30 November 1739 at the medieval church of St Thomas in the centre of Salisbury.

The following year Robert was raised in rank from captain to captain lieutenant. The regiment continued on the British mainland, mainly around the Salisbury area, until the spring of 1741 when it was sent as part of the force to relieve the Siege of Cartagena and to reinforce the regiments already there that had been decimated by action and disease.

The Battle (or Siege) of Cartagena was a disaster: in total it lasted sixty-seven days and resulted in the British forces ignominiously withdrawing in defeat to Jamaica with the hope of gaining reinforcements to replace the 18,000 men who had died.[26]

On 12 April 1741, while in the Spanish Caribbean, Captain Robert Brown was transferred from the 34th Regiment into 'the Americans', one of the newly-raised Marine regiments. Due to the high death toll promotions were to be gained and he was quickly raised to the rank of major in this regiment and shortly afterwards to the rank of lieutenant colonel: 'Robt. Browne Esq. to be Lt. Colonel to the American Regt. of Foot commanded by Col. Wm Gooch, Port Royal Harbour [Jamaica], 16th June 1741.'[27]

The regiment Robert Brown transferred into was the 43rd Foot, first Spotswood's and later Gooch's Marines, formed from American colonists but serving alongside the British Marines. Lawrence Washington, the half-brother of George Washington, served in this regiment at the same time as Robert Brown.

Helen Ker, née Brown, died in 1741 while her nephew was gaining promotion abroad and the following year Robert began the journey back to
England. He had prospects now: he was a lieutenant colonel in the British
army and his eldest son stood in line to eventually regain possession of the
family estate at Blackburn but the wheel of fate now turned once more.
Either suffering from disease or injury sustained in the course of duty, Lieutenant Colonel Robert Brown died in October 1742, shortly after making it
back to the shores of England: 'Last Week died at Portsmouth, soon after he
landed there from Jamaica, Col. Browne, Lieutenant-Colonel of one of the
Regiments of Foot at that Island; he went from England a Captain.'[28]

His remains lay in the churchyard of Domus Dei, the Royal Garrison
Church in Portsmouth, where he was buried on 17 October 1742.

A year after his death an auction was held at Gloucester Street, London
for the sale of the belongings of Mr Henderson and added to this sale was
'The Wearing Apparel and Linnen, Fire-Arms and Field-Equipage, of the
Hon. Col. ROBERT BROWN, who died at Portsmouth, in his Return from
the Expedition of Carthagena.'[29] It is interesting to note the inclusion of
the prefix 'Honourable' to Colonel Robert Brown's name, in respect of his
recently-gained military rank.

As Helen Ker had died the year before her nephew and with only the
eldest daughter of Colonel and Mrs Robert Brown married, the six younger
children were left to the care of their mother and the guardians appointed by
their great-aunt's will, and the youngest Brown son died around this period.

On the death of her great-aunt, Lady Blackburn, the new Mrs Helen
Dundas received her inheritance of £100. Lady Blackburn's will had provided
this money for her niece Helen only, as she was the eldest by some years, the
remaining children still being minors and having no immediate need. If
Blackburn House could be secured for George Cornwallis Brown, he would
then be able to look after his remaining sisters until they married and Lady
Blackburn had assumed that Robert Brown would survive many more years to
provide for his family too.

Only in the event of this plan not being put into effect was Helen to
receive anything further; if Blackburn was not bought then the remaining
money would be shared between the Brown siblings. In this case Helen, as
eldest daughter, would receive a further £100. Robert Brown's early death
threw everything into disarray, and for two years from 1743 Helen and her
husband John Dundas were in contact with the trustees of Lady Blackburn's
estate, who were also the guardians of the younger Brown children, to ask for
the remaining money due to them to be paid as the purchase of Blackburn
had not been accomplished. This wasn't Lady Blackburn's plan at all! She

had wrongly assumed that more time would be given for the money to accumulate and in such a short space of time it wasn't viable to purchase the estate. Helen Dundas must have known this and known that she was cheating her brother out of his intended inheritance, but she wanted to force the trustees into paying her the extra sum and legally she was within her rights to do so.

Her need for the money was hastened because John Dundas had borrowed £300 from his brother Charles, assuming that his wife's extra inheritance would soon be available for him to partially repay this loan. The trustees, trying to act fairly to the children to whom they were tutors and guardians, declined this request and the matter was taken to the courts to get a decision. As Blackburn did not pass to George Cornwallis Brown, the Dundas's need for their additional £100 denied George the chance to become Laird of Blackburn.[30]

Blackburn, by this time owned by the guardians of Mark Ker junior (who was a minor and overseas), seems to have been run inefficiently and was possibly becoming something of a liability. With nothing to give George's views on Blackburn but only those of his trustees and guardians who were trying to act in his favour, it is impossible to say if losing the chance to be Laird of Blackburn was a disappointment for him or not. Possibly taking the money and having the chance to make something of his life without the encumbrance of a mismanaged estate hanging round his neck was the better choice?

George Cornwallis Brown's distinctive middle name was given in recognition of the Honourable Stephen Cornwallis, colonel of the regiment in which his father Robert Brown served, the 34th Regiment of Foot. Robert chose to honour his commanding officer by bestowing his surname as a middle name on his son. Indeed, as he bears his name, it is very possible that Stephen Cornwallis stood as godfather to the little boy.[31]

During 1754, around the time Grace was born, George, by now in his early twenties, made a failed attempt to establish himself 'in business' in London, working as a merchant. We know this from the letter sent by John Murray to Grace's father Hugh. John, a merchant himself and in London after a recent return from his own business affairs in South Carolina, expressed to Hugh his regret that his brother-in-law George, who seemed to have made every effort to establish himself, was obliged 'by the importunity of his friends' to return to Scotland after a failed attempt to 'get into business' in London. Murray, with his mercantile experience, believed that George Cornwallis Brown should have been given longer to prove himself before returning, saying that 'I never saw or met with a young man who gave stronger proof of an inclination to do well than he ... that he wanted success was not the effect of neglect so cannot be imputed to him.'[32]

With Blackburn House no longer an option and his attempt at establishing himself in business a failure, George turned to the only other option he knew. His inheritance from his great-aunt allowed him to purchase a commission and so George joined the army in January 1756, following in the footsteps of his father, with an appointment as ensign in the newly-raised 55th Regiment of Foot, serving with them until appointed adjutant to the 36th Regiment.[33] The *Public Advertiser* newspaper mistakenly gave the details minus his surname: 'George Cornwallis, Gent. to be Adjutant to the 36th Regiment of Foot, commanded by Lord Robert Manners.'[34]

Just three of the Brown sisters now remained in Scotland. The Berwickshire minister George Ridpath recorded a visit to John Mow's house at Mains in Chirnside, a small village in the Berwickshire Merse not too far from Blackburn.[35] Ridpath stopped to drink tea with his friend John Mow on Thursday, 27 October 1757 and at Mow's house met with 'two fine women, sisters-in-law to Mains, the one, lady to Major Dundas, the other to young Dalrymple of Dreghorn, the Advocate. The latter in particular is a celebrated beauty, but I did not see her to advantage.'[36] The 'celebrated beauty' is easily identifiable as Grace Dalrymple's mother Grissel, and she must have been every bit as striking as her daughter.

John Mow of Mains paid the costs associated with a marriage at Chirnside on 1 April 1753; unfortunately the name of his bride was not recorded. The baptism of Mary, daughter of John Mow, took place at Chirnside on 18 February 1754, just ten months after the aforementioned marriage, with no name given for the mother. However, the burial charges and collection registers for Chirnside list a payment of two shillings on 22 December 1754 for a mort cloth and bell for Jean Brown.[37] Scottish customs assign the maiden name to a woman where we would in England expect to see a married name and so this is Grace's aunt, dying while still a young woman, around the same time that Grace was born, leaving her own poor daughter motherless before her first birthday.

It is also likely that Jean died in childbirth, for at Chirnside on 8 January 1755 there is the baptism of John, the son of John Mow, but if so, it would seem that this son soon followed his mother to the grave as there is no further mention of him. Grissel and Helen were therefore on a visit to their widowed brother-in-law John Mow of Mains in October 1757, visiting their 3-year-old motherless niece who would have been around the same age as Grace; surely Grace was there with them, happily playing with her cousin while the adults talked?

Grace was consequently growing up in a very matriarchal environment. Her widowed grandmother Janet Brown was still alive and living close by in Edinburgh while Grace was a young child.

Richard Cooper was an engraver. Born in London, he had moved to Edinburgh in 1725 and remained there for the rest of his life, founding a successful business producing maps, portraits and music tickets.[38] On 28 July 1758 he sold a flat 'being the east-most half of the second story in a "great tenement of houses" on the south side of the Canongate opposite to the Church, to Janet, widow of Lt. Col. Robert Brown of General Gooch's Regiment of Foot.'

The sale was witnessed by two men known to and trusted by her daughter Grissel's father-in-law, Robert Dalrymple, and also by Alexander Orr, Clerk to the Signet.[39] It is tempting to think, as the sale was authorized by Robert Dalrymple's business associates, that Grissel, who had by now been abandoned by her husband Hugh, moved into this Edinburgh flat with her mother, taking her young daughter Grace with her and this Edinburgh apartment was Grace's early home.

While Grace's aunt Helen was a prominent figure in her life, Helen's husband John Dundas, who died during the summer of 1759 at his house in Fountainbridge, Edinburgh when Grace was only around 5 years of age, was hardly remembered by her. Dundas, who was laid to rest in the Greyfriars Kirkyard, had died a major in Lord Effingham's Regiment of Foot and had been living in St James's in Westminster, London when he wrote his will four months before his death.[40] Helen, who inherited her husband's estate, chose to live in Edinburgh after his death and during her widowhood.

What of Hugh? In early January 1757 a burlesque of the Scottish minister and writer John Home's tragedy *Douglas* was performed in Scotland, and it was suggested that 'both it and the prologue were from one hand' and that hand was suspected of belonging to Grace's father.[41]

Chapter Three

The Pen of Hugh Dalrymple

Hugh Dalrymple was now resident in London, either with or without his 'lady of fortune' from Dumfries.

Although Hugh had qualified as an advocate in Scotland, this did not mean he could practise law in England, the Scottish and English legal systems being so different, and so he enrolled in the Middle Temple in London, admitted on 17 May 1759 and intending to qualify to practise as a lawyer in England.[42] However, far from gaining any legal qualifications, or indeed being noted as practising law at all, instead Hugh gained notoriety for his writing. In 1761 he published a poem, *Woodstock: An Elegy* and in 1763 Cantos I and II of *Rodondo; Or, the State Jugglers*. Both were published anonymously but were known at the time to have sprung from the pen of Hugh Dalrymple. *Rodondo* was a political satire, an attack on William Pitt the Elder for his three-hour speech against the First Lord of the Treasury (the position we know today as prime minister), John Stuart, 3rd Earl of Bute.[43] Bute, like Hugh Dalrymple, was both a Scot and a Tory, and *Rodondo* proclaimed Hugh's allegiance to both his native country and his political party, although it ultimately did not save the career of Bute who resigned and was succeeded by the Whig, George Grenville.

Rodondo received critical acclaim at the time of its release. *The Critical Review, Or, Annals of Literature*, edited by Tobias George Smollett, in February 1763 gave its opinion on Cantos I and II:

> If the political disputes of this æra have produced abundance of illiberal abuse and dull scurrility; it must be owned, they have also given rise to some productions of true genius ... The play is a satire upon a late m[iniste]r and some of his supposed emissaries, who have lately exerted their talents in raising disturbances in the commonwealth; and, in particular, have poured forth a torrent of unprovoked abuse against the Scotch nation. *Rodondo* seems to be the revenge of some Caledonian bard, who, in our opinion is not unequal to the contest ... On the whole, we think this author's turn for satire and altercation so keen, lively and diverting.

Rodondo would, Hugh's friends judged, be sufficient recommendation for the Earl of Bute to make some provision for Hugh and to gain him a position, but apparently the earl objected to Hugh's moral character, perhaps with reference to the reputed Dumfries nocturnal adventures!

Hugh was also busy in another literary vein in the 1760s for he was the author of a flurry of political letters sent in to the newspapers, signed only as 'Modestus'. It was not long before his identity was guessed, and he was certainly fully acknowledged as the author some years later. In the late 1760s and early 1770s the letters became less frequent, indicating that Hugh was engaged in other activities with little time to spare for his writing, or absent from the political arena.

Robert Dalrymple, Grace's grandfather, had died in 1765. He left a lengthy will behind him, almost interminable in parts, but he did mention his family and specifically Grace, her siblings and her parents.[44] He referred to Grace and Jacintha by their proper names, calling them Grizel [sic] and Janet, and acknowledged the rift between his eldest son and daughter-in-law by providing an annuity of £50 a year for Grissel which was not subject to Hugh's control. Robert made Henry Hew Dalrymple, his eldest grandson, the main beneficiary, cutting out Hugh and telling us all we need to know about the relationship between the two men. Robert Cornwallis Dalrymple was bequeathed £500 and the two girls £350 each, to be payable either when they married or came of age.

Robert Dalrymple, a legal expert, must have died secure in the knowledge that he had used all his professional abilities to draw up a watertight last will and testament that would see his estate directed to those of his family he felt deserved it. Sadly, it seemed he had instead left a legal minefield behind him. Many, many people were mentioned in the document, with debts due and those owed all itemized and the wrangles between all concerned raged for some thirty years after Robert's death, not being finally sorted out until 1796. This was a tragic precursor to Grace's own experiences: she would be a named beneficiary in three further wills that took years to be proved at a time when she, like her mother Grissel before her, had been abandoned and was sorely in need of the security that a substantial annuity or bequest would have brought.

Chapter Four

The Military Uncle

George Cornwallis Brown, with his regiment, spent the winter of 1759 camped at Salisbury.[45] The regiment remained there until the middle of May the following year, at which time they broke camp to march to Berkshire, but not before George had made the acquaintance of a young Dorset girl.

No doubt the presence of an army camp provided a welcome diversion for the girls from the surrounding area and heralded the occasion of many balls and social gatherings, providing the opportunity to flirt and dance with a gentleman in uniform. Susannah Margaretta Coker, a young girl from a Dorset landed gentry family, must have been one of those who, during the early spring of 1760, travelled to view the spectacle of the army camp, for she became sufficiently well acquainted with George Cornwallis Brown for him to propose marriage to her.

Susannah was aged around 17, a noted beauty and the eldest daughter of William Coker, Esquire, and his wife Susannah, née Saint Lo. Many in George's family were described as being elegant and blessed with particularly good looks, so it's not improbable to think that George too had inherited his fair share of attraction and cut a very fine, dashing and handsome figure in his military uniform, enough to turn a young girl's head at any rate.

The Coker family had previously owned Mappowder Court, a fine mansion in the small village of Mappowder near Sturminster Newton, Dorset and had made their fortune through investing in the slave trade but, by the mid-1700s, their fortunes had reversed and they found themselves in debt, necessitating the sale of the estate in 1745.[46] William Coker moved to Wimborne Minster, a small town a few miles away from Mappowder, and it was there, on 6 June 1760 in the fine Norman church serving the parish, that his daughter Susannah married George Cornwallis Brown.

Back in Scotland, Helen Dundas moved to Canongate in Edinburgh where her mother lived (it is likely that Helen, her mother, her sister Grissel and Grissel's children were all living under the same roof), and it was there, on 29 March 1764, that she wrote her will in the presence of Alexander Orr.[47] She named as her executors and trustees her brother-in-law Richard Dundas of Blair, Esquire, and her brother George Cornwallis Brown, lieutenant in Lord Robert Manners' Regiment of Foot, before specifying that a debt of nearly £200 sterling was to be repaid to Sir Lawrence Dundas, Baronet, and also asked that £10 sterling be given to 'Mrs Janet Brown my mother' and 'Grissel Brown alias Dalrymple my sister wife of Mr Hew Dalrymple Advocate'.

Helen also bequeathed to her sister Grissel 'all my bed and table linnen and china and one of the two pictures done for myself, with all my body cloaths wearing apparel towels and paraphernalia with my mahogany cloaths chest', plus her large prayer book. The second picture Helen left to Miss Ogilvie Dallas, daughter of James Dallas, a singing master at Edinburgh.

George Cornwallis Brown was bequeathed

two pairs of candlesticks, twelve soup spoons, a turine spoon, a marrow spoon and milk pot, twelve tea spoons, tea tongs and a strainer all of silver, two cases of china handled knives and forks, with a picture of my mother and all my books of different languages (excepting the prayer book).

He would also inherit £200 sterling, and his wife Susannah was bequeathed a diamond ring.

Three of Grissel's children also received bequests: her son Henry Hew was left 'a miniature picture of the said Grissel Dalrymple his mother' and the two girls, Grace and Jacintha, referred to as Grissel and Janet by their aunt, were left monetary bequests of £200 sterling each.

Among various other bequests to friends and family members, Helen also stated 'my gold watch which I leave to Mary Mow my niece in token of my affection for her seeing she stands in no need of any addition I could afford to make to her fortune tho' my affection for her is not the less.'

The money left to her nieces Grace and Jacintha was 'life-rented' to their mother 'during all the days of her life if she does not marry a second time which if she do this life rent is from thenceforth to cease', giving Grissel a little in the way of independent means to live on while she had her children to care for.

In a neat reflection of the views of the Brown family on the errant Hugh Dalrymple, husband to Grissel, Helen did

hereby exclude and debar ... the said Mr Hew Dalrymple advocate over the donations and legacies above mentioned given by me to the said Grizle [sic] Dalrymple his spouse and their children which they shall be of themselves intitled to uplift receive enjoy and discharge without his consent or approbation and to this end so nominate and appoint the said George Cornwallis Brown my brother and Alexr Orr writer to the signet to be tutors and curators to the said Janet and Grissel Dalrymple my nieces during the whole years of their respective pupillary and minorities for the management of the legacies hereby bequeathed to them.

In other words, Hugh had no rights over his daughters' inheritance and, moreover, was not even to be their guardian. This will has echoes of the one made some thirty years earlier by Helen Ker, Lady Blackburn. It therefore becomes clear that Grace Dalrymple was descended from a family of strong-willed women who liked to have their own way.

Despite her challenge to Lady Blackburn's will nearly twenty years earlier which denied her brother the chance to inherit their ancestral home, there was no ill will between the two siblings by 1764. Indeed, Helen seemed to rely very much on her brother and to trust him implicitly to act in the best interests of his sister Grissel and her children. Helen was not to live long after writing her will and on 18 April 1764, the *Gazetteer* newspaper reported her death: 'Died. At Edinburgh, the relict of Major John Dundas, of Lord Effingham's regiment and eldest daughter to the late Col. Robert Brown.'

George Cornwallis Brown's wife Susannah had continued to base herself in Wimborne Minster after their wedding. The baptisms of the three children she bore to George are all recorded in the parish register of the minster: Susannah Robiniana in November 1761; George Robbins in September 1763 (who died young); and Janet Lawrence in January 1767. The middle names of the two eldest were given in honour of George's sister, Robinaiana.[48]

George was promoted to captain lieutenant within the 36th Foot and in 1764 the regiment sailed to the West Indies, not to return until 1773. That George returned early is clearly proved, however, by Janet's baptism in 1767. His commanding officer, Lord Robert Manners, travelled home to England in 1766 following his transfer to the command of a different regiment, and George may have sailed home with him. Shortly after little Janet's baptism, he was promoted to the rank of captain in the 36th Foot and by June was at an army camp located at Kingsdown on the outskirts of Bristol, preparing to sail to rejoin his regiment in the West Indies.

George Cornwallis Brown's life came to an end at the camp on Kingsdown. How or why has not been recorded, but the *London Evening Post* of 4 July 1767 carried the following notice: 'Friday last died, on Kingsdown, near Bristol, George Brown, Esq; a Captain in one of his Majesty's regiments of foot now in Jamaica.'

George was buried in the crowd (crypt) of the Church of St John the Baptist in Bristol, a fourteenth-century church in the city centre. His death left the Brown family without an immediate male heir and, more importantly, deprived his sister Grissel's two daughters of their tutor and protector as appointed in the will of Helen Dundas. The Brown sisters seem to have relied on George to a considerable degree and had trusted him to take care of the young Grace and Jacintha. As the head of their family his untimely demise must have had an enormous effect on their lives, not least because Grissel only survived her brother by just three months, dying in Edinburgh at the end of September and turning the world of her two young daughters upside down.

Had George Cornwallis Brown lived, would Grace have been taken into his household after the death of her mother, to be brought up alongside his two young daughters? Her history could then have been a very different one indeed.

Susannah Brown remained in Wimborne Minster after George's death and on 30 November 1769 she married Captain Richard King of the Royal Navy, a man from Titchfield in Hampshire, marrying in the same church where she had wed George some nine years earlier. Captain King was a rich man by the time of his marriage to George's widow, having taken a share of the prize money for his capture of the galleon *Santissima Trinidad* from Manila and he was to rise through the ranks of the navy, becoming Admiral of the Red (of the Fleet) by 1805. In 1784 King received the honour of a knighthood, enabling the couple to be known as Sir Richard and Lady King, and in 1792 was created a baronet. The couple were to have several children, giving the two Brown sisters plenty of half-brothers and sisters, but the two young Brown girls did not live with the Kings. Instead, they were taken into the household of their aunt, Robinaiana, Countess of Peterborough.

Although the Browns were not to regain Blackburn House, one of the daughters of George Cornwallis Brown later proudly displayed the arms belonging to her family, recognizing the nobility of her ancestry. The surname of this branch of the family died with George Cornwallis Brown although their descendants live on to this day, with several notable English families able to claim the Browns of Blackburn House as their ancestors.

Chapter Five

Robinaiana and Janet Brown: Mistress and Wife

Normally the birth of a firstborn son for a peer of the realm would be a cause of great celebration. One could expect an announcement of the birth in the newspapers and a grand baptism. However, the birth of the 4th Earl of Peterborough and Monmouth's eldest son went by largely unnoticed and his baptism entry at St George's Chapel in Mayfair, London merely records, on the date of 15 May 1748, the name of 'Charles Mordaunt son to Lord Peterborough'. There is, however, a very good reason for this: Mary, Countess of Peterborough and Monmouth, née Mary Cox, was not the mother of this infant. His mother was Robinaiana Brown, mistress to Charles Mordaunt, the 4th Earl, and the maternal aunt of Grace Dalrymple.

The 4th Earl of Peterborough was born in 1708 and Robinaiana was around twenty years his junior, possibly still legally a minor when her son was born in 1748.[49] His father John, Lord Mordaunt, Brigadier General of the Scots Fusiliers, had succumbed to smallpox in 1710, leaving his widow Frances, daughter of the 2nd Duke of Bolton, with two sons under 3 years of age (Charles, the future 4th Earl, and his younger brother John) and little else as Lord Mordaunt died intestate and with many debts outstanding.[50] The 3rd Earl of Peterborough, another Charles Mordaunt and a celebrated military hero, stepped in to look after his two infant grandsons and installed them in Paris where they were schooled. They were orphaned five years later when their mother died in 1715 and the two boys were later brought back to England and enrolled at Westminster public school, Charles later going up to Balliol College at Oxford.

An account of his later life, published in 1777 by the *Town and Country Magazine* within one of its scurrilous *tête-à-tête* articles, recounts his youth. He was 'at a very early age ... by turns, the cicisbeo of many women of rank and fashion ... particularly distinguished by a certain amorous duchess for his athletic form and manly appearance. In his travels abroad he was afterwards very successful in his amours.' Referring to his noted grandfather, the publication continues, describing Charles as 'descended from a great general, who had eminently distinguished himself in the wars of queen Anne and obtained considerable renown, [and] our hero approved himself as great a conqueror in the field of Venus, as his grandfather had in that of Mars.'[51]

He seems to have spent a great deal of time in France where he made many conquests and 'it is said, that Madame Pompadour herself, in the early part of her life, entertained a strong predilection for him.' Jeanne Antoinette Poisson, known as Madame de Pompadour, was born in Paris on 29 December 1721. Even allowing for extreme youth, if this statement is true it must place her predilection for him in the mid to late 1730s, certainly after the young man had attained his earldom.

Charles Mordaunt, 3rd Earl of Peterborough and Monmouth, died in October 1735. His will dated 9 September of the same year gives evidence of a rift in the family.[52] This document starts by stating that 'taking into my serious consideration the present circumstances of my family and to the end to preserve some estate to my posterity' but does not elaborate on what those present circumstances were, although the rest of the will seems to suggest that the earl believed his eldest grandson was something of a wastrel and his estate somewhat in debt.

Placing his estates in the hands of trustees, he left legacies and bequests to several members of his family, including his mansion known as Peterborough House at Parson's Green in Fulham to his younger grandson John and John's soon-to-be wife Mary, Countess Dowager of Pembroke, and there was only one mention of his grandson Charles.[53] Towards the end of the will he directed that the yearly rent of £500 from his estate should be

> for my grandson Charles Lord Mordaunt [and] shall be in lieu and satisfaction of all claims and demands whatsoever which he might have upon or out of my real or personal estate and in case he shall by any suit in law or equity or in any court temporal or spiritual or otherwise controvert or contest my said settlement above mentioned or this my will or obstruct or hinder the execution of either of them then the said rent of five hundred pounds shall from thenceforth cease.

So Charles, now the 4th Earl of Peterborough and Monmouth, inherited his grandfather's titles but precious little else, although provision was made for the maintenance and education of any legitimate sons he may have. One wonders if the 3rd Earl would have barred him from the titles had he been able to, as Charles, it appears, was a complete spendthrift. Again, the 1777 account gives us information:

> As our hero's views were never mercenary, but, on the contrary, his generosity almost unlimited with respect to this ladies; these pursuits greatly

diminished his finances and often drove him to disagreeable expedients to raise the supplies. These ways and means were generally of the usurious kind, whereby his fortune daily decreased and at length his distress was very visible, as he was under the necessity of laying down his equipage and for a time became an itinerant peer.

Charles needed a rich wife to bolster his finances and he needed one quickly. This was probably the main consideration for the marriage he contracted sometime around 1734 or 1735 when he secretly married Mary Cox, daughter of Thomas Cox of St Botolph's Aldgate, London, a wealthy Quaker grocer; another slightly irregular marriage from a son of the house of Mordaunt for both his father and grandfather had eloped with their prospective wives and after being widowed the 3rd Earl had also made a secret second marriage to his long-term mistress, the opera singer Anastasia Robinson.

Charles, 4th Earl of Peterborough, and Mary had three daughters: Frances, born c.1735; Caroline, born April 1736 (who died just months later); and Mary Anastasia Grace, born 25 June 1738. Caroline, born after Charles had attained the title of Earl of Peterborough, had her birth announced in the newspapers, which also shortly after contained news of her grand baptism at which Queen Caroline, wife of George II, stood godmother via her proxy the Countess of Bristol, with the Duchess of Bolton and the Duke of Gordon also being godmother and godfather. Unfortunately, the newspapers would also shortly announce the death of the infant at her grandfather Thomas Cox's house at Hendon.[54]

A turning-point in the marriage of the Earl and Countess of Peterborough is hinted at by a report in the *Penny London Post* of 28 August 1747: 'His Majesty has been graciously pleased to grant a Pension of 400l. a year on the Irish Establishment, to the Countess of Peterborough, to enable her to educate the young Ladies suitable to their Dignity.'

The Irish establishment was used by successive sovereigns as a special institution for providing for their royal mistresses, illegitimate children and for court favourites. It is intriguing that the Countess of Peterborough needed to be granted a pension at this particular time and suggests that the earl was unable (or unwilling) to provide financially for his wife and two daughters.

The 1777 *Town and Country Magazine* informs us that, during the summer of 1747, he was a 'very pressing suitor' of the opera singer Miss Falkner when she sang at Marylebone Gardens.[55] His suit was not successful, the magazine unkindly pointing out that he was not a young man any more and anyway, the lady had other, more flattering offers of marriage. Also, probably most importantly, 'she was, moreover, not unacquainted with the state of the count's tattered fortune.' Charles was annoyed; Miss Falkner 'was the first female that had ever slighted his advances'. It was rumoured that had he not already the encumbrance of a wife, he would have offered his hand to her. Whatever the attractions of Miss Falkner at this time, Charles was actually involved elsewhere. Maybe she was even a handy cover for what was really going on, for at around the same time that the countess was being granted her pension and Miss Falkner was performing at Marylebone, the earl was fathering a son by his mistress, Robinaiana Brown.

No sources have yet been discovered to tell how or when the earl met and became enamoured with Robinaiana. Annoyingly, the *Town and Country Magazine*, which tells us so much of his life, remains silent on hers. That she was regarded as a beauty is a fact and she can hardly have been more than 21 years of age when they met and possibly still in her teens but, however she came into the orbit of Charles Mordaunt, she captivated him. She also managed to provide in one way in which the countess had been sadly lacking; she gave the earl sons as well as daughters. Quite what Mary, Countess of Peterborough and Monmouth, thought of this extra-marital family is unknown, but as Lord Peterborough had acknowledged himself the father in the baptism records they could hardly have been kept as a totally secret family. The Earl of Peterborough paid land tax for a property on North Row, St George's Hanover Square, London between 1744 and 1754; from 1750 his wife, the countess, is listed as the occupier of a house in Park Street in the same area. It seems then, from 1750 at least, if not before, the earl and his countess were living very separate lives.[56]

Robinaiana's forename is an unusual one, almost unique, contrasting oddly with the more solidly traditional names of her siblings and is possibly a later affectation, similar to the fanciful names adopted by her nieces Janet and Grissel Dalrymple who used Jacintha and Grace instead. Robin was a common nickname for Robert, the name of her father, and a popular feminine version of this, in use in Scotland in the seventeenth and eighteenth centuries, was Robina. The French style was to use a diminutive at the end of names to create nicknames or to feminize names, for example adding 'ine' to Paul to make Pauline. The Scottish then 'Latinized' these diminutives by adding an 'a' on the end, hence Paulina. Robinaiana therefore looks to have been given her name as an inventive attempt to make a more interesting feminine variant of her father's forename.

At this point we return to the baptism of Charles, son of Lord Peterborough, in 1748 at St George's Chapel on Mayfair, a place renowned for clandestine and private ceremonies. Over the ensuing few years more children of the couple were brought there for baptism: 'John Mordaunt, son to

Lord Peterborough' on 15 May 1749 and two daughters, both named Harriat, on 30 January 1752 and 11 June 1753 respectively (the first dying young and certainly before the baptism of the second). There was also another son, Henry, born c.1754–55, around the same time that his cousin Grace was making her entrance into the world in Scotland.[57]

Whatever the private gossip of the day, not a whiff of scandal permeated through to the newspapers of the period relating to the Earl of Peterborough's second family. Robinaiana, with her own London town house at 12 New Burlington Street in Mayfair near Piccadilly, seems to have brought her children up quite privately.[58]

It must have been frustrating to the 4th Earl to have three sons, none of whom would be able to inherit his titles due to their illegitimacy, nor able to be provided for, in respect of their education and maintenance, by the trustees of his grandfather's estate. In light of this, one wonders if he viewed his wife's death on 18 November 1755 with some relief. The *London Evening Post* reported her death two days later: 'On Tuesday Morning died at Northaw in Hertfordshire, the Lady of the Right Hon. the Earl of Peterborough.' Far from entering a period of mourning for his wife, the earl instead applied almost immediately to the Faculty Office of the Archbishop of Canterbury for a marriage licence for himself and Robinaiana, the licence bearing the date of 3 December 1755.

Two days later Charles and Robinaiana married at St James's Church in Piccadilly, Westminster.

Again, the marriage of a peer of the realm ought to have attracted some publicity but this particular wedding seemed to pass unnoticed by the world at large, the only witnesses noted on the register being a Christopher and Lucy Oliver. Speculation as to why could encompass several different reasons but, with his previous marriage to the daughter of a grocer, albeit a wealthy one, Charles could hardly have felt he was marrying beneath him and so kept the marriage secret, as had his grandfather with his own marriage to the opera singer Anastasia Robinson some decades earlier. Indeed, Robinaiana's family were of more noble stock than poor Mary Cox's family, and it was hardly unknown for a man to marry his mistress. Perhaps it was just to do with the indecent haste with which they wed, ignoring any conventions regarding a decent period of mourning for his first wife?

Indecent haste indeed, for less than three weeks after Mary's death Robinaiana was Countess of Peterborough. However, there was good reason for this as Robinaiana was once again pregnant, probably by about ten weeks, and there was every possibility that Charles could, at last, have a legitimate male heir.

On the face of it, it seems unlikely for Robinaiana to have been the mistress of such an aristocratic man. Yes, she was a beauty and yes, she came from a good, albeit dispossessed, Scottish noble family, but her experiences and path in life were the polar opposite to those of her sisters Grissel, Helen and Jean. One sibling did emulate Robinaiana's experiences though, and this was Janet, born c.1725 and the elder of the two reprobate sisters. Janet Brown made her way in the world by virtue of the fact that she outlived all her husbands and ended up a wealthy widow. However, she was first a mistress for many years and, having no immediate prospects, perhaps the life of a cossetted mistress was preferable to a more sedate one spent living in dependency upon surviving relatives in Edinburgh?

Peirce A'Court Ashe, born in 1706, was almost twenty years older than Janet. He was the eldest son of Peirce A'Court, the owner of the estate of Ivy Church, an old Augustinian priory in Alderbury, just to the south-east of Salisbury and also of estates in Rodden, Somerset, the inheritance of his mother, Elizabeth Ashe. After the death in 1750 of his cousin William Ashe, he became heir to the estate of Heytesbury near Warminster in Wiltshire and took the additional surname of Ashe from this date.[59]

In 1725, around the same time that his future wife was making her appearance into the world, Peirce entered Wadham College, Oxford but did not complete his degree. In 1731 he was a page of honour to Queen Caroline of Ansbach, wife of King George II, a ceremonial position requiring attendance only on state occasions, usually for duties such as carrying the train of the Queen's gown, but he was obviously close to the royal family at this time as he hunted in Windsor Great Park with them:

> On Saturday last, about Eight in the Morning, the King, together with the Queen, Prince of Wales, the Duke and the three eldest Princesses, went from Court to Old Windsor, where a Stag was unharbour'd and ran but a short Chace in the great Park before it was kill'd: Major Selwyn, Equerry to her Majesty and Mr. Acourt, Page of Honour to her Majesty, fell from their Horses, but got no Hurt; many others of lesser Note had also Falls and a Youth, Son to one of the Huntsmen, broke his Neck and died on the Spot. The Royal Family returned between Twelve and One o'clock to Hampton-Court.[60]

The following year, after giving up his position as page of honour, he was reported by the *Gentleman's Magazine* to have joined the Foot Guards as an ensign but his military career progressed no further.[61] Peirce later represented the family borough of Heytesbury as Member of Parliament between 1734 and 1768 and he was also equerry to King George II in 1739. In 1753 he was granted a Secret Service pension of £500 per year but 'seems to have been so indifferent to money that sometimes he did not trouble to draw it'.[62] This pension ceased in 1762 when he remained with the Duke of Newcastle in opposition to the government.

Janet had been Peirce's mistress for some time before their marriage; her sister Robinaiana had been mistress to her beau since the late 1740s and it is entirely feasible that Janet had made the acquaintance of Peirce at the same time, or very shortly after. The couple did not, however, apply for a marriage licence until 25 January 1762.

The marriage seems to have been conducted with an element of secrecy but had taken place by 22 June 1762 when Peirce drew up a new will which was extremely beneficial to his new wife, Janet Ashe.[63] Indeed, the reason for marrying after so long an attachment had probably been with the sole aim of providing for Janet after Peirce's death and, if Janet had pushed for marriage for just that reason, one can hardly criticize her for her actions. She had possibly been his mistress for up to fifteen years and had given her youth to him; with Peirce approaching 60 years of age the prospect of being turned out of the house she had come to regard as her home in the event of his death would have been a frightening one.

Peirce and Janet had no children and Peirce's brother, General William A'Court, assumed that his son (and Peirce's godson and presumed heir) William Peirce A'Court Ashe would be named as an immediate beneficiary. Instead, Peirce left everything he owned including his estates, his London town house on Upper Brook Street and all his jewels, plate, furniture, pictures, ornaments, books, carriages, etc. to his wife for the term of her life, his nephew and godson only to inherit after Janet's death. He also asked for a sufficient extent of his property held in Somerset, Wiltshire and elsewhere to be sold to cover his funeral expenses and any debts. His wife was the sole executrix named in the will, to which a codicil was added on 16 June 1768:

> I find on computation that my debts amount to a very considerable sum in the whole and that the money arising by the sale of my said estates will after payment of the same be a very scanty if any provision for my said dear wife supposing the same to be her absolute property. In full consideration whereof I do hereby confirm my said recited will so far as relates to the devise of all my said manors messuages farms lands tenements and hereditaments therein mentioned to my said wife and her heirs, it being my full intent that the whole thereof should be sold forthwith and I do hereby give and bequeath all the money arising by the sale of the same after payment of my said just debts and funeral expences to my said dear wife Janet Ashe her

executors and administrators full and absolutely to and for her and their own sole and absolute use and disposal.

He went on to revoke and annul the part of the will that specified his nephew and godson should be entitled to his estates after Janet's decease, stating instead that he should have 'no estate or interest therein or benefit therefrom'. Janet was entitled to everything and might sell it as she saw fit to discharge her husband's debts and leave her enough to live on, without having to worry about having merely a life interest in the estates and property. Peirce died later that year and was buried on 19 September 1768 in the A'Court family vault at Rodden in Somerset.

Legal papers giving the opinion of Peirce's brother, who contested the will, asserted that Janet had become dissatisfied with the arrangement of only a life interest in her husband's estates, demanding to know 'What she was expected to live on?' General William A'Court Ashe further swore that, during his last illness, Peirce had fallen entirely under the domination of his wife and it was she who persuaded him to add the codicil to his will. One can understand William's desire to save the family estates; it is, after all, a partial echo of the fate that befell Janet's own family estate of Blackburn in Berwickshire, which tumbled out of the family hands. However, if Peirce's debts were of such an extent that his wife would be left impoverished, one can also understand her wanting to safeguard her future.

Janet was just over 40 years of age at this time and, while she had every expectation of a long life in front of her, at such an age and with no fortune, she would also have presumed a subsequent marriage to be unlikely. Her brother-in-law's statements during the case baldly declared that Janet had 'lived in sin' with his brother for some years prior to their marriage; William regarded his sister-in-law as nothing more than a gold-digger.[64]

Fortunately for Janet, she was granted administration of Peirce's will and took possession of the estates, including the London town house at 27 Upper Brook Street. The legal case between Janet and her brother-in-law, who continued to contest the codicil to the will, dragged on for many more years, during which time Janet had sold the burgages on the estate to the Duke of Marlborough for the not inconsiderable sum of £14,000.[65]

Thus Janet had been left a very wealthy widow and Robinaiana had gained the title of countess as payment for their time as mistresses, while their sister Grissel, who had married in conventional fashion, had been left an impoverished and deserted wife. These were powerful lessons provided by her maternal family for the young Grace Dalrymple to learn from, ones that would significantly influence her later life.

Chapter Six

The Doctor's Wife

The death of Grace's mother, Grissel, was perhaps hastened by grief at the loss of so many people close to her, combined with worry about her financial situation. Grissel was buried at the Greyfriars Kirkyard in Edinburgh on 30 September 1767 and her cause of death, in an era when life expectancy was considerably shorter than it is now, was given as 'old age' in the burial registers; she was probably around 43 years old when she died, prematurely aged by her experiences.[66]

Was Janet, widow of Colonel Robert Brown, still alive? She was definitely still living in March 1764 when she was mentioned in her daughter Helen's will, so it is highly likely that she survived her daughter Grissel also, and initially had responsibility for the welfare of her four Dalrymple grandchildren. Of the two tutors and curators (i.e. guardians) appointed by Helen Dundas for the children until they came of age, only Alexander Orr, Writer to the Signet and close kin by marriage to the Dalrymple of Waterside family was still living, so the burden of care of Grace and her siblings should have fallen to him.[67]

The oral tradition, given in the preface to Grace's journal, states that Grace, on being returned to her father's care after the death of her mother, was then placed by him into a convent school situated in either France or Flanders. However, we have no proof that it was Hugh Dalrymple's decision to send Grace abroad and it is equally likely to have been the decision of her grandmother and Alexander Orr, perhaps designed to keep her away from her father as intimated in Helen's will.

In September of 1769 another letter from Modestus was published, in which the writer (Hugh) stated that he had been abroad for some time.[68] There had been no letters between March 1766 and September 1769; was he even in the country then when his estranged wife died? On the basis of the available evidence, if we accept that Grace was sent to the convent after the death of her mother, it seems that the decision rested with her guardians in Scotland and not, as previously thought, with her father.

However, another scenario should also be considered: it is quite feasible that Grace and her sister Jacintha had been sent away to school while their mother was still alive. We do not know for sure that Jacintha attended the same convent school as her younger sister Grace – there were possibly as many as six years separating the two sisters – but we do know which convent Grace attended: the Ursuline Convent in Lille, Flanders. Henry Angelo, son of the famous London fencing master Domenico Angelo Malevolti Tremamondo, remembered her being there.[69]

Henry Charles William Angelo, a couple of years younger than Grace, recalled that she attended the same convent school as his younger sisters, Florella Sophia and Anne Caroline Eliza. Henry Angelo was sent to Eton in 1764 and, during his school holidays in 1767, if we accept the accuracy of his reminiscences, he accompanied his parents to Flanders to place his sisters in the convent:

> During the August holidays, when I was a school-boy, my father and mother took my two eldest sisters to place them in a convent in French Flanders, having fixed on The Ursulines, at Lisle. On our arrival there, a grand fête was given (that lasted during our stay), on the occasion of its being the completion of the first hundred years subsequent to the city being re-taken from the Spaniards. The festivities consisted of fire-works, *jets du vin* (fountains of wine) for the populace, firing of cannon for prizes, a general illumination, &c. On our visit to the convent, we were received at the gate by the prioress, a tall handsome English lady, a Mrs Skerratt, whom they called St. Edward and there my sisters were left.[70]

Lille had been retaken by Louis XIV of France during the Siege of Lille that lasted from 10 to 28 August 1667, so this would seem to date Angelo's recollection of his sisters entering the convent to August 1767. Was Grace a pupil there already, or did she join just a few weeks later, following the death of her mother? The latter supposition would fit the oral tradition that she was not sent to school until Grissel died and would also give reason for her to become friendly with the Angelo sisters, who were much younger than her, if they were all the 'new girls' at the school together.

The *Town and Country Magazine* later said that, at this time, Hugh made 'a tour' to visit Grace at her convent school because 'he greatly loved' his daughter although, inaccurately, the publication does claim that Grace was the only daughter of Hugh, ignoring Jacintha. Perhaps then, when Hugh was abroad in the late 1760s, he was on mainland Europe and able to re-acquaint himself with his youngest daughter?

It was during September of 1769, shortly after Hugh had returned from his trip abroad, that the letters from Modestus began to increase in volume. They were mainly directed at another writer who signed himself as 'Junius' and a war of words erupted between the two men, Junius taking the Whig stance and Modestus the Tory viewpoint. The identity of Junius has never been fully resolved but he is thought most likely to have been Sir Philip Francis, an English politician and pamphleteer.

Someone signing themselves only 'A British Spy' inferred that Modestus was really Sir William Draper, a claim denied by the *Gazetteer* newspaper.[71] The letters continued to appear intermittently and, by November of 1770, the true identity of Modestus was obviously becoming known. The *Gazetteer* published a letter on 1 November 1770 from 'Anti-Modestus', addressed to Modestus:

> So Mr Scotch Modesty, you appear again; old men like you have a right to be garrulous; but you tiresome rogue you, would not a pamphlet be a better way of conveying your *through the nose Scotch* to the world? It is true, not a mortal would buy it, but no matter for that; you might totter on your crutch to the Treasury and wheeze out of your hoarse throat to the door-keeper, what a *grate rin* your *guide wairk* has had.
>
> But Mr Old Squaretoes, what do you mean by your unconscientious letter of today? I have been told by a drudge at a coffee-house, who, God forgive him, read your *wairk* through, that you endeavour to prejudice us English against juries. I am told that your slavish countrymen have no juries, but when they are to be hanged; but your Scotch *preachment* will not make us give up juries, the greatest blessing a free nation was ever possessed of.
>
> As my mentioning you may be of service to you with your masters, I am resolved out of charity sometimes to honour you with my notice. I have more humanity, than to wish to see a poor meagre old man dying with hunger, be he ever so depraved and worthless. Eat, live, time will soon pre-vent the hand of the executioner; and the hemp, which your bad inten-tions ought to place round your neck, will be soon unnecessary. In the meantime write on, I respect your dullness on account of your years and I never wish to see a better defence made by your party, than the dullest of all Scribblers Modestus makes. The printer of the *Gazetteer* will execute this notice of you, though I hope, for the sake of his paper, he never will admit such detestable stuff as your's.

Is this merely scurrilous or an accurate description of Hugh? Wheezing, with a hoarse throat, speaking in a thick Scottish brogue and walking with a crutch? For all that the writer disparages Modestus this is just tit for tat; the letters written by Hugh are erudite, articulate and demonstrate both his learning and wit.

During 1770 Hugh published the third and last canto of his poem *Rodondo* and, by the end of the year, had managed to dispose of two of his children, for Robert Cornwallis Dalrymple had entered the East India Company's Bengal army as a cadet and his eldest daughter was about to marry.

In 1770 when Jacintha encountered Lieutenant Thomas Hesketh of the 7th Regiment of Foot, eldest son of Robert Hesketh, she was living not in London with her father but in Kent with John and Elizabeth Pitcairn (née Dalrymple), her uncle and aunt.[72] As John Pitcairn was a military man his family were living in the Chatham area, close to the garrison there, and Jacintha, a beauty like the other women in her family, soon attracted the attention of a dashing officer from the barracks. Although Thomas Hesketh had future expectations, his immediate ones were not the best: his mother was reportedly insane and his father was living in reduced circumstances with a mistress in London, a Miss Ann Townsend, nominally his housekeeper but with whom he had two young illegitimate children.[73]

On 31 December 1770 the couple applied for a marriage licence in the names of Thomas Hesketh and Jennet Dalrymple and they married the next day, the first day of the new year of 1771, at Rochester St Margaret's, just a short hop away from the Pitcairns' Chatham base. The witnesses to the marriage were Jacintha's cousin, Catharina Pitcairn, Charles Churchill (a fellow officer in the 7th), and Thomas Hesketh's sister, Ann Byne, together with her husband Henry.[74] With the groom in full military uniform and Jacintha a beautiful bride in her best gown, they must have been a truly handsome couple on their wedding day.

Grace was probably not present at the wedding as she was likely to still be at the convent school in Lille, and neither was Hugh Dalrymple in all probability (one would have expected him to sign the marriage register as a witness if he were there). It appears that Jacintha had little to do with her father at this time; as the eldest of his children she no doubt had more awareness and recollection of her parents' unhappy marriage. It's also possible that Hugh Dalrymple didn't approve of his daughter's marriage to Lieutenant Hesketh as the couple had little other than the salary he drew from the army on which to live.

In the absence of any portrait of Jacintha yet being found, a later description of her from one of her daughters must suffice: 'My mother had a charming personality and was perfectly beautiful, with the celebrated "Dalrymple brow," so well known in Scotland. She was, of course, very proud of her Scottish descent ... She was devoted to dress, cards and the world, was often absent on pleasure bent.'[75]

From this description of Jacintha it becomes obvious that the two sisters, Jacintha and Grace, when younger were very much two of a kind, both beautiful young ladies devoted to the pursuit of enjoyment. Inheriting the beauty so associated with the daughters of the Browns of Blackburn, it is no wonder that Thomas Hesketh fell under Jacintha's spell and, regardless of Robert Hesketh's precarious financial condition in the early 1770s, the Heskeths were a landed-gentry family of Lancashire who owned Rufford Hall and its surrounding estate.[76]

Sir Thomas Hesketh, the head of the family, was childless and so his eldest nephew, Jacintha's husband, had every hope of succeeding to the baronetcy and the estate of Rufford in due course. By making this marriage Jacintha Dalrymple expected, in the future, to become Lady Hesketh and châtelaine of a large country estate. In the meantime, however, her husband was a mere lieutenant in the 7th Regiment of Foot, otherwise known as the Royal Fusiliers, still aspiring to a captaincy and dependent upon his military wage.

With a change of government and with Frederick North, Lord North, at the head of the ministry, the Tories were once again in the political ascendancy after years of Whig dominance and Hugh no doubt hoped for some benefits to come his way in return for his steadfast propagandist efforts for the Tories under his pen name of Modestus. However, his reward, when it came, was bittersweet. He was offered the position of attorney general of the island of Grenada in the West Indies, a good position but an unwanted posting. The climate in Grenada was not suited to a dour Scotsman and, already gouty, he must have dreaded the prospect of disease and fever, but the posting was not to be refused and preparations were laid for his departure.

Hugh, however, did not plan to travel alone and to find out the identity of his travelling companion, we must return once again to Henry Angelo.

When Grace had visited at Angelo's father's house in Carlisle Street, Soho, aged about 18 and, as dated by Angelo, shortly before her marriage in 1771, she was accompanying her father and his wife!

> Mr. D___ and his wife were constant visitors at my father's house and with them their daughter, a tall, handsome girl, about eighteen, who had been at the same convent with my sisters, at Lisle; though I was too young then to attract her notice, yet at all times she was glad to have me near her. Soon after, she was married to Dr. E___, M.D., her parents leaving this country for Barbadoes [sic], where her father had a place under Government.
>
> How long the Doctor's honey-moon lasted I know not, but that Lord V___ supplanted him; after that the Duke de Chartres (*égalité*); then Lord C___.

Undoubtedly Grace then! So Angelo has got the destination wrong but this is an easy mistake to make; he was writing some years after the event and one can accept him mistaking one West Indian island for another. However, if Hugh was a constant visitor to his father's house, then it would be very odd indeed to remember a wife who was not there. Not only that, but he refers to the couple as Grace's parents.

With Grissel living in genteel obscurity up in Scotland, did Hugh live with another woman whom the world at large (and especially a young boy aged about 15) accepted as a legitimate Mrs Dalrymple? If Angelo's reminiscences are correct his sisters did not go to the convent until 1767, just weeks prior to Grissel's death, but this does not preclude the family knowing the Angelos before that, or Grissel herself being present in London with her husband shortly before her death. While the Mrs Dalrymple present with Hugh visiting the Angelo family could, just possibly, be Grissel, it is, however, much more likely that Grace acquired a stepmother after her mother's death.

On 8 February 1771 Hugh Dalrymple was 'called to the bar'; in other words he was now qualified to practise law in England. The following day he surrendered his chambers at 1 Brick Court in the Middle Temple in London, which he had shared with a man named Charles Hopkins. In April Hugh learned of his appointment to be attorney (or solicitor) general of the island of Grenada and, as his son Henry Hew Dalrymple had turned 21 years of age, he just had his youngest daughter left under his care and he knew that he would soon be required to set sail for the West Indies.[77]

Home from her convent school, Grace was a beauty and tall as well in an age when the average height was much shorter than it is today, and with good family connections even if there was a hint of scandal in the background of two of her aunts. Her one stumbling block was probably the fact that while she could bring youth, looks and connections to a marriage, she probably could not bring much in the way of a fortune, for though it is not known whether Hugh was a wealthy man or not, it has generally been accepted that the latter scenario is the more accurate. Coupled with his obvious interest in politics, his eloquence in writing and wit, Hugh, we can safely assume, was good company around a dinner table and possibly entertained a wide circle of acquaintances; plenty of opportunities for people to meet his equally well-educated and beautiful daughter before he sailed for pastures new.

Over the following centuries people have speculated as to why Grace chose to accept the proposal made to her by Dr John Eliot. Older than her and reputedly also shorter in height, he made up for these 'flaws' by virtue of his wealth and charming manner. John Eliot was born c.1733–39 in Scotland, the son of Thomas Eliot Esquire of Peebles in the Scottish borders, a Writer to the Signet like Grace's grandfather Robert Dalrymple, who also acted as an agent and solicitor to Frederick, Prince of Wales. His father died young and John was brought up by his mother Mary (née Davidson) and step-father, the Reverend Thomas Randall. John trained as a surgeon and made his fortune by acting in this capacity on board a privateer vessel and sharing in the prize money the ship received, enabling him to set up a medical practice in London.

His fortunes received another advance when Sir William Duncan, another Scotsman and a very fashionable doctor in London who was physician to King George III, moved abroad, transferring his practice to John Eliot and introducing him to many of his high-society patients. By 1771 Eliot was well-known among his aristocratic and well-born London patients, not only for his medical care but also as a raconteur, a man who charmed the ladies and was a genial dinner guest and host. He was also wealthy, an important consider-ation for a father with little fortune of his own to pass on to his children.

By this time John Eliot had at least two illegitimate children: a son, named John for his father, by an unknown mother; and a daughter Elizabeth by Jane Jackson, a tea dealer from Tottenham Court Road. Both children were born around 1763.

Viewed from a modern perspective, Eliot doesn't appear to be ideal hus-band material for Grace and it is difficult not to wonder whether she could have done better for herself. However, viewed through eighteenth-century eyes it was a perfectly good match: Eliot would provide Grace with a status in society at least equal to that demanded by her ancestry, she would have a good London town house, a carriage, all the gowns and hats she could wish for and a secure future.

The fact that he was Scottish may also have played a part in the decision and perhaps influenced Grace's Caledonian relatives. Eliot's mother hailed from Whitekirk in East Lothian, not far away from Grace's ancestral home of Blackburn in the Berwickshire Merse, so it is entirely possible that the two families had been known to each other for a generation or two. Was the Scottish clan system in operation once again and there was some remote link between the two families? As to the age difference, Eliot could have been as many as twenty-one years older than his teenage bride, but perhaps it was suggested to Grace that a few years of marriage could leave her a wealthy and independent widow while still young enough to enjoy her freedom? The *Town and Country Magazine*, writing retrospectively about the marriage in August 1774, said that:

[Grace] attracted the attention of the men and had many suitors, though she was not yet seventeen years of age. Her prudent kinswoman pointed out to her such as she judged eligible and those she thought improper. Dr. E___ was among the number of her admirers and her faithful monitress counseled her to listen to his addresses, as he was at that time in very considerable practice and was judged to have already acquired an easy fortune.

Who was the prudent kinswoman in question? The *Town and Country Magazine* said that Grace, 'being returned from abroad, lived with a distant relation', and one has to think that this 'distant relation' was one and the same as the 'prudent kinswoman'. Jacintha was newly-married and possibly not immediately available to help her younger sister but Grace's grandmother, Mrs Janet Brown, has to be a possibility as, if she was still alive, she would no doubt want to see her young granddaughter well-married, preferably to a Scotsman.[78]

Her aunt Janet, Grissel's sister, seems the most likely candidate: widowed in 1768 and with no children of her own, she could well have taken a maternal interest in her young niece, as also could Robinaiana, Countess of Peterborough. Grace's home on Berners Street in the parish of Saint Pancras was just minutes away from Robinaiana's Soho town house, and also from the house on Percy Street in which Janet was certainly living just two years later.

We also have to consider the shadowy third Dalrymple sister and the possible stepmother who, if either of them existed, would also have been on hand to counsel Grace. Hugh Dalrymple had his own reasons for wanting a hasty marriage arranged for his beauty of a daughter. Knowing he had to leave the country for a position abroad by the end of 1771, it would have been a weight off his mind, no doubt, if he could have left his daughter safely in the hands of a husband. The *Ramblers Magazine*, writing even further after the events in question in August 1784, certainly took this view:

> [Dr John Eliot] was the particular friend of Mr. Dal___ ... To this friend Mr. Dal___ produced his daughter, communicated his difficulties and besought his advice – but all difficulties soon vanished – for the Doctor was instantly smitten and immediately offered to take charge of that lady's reputation and fortune and provide for both by making her the wife of his bosom.

A Hugh Dalrymple gained an LL.B. law degree from Edinburgh University on 14 October 1771; it has always been presumed that this was Hugh Dalrymple, father of Grace. There is, however, the son Henry Hew, and in the absence of any further evidence it cannot be fully proven which of them attained this qualification. Hugh Dalrymple is not known to have been in Edinburgh at this time and in any case he would have been a very mature student at this period, while Henry Hew would almost certainly have attended a university somewhere, and if not Oxford or Cambridge then Edinburgh would be the most likely option and it is probable that he would have initially followed in his father's footsteps in choosing law as a profession. Whichever Dalrymple attained the LL.B., father or son, we know that the father was in London five days later as his name appears on the marriage licence allegation, dated 19 October 1771, together with Dr John Eliot's, giving his permission for his young daughter, still legally a minor, to marry, the two men also the signatories to a bond in respect of the nuptials.[79]

The marriage took place on the morning of the same day at the church of Saint Pancras, an ancient building then in a rural setting with the River Fleet running alongside.[80] The *General Evening Post* of 24 October 1771 contained the following simple announcement of the marriage: 'MARRIED – At St. Pancras church, Dr. Eliot, to Miss Dalrymple, of Berners-street.'

Grace's father, Hugh Dalrymple, signed his name on the marriage register as a witness to the wedding, along with a Mary Dalrymple. There is no known relative of Grace bearing this name, leaving only two real possibilities for her identity: she is either the missing third sister or, much more likely, Hugh Dalrymple's second wife and Grace's stepmother.

Shortly afterwards Hugh Dalrymple took a ship for Grenada to take up his position as attorney general of that island, granted as a reward for his propagandist letter- and poem-writing now the Tory party was back in power. If Mary Dalrymple was his wife then she left too, as Henry Angelo in his *Pic Nic* recalled that both of Grace's parents departed. The sea voyage would have taken just over a month and although Hugh's reaction to seeing Grenada for the first time has not been recorded, the 1st Earl Macartney, who became governor of the islands of Grenada, the Grenadines and Tobago late in 1775 and arrived there in May 1776, said of Grenada on his arrival: 'With regard to the fact of the country, it is impossible for the most lively imagination to figure anything so beautiful.' He did, however, have problems with 'the strange discordant mass of English, Scots, Irish, French, Creoles and Americans of which this colony is composed, heated by various passions and prejudices far beyond any European idea.'[81]

So, Grace began life as Mrs Eliot. Dr Eliot's home was a fine house in Cecil Street, close by the Strand and in the parish of St Clement Danes where he had lived for at least some four or five years prior to his marriage. At its sale some years later, after the death of John Eliot, the house was described thus:

THE ELEGANT LEASEHOLD HOUSE with convenient OFFICES, &c, desirably SITUATE on the EAST SIDE of CECIL STREET, in the

STRAND; with beautiful Command of View of the RIVER THAMES, the BRIDGES, SURREY HILLS, &c.[82]

At this house, soon after her marriage, Grace met her two little illegitimate stepchildren, John and Elizabeth, who were around 8 or 9 years old. We have no way of knowing if she knew they were her husband's offspring but Elizabeth, writing some years later in 1806 to her brother, recalled the visit:

> ... there is a circumstance I mentioned in one of my former letters that took place many years past when we were children. I went to Cecil Street one day, I think it was Sunday and was introduced into the parlour where you and Mrs. Eliot were sitting, eating fruit. The instant I entered she exclaimed, 'Good God! What a striking resemblance there is in these children.'[83]

It is extremely tempting to read this and think that the penny had just dropped with Grace as to the true identity of these two children. Grace was to bear one child to her husband and she must have fallen pregnant quite soon after her marriage as the birth took place in the house on Cecil Street on 25 September 1772.[84]

This son was named William Duncan Eliot and was baptized on 15 October 1772 at the parish church of St Clement Danes. The choice of names seems strange; one would have expected Thomas for Dr Eliot's father and stepfather, John for himself or either Hugh or Robert for Grace's father, grandfather and brothers. Duncan harks back to the couple's Scottish roots though and the name was given in remembrance of Sir William Duncan, the king's physician, who had helped Dr Eliot early in his career. The child died as an infant, certainly within the first two years of his life.

Horace Bleackley, in his biography of Grace contained within *Ladies Fair and Frail*, described John Eliot's father as a 'roistering Writer to the Signet' and went further to say of John Eliot that he possibly

> had no great reverence for his marriage vows. It was well known that, like a true son of the riotous Writer to the Signet, he had wallowed deeply in the mire and when Grace became aware that many of his patients were disreputable sirens, such as Sophia Baddeley, it is not improbable that she imagined his heart was as inconstant as her own.[85]

In light of this and of events about to unfold, it is impossible to read the letters now written by Modestus as anything other than an attack on Dr Eliot. Hugh Dalrymple was by now overseas in Grenada, so who was writing the letters signed Modestus? The likelihood is this was Henry Hew Dalrymple, taking on the mantle of his father and defending the honour of his sister, although it's not to be discounted that Hugh wasn't being advised on affairs back home in England and was continuing to write from Grenada. From the 29 August 1772 edition of the *Gazetteer and New Daily Advertiser* newspaper:

> To the PRINTER of the GAZETTEER
> The lewd and abominable practice of keeping mistresses, not only by persons of quality, but citizens of as bad and infamous lives, though not possessed of their wealth and estates, is become so common, that it is a matter of doubt whether *tradesmen* or *trading women* mostly abound in the metropolis. The commonness of the vice hath occasioned many to look upon it to be no vice at all and fashion and gaiety have taken away the sense of the folly and wickedness of the sin. The gentleman of distinction and spirit, instead of being out of countenance for keeping a girl, is rather ashamed of having it known, that he doth not keep one and the rakish Cit considers it not a disgrace but an honour to imitate a Lord. Whoredom is arrived to such a height as to scorn the censure of man and defy the vengeance of heaven. From the number of offenders and the public manner in which they expose both their persons and vices, at all places of resort and entertainment, chastity might be accounted a sin and libertinism a cardinal virtue. No man's wife or daughter is safe and secure from the gay intriguing villain. When lust hath conceived, gold and flattery are artfully and too successfully, employed to corrupt the fidelity of the one and to debauch the virtue of the other. ... MODESTUS

What to make of that letter, then, written about a month before the birth of Dr Eliot and Grace's son? With Grace heavily pregnant, was the good doctor taking his pleasures elsewhere, to the disgust of his wife's family? Modestus again returned to the theme of immodesty in a most bizarre letter published in the *Morning Chronicle* on 26 November 1772, addressing an 'eminent Tradesman in Fleet-street', asserting that '"Immodest" actions "admit of no defence"'. He railed against a man who exhibited himself naked at his window, to the shame and confusion of his modest and offended neighbours, while 'brandishing what decency does not allow a mention of'. The tradesman was newly-married to a wife thirty years younger than himself and his 'fair, but unhappy partner, is greatly pitied by her friends, in being sacrificed (contrary to her own inclinations) to such a lump of pride, ill nature and filthiness.' Trying to unravel the riddles in which eighteenth-century gossip was composed is often nigh on impossible, but knowing that the letters from Modestus spring from the pen of Hugh or Henry Hew Dalrymple and that Grace had been recently married to a man much older than herself, knowing also that pride was a failing to which Dr Eliot was prone, then perhaps Grace's menfolk were suggesting that Dr John Eliot was causing his new wife some anguish by indulging in some not very well hidden extra-marital affairs?

On 18 March 1773 Henry Hew sat down and wrote his will, simply signed as Hew Dalrymple Esquire of the parish of St Martin in the Fields in Middlesex. Trying to act fairly in the distribution of his property, he left the sum of £500 to his sister Jacintha (named as Janet in the will), wife of Captain Thomas Hesketh, 'in case the said Captain Thomas Hesketh shall not at the time of my decease have succeeded unto or become intitled unto the Estate of Sir Thomas Hesketh Baronet'. A bequest of £100 was made to Robert Douglas of St Martins Lane who was also nominated as the executor of the will and everything else was left to 'my brother Robert Dalrymple now an Ensign at Bengal in the East Indies'.[86] Should Robert predecease his brother, then Jacintha and her children would inherit next but only if her husband had not succeeded to his own inheritance.

Once Thomas Hesketh had inherited his father's estate, then Henry Hew knew his sister would have no great need for any extra money, but would while she was merely Mrs Hesketh and not Lady Hesketh as she had no absolute surety of inheriting that estate. Should Jacintha have become Lady Hesketh before Henry Hew died and should Robert Cornwallis Dalrymple also be dead, Henry Hew willed that his estate should go to the children of his uncle by marriage, 'Major John Pitcairn of the Marines now living at Chatham in the County of Kent', to be shared equally among them, proving the regard in which the Dalrymple children held this family. Henry Hew obviously bore the Pitcairns a lot of affection and perhaps had spent some time living in their household. However, his sister Grace is strikingly conspicuous by her absence from his will. Without further evidence it is impossible to truly conclude the reasons why, but as Jacintha was only to inherit if her husband had not come into his own estate, then he may have assumed that Grace, secure in the wealth of her husband, had no need of any inheritance from her brother and so her absence from his will was purely down to logical financial decisions rather than any personal disagreements. Henry Hew did not amend this will made so early in his life and when he eventually did die, over two decades later, Grace, who by then did indeed stand in need of financial help, remained excluded from it.[87]

The letters columns of the newspapers, in particular the *Public Advertiser*, seem at this time to be filled with inveterate hatred towards the Scots, interspersed with some spirited defences. Dr John Eliot came in for his own share of abuse:

[Letter signed by a writer named TOBY] ... Can any Thing be more wonderful or diverting than the next Phenomenon, the dapper, FAWN-ING Dr. E___t, emerging from the Cock-pit of a Man of War and start-ing up, as by Enchantment, a great Physician at the Court End of the Metropolis in less Time than an Englishman of the first Merit would have gained a dozen Acquaintances.[88]

A further letter from Modestus followed, found in the *London Chronicle* news-paper dated 6 July 1773:

I was the other day in company where modesty was the topic of conver-sation ... that the most abandoned men of the town are often preferred; even by the most modest women; and in excuse we are told, 'that reformed rakes make the best husbands'. If this maxim were true, it might perhaps be hard to judge when a rake was reformed; but I fear the contrary is generally the case: for, in the first place, it is hard, very hard, to wean such persons from their evil courses; and, in the second place, when they have at last been brought to abandon ill women, it is a great chance indeed if they do not also quit all thoughts of the whole sex. Accustomed as they are to the worst of females, they generally get an ill opinion of all; and surfeited as they are with fictitious charms, they seldom retain any relish for real ones. In short, the consequence of a woman's joining herself in wedlock with such a man, is generally that he brings her a fortune and constitution equally broken and impaired and often despises his wife for no other reason than because he himself is really an object of supreme contempt.

Is Dr John Eliot the reformed rake and Grace the modest woman who thought such a reformed rake would make the best husband, only to find herself despised? It is just at this period when Grace began to look for company and solace outside of her marital home. Could this be the reason for which Grace set herself on the path which led, ultimately, to her divorce? Bleackley asserted of Grace that 'Just as some women are "born married," so was she a courtesan at heart from her birth – not wholly through wantonness and sen-suality, but because she loved adventure and aspired to dominate mankind', and he's probably not too far away from the truth with that statement. Brought up in a strongly maternal family, filled with beautiful women, she had before her both the example of her aunts who, as mistresses, had made their fortunes, and the example of her mother who had followed a more respectable path only to be abandoned. Grace, beautiful herself and clever too, initially followed that respectable path and perhaps her husband's behaviour led her to fear that, like her mother before her, she risked being cast aside; there could even have been an element of 'tit for tat' involved, what being 'good for the gander' obviously being 'good for the goose' too, to paraphrase an old saying.

At around this time Henry Hew Dalrymple sailed for Grenada to make a visit to his father and to look around the plantation Hugh had purchased there and, while he was away from England, a writer signing himself as 'Regulus', in continuing the abuse of the Scots, took the opportunity to both deride and unmask Modestus. In the *Public Advertiser* of 13 September 1773, Regulus wrote:

> But to carry the Outrage of the Court and its hireling Writers still farther, I will produce another hungry Champion, the SCOTCH MODESTUS. This Man, having failed in the Professions of a Soldier and a Lawyer in his own Country, brought his two only Qualifications to the ministerial Market; and UNFEELING PRESUMPTION, which no Infamy could discountenance and a Prostitution which no Drudgery could tire. Thus equipped, he took the Field against JUNIUS and soon distinguished himself for passive Valour and the many sound Baitings and Drubbings which his callous Hide received. But after many heavy Essays, finding nothing could be done, by the Sophistry of the Lawyer and Government being then hard passed by Opposition, he advised a more summary and military Mode of Proceeding.
>
> When Sir George Savile, with the Virtue and Spirit of a true Englishman, severely reproached the corrupt Majority of the House of Commons, 'with BETRAYING THEIR CONSTITUENTS,' this hireling Slave endeavoured openly in the *Public Advertiser*, to instigate some practis'd Ruffian to cut him off, for daring to do his Duty to the Public, as became an honest Man and uncorrupt Senator. And for thus STRIKING, with a trayterous Hand and the Freedom of parliamentary Debate, during the very Session and consequently at the Root of public Liberty, this Scotch Vagabond has been promoted to the Attorney-Generalship of the Gr___s.

It is quite clear to whom the writer is referring: a Scotsman, a former soldier and failed Scots lawyer, writing letters as Modestus against Junius and the final proof, he is now attorney general of the Gr[enade]s, as Grenada was then known. Given that we know next to nothing of the true relationship between Hugh Dalrymple and his children, it is both interesting and heartening to know that his eldest son, just arrived home from Grenada, jumped to his father's defence after the above letter and did not on this occasion scruple to attach his name to his letter. He also provided us with absolute confirmation that his father was Modestus.

From the *Public Advertiser*, 30 September 1773:

To the WRITER who signs himself REGULUS.
Struck with the Spirit and Elegance of your Letter of the 13th instant, which was put into my Hands upon my Arrival from the Grenades, I made all the Inquiry possible for you. Hitherto I have been unsuccessful, though I have dived into every Cellar and ascended into almost every Garret, in the genteel Purlieus of White Friars and Saint Giles's.

In the Course of my Search I waited upon a Reverend Gentleman (Mr. Northcote) who I was well assured, had boasted in many Coffee-Houses about Town of his being the Author of the Letter in question. However, upon my advancing towards him, in order to pay him such Acknowledgements as the Nature of the Obligation required, he *modestly* waved any Degree of Merit on that Score by protesting in the most solemn Manner, 'that he was NOT the Author of that Letter signed REGULUS'.

I have nothing now left but this public Application to yourself and I hope you will overcome your natural Shyness so far as to make yourself known to a Person who wishes to give you some *striking* Proofs of his Admiration. The kind Notice you have been pleased to take of *my Father* has excited in me a great Desire of giving you substantial Marks of Esteem; and as very probably some of your Friends are not so indifferent about Interest as you seem to be, I have left at the Bar of the Somerset Coffee-House a Reward suitable to the Information they shall be pleased to give of your Residence.

Though the Sum left is not adequate to your Panegyric upon a Gentleman now Two Thousand Leagues distant from London, I should be glad to bestow it upon you with Addition, if you will favour me with Tidings concerning yourself. But if you are determined to continue in Obscurity, I must continue my Search. My Curiosity shall rise in Proportion to *your* Modesty; and the longer the Hand of Gratitude is suspended, the heavier it must fall.

If you are by Trade a Writer, I expect no explicit Answer to this; but if you are a Gentleman, you will save me further Trouble by sending a Line to the above-mentioned Coffee House addressed to H. DALRYMPLE, jun.

Henry Hew's letter leaves us in no doubt that he was sincerely attached to his father and confident enough in his own personality and abilities to put his name to his letter. He is also, quite clearly, more than a little feisty in his opinions. In the absence of any other information regarding Hugh and his children, we have to conclude that, with his eldest son at least, he enjoyed a good relationship and that there was a great deal of affection and respect between them.

Hugh Dalrymple died in Grenada on 9 March 1774. The Treasurer of Grenada, Mr Townsend, was appointed the trustee of Hugh's estates on that island, which were in the possession of a mortgagee, and Henry Hew eventually took possession of some of his father's plantations.[89] The news of Hugh's death reached England towards the end of April, and by the beginning of May Grace had separated from her husband.

We cannot leave Hugh's story without sharing what little information we have regarding his possible second wife. While we have no tangible evidence that she ever existed, a very interesting set of circumstances has come to light that hint at her partial identity. We return to the Mary Dalrymple who witnessed Grace's marriage in 1771 and Henry Angelo's recollections of Grace's parents (plural). On 31 August 1776 a widowed lady named Mary Dalrymple was married, by licence, in the parish church of St Marylebone in Westminster, London to a widowed gentleman named John Dumaresq Esquire. The marriage was witnessed by a Thomas Bird (who witnessed many marriages in that church), and a gentleman named PFM de Court, otherwise Pierre François Maurice de Court de Sorlut, a French wine merchant.

All pretty ambiguous until one realizes that there was a John Dumaresq in Grenada at the same time that Hugh Dalrymple was attorney general there. John Dumaresq was an officer in the 70th (Glasgow) Regiment of Foot and this regiment sailed to the West Indies in the mid-1760s. He was promoted to the rank of captain within this regiment on 25 May 1772. A deed survives, a purchase agreement, between Alexander Campbell, Hugh Dalrymple and John Dumaresq dated 22 May 1772. The 70th Regiment of Foot returned from the West Indies in 1774, Captain John Dumaresq resigning his commission the following year.[90] Dumaresq is an unusual name and we hypothesize that the widowed Mary Dalrymple travelled home under the protection of the officers of the 70th, subsequently marrying John Dumaresq two years later. We leave it up to the reader to decide, on the basis of this evidence, whether Mary was wife to Hugh and stepmother to Grace. Could Grace and Jacintha's speculated-upon third sister, if she did indeed exist, be a daughter of this second union of Hugh's and a stepsister?

Chapter Seven

Viscount Valentia and a Trip to a Bagnio

Arthur Annesley, Viscount Valentia, Baron Altham and later Earl of Mount-norris, was born in 1744, the son of Richard Annesley, 6th Earl of Annesley. On 10 May 1767 he married Lucy Lyttelton at St James, Westminster, the daughter of George Lyttelton, the 1st Baron Lyttelton of Fortescue. Valentia also had a claim to the earldom of Anglesey but he could not prove that he had been born legitimately due to his father's tangled love life and so had succeeded to his father's Irish titles only. Baron Lyttelton had both money and influence and Valentia hoped, with his father-in-law's help, to rescue his earldom as Baron Lyttelton was anxious to see his daughter a countess. This was not to be, as a further legal challenge resulted in the final decision that Valentia's claim to the earldom of Anglesey was not valid.

Meanwhile, Grace was reportedly becoming bored with her affluent husband, John Eliot, finding him dull company. Perhaps he had little free time, focusing instead on his medical practice and his patients, keen to build both his reputation and fortune even further and so, to keep his young wife happy, he allowed her to attend all the routs and drums she pleased, escorted by people he considered to be his friends.

The *Town and Country Magazine* declared that, at this time, Grace was 'one of the happiest women in the metropolis, she was envied by all the married women who knew her and courted by all the men who saw her.' Grace had her carriage, jewels and fine clothes but it wasn't enough. If Eliot was basking in the glory of having a beautiful young wife who was desired by the young men of the town but available only to himself, then he was ultimately playing a dangerous game.

Grace had recently suffered the loss of her only child and possibly it was the death of her son that proved to be the catalyst which tipped her over the edge. However, now her eyes were fully open to the world, seeing both its charms and its tragedy, and she wanted more for herself than she had at the time. Dr Eliot soon began to suspect his young wife of preferring the company of other men to his own:

> She [Grace] was peevish and fretful whenever in his company; at other times she was the soul of mirth and gaiety. This he was perfectly

acquainted with and though he could not tax her with any infidelity, he had great reason to believe there was some rival, who had ingrossed her affections.

Eliot now looked elsewhere himself, allegedly through a wish to revenge himself on Grace; if she didn't enjoy his presence, he would find someone who did. His choice was a milliner who lived nearby, a decent woman with a reputation to uphold and so his affair with her was conducted with the utmost secrecy. We know her only by the initial of her surname, Mrs G___.

Although it was rumoured that Grace may have formed relationships with more than one man during her marriage, only one man, Viscount Valentia, was named and he was described as a 'very particular acquaintance'.

In the article that appeared in the *Town and Country Magazine* in August 1774, 'Histories of the *Téte-à-Téte* annexed; or, Memoirs of L___ V___ and Mrs. E___t', we learn more of Valentia's character and are provided with an engraving of the notorious couple. Supposedly the attitudes in which the subjects of the '*Téte-à-Téte*' were pictured (either looking towards each other, away from one another or face on) denoted their feelings towards one another. If so, the illustrations of Grace and Valentia appear to suggest that he thought less of her than she did of him. Grace was pictured, looking rather demure and wearing what would become her trademark ribbon choker around her neck, gazing at Valentia who was staring straight ahead.

> Born with a lively fancy and disposed to gaiety, lord V. soon distinguished himself as a young fellow of spirit and whilst he was still at school, his boyish pranks made him be considered as a clever lad amongst his school-fellows ... he constantly fleeced his companions; but his natural generosity induced him to let them partake of the spoils and he seemed only their temporary banker and benefactor, instead of their successful antagonist. As he advanced towards manhood, his pursuits taking a different channel, he displayed the man of taste and pleasure; and being favoured by the Graces, he was greatly admired by the ladies, who seemed ambitious of bestowing their attentions upon our young hero, who was not less emulous of being thus partially distinguished. An athletic form and an agreeable countenance were no small recommendations in his favour and his natural complexion strongly prompted him to avail himself of his good fortune.

The polar opposite to Dr John Eliot, Valentia was closer to Grace's age, still a young man when the couple met either in the latter half of 1773 or the early spring of 1774. With both being married, Valentia viewed Grace as little more than an interesting distraction; how Grace viewed him is unknown but she could hardly have been hoping for a legitimate union with him. Grace, although still so young, knew the rules by which society played and she knew what the consequences could be. The *Matrimonial Magazine* (admittedly sympathetic to Eliot) later referred to Grace as the 'fair Elliotina', a sweet seducer who happened to cross Valentia's eye and fatally led his steps astray.

We can only guess at the reasoning behind her actions and, while it is understandable, if reprehensible, that she would be tempted, Grace either felt secure enough in her position as Eliot's wife to think that he would look the other way at her indiscretions, or she simply did not care and followed her heart rather than her head. It is even possible that Eliot was regretting his marriage, maybe finding his wife to be more of an expense than she was worth, and deliberately put her into temptation's way by allowing her to be escorted around London by men other than himself, knowing full well what the likely outcome would be and that he would then be able to rid himself of her.

Valentia had, before his own marriage in 1767, been known to keep mistresses and court the demireps of the day but, once married, had proved faithful to his wife, the *Town and Country Magazine* describing him in the early days of his marriage as 'uxorious' or a perfect and doting husband. He changed after losing his final legal challenge for the earldom, becoming cooler towards his wife and preferring to associate more with others. A cynic might suggest that he had merely played the part of devoted husband to please Lucy's father while he was funding Valentia's attempt to reclaim his earldom and, when that failed, he had no further need to appease the Lyttelton family:

> [Viscount Valentia was] now talked of for having formed some connections in the female world of a very intimate nature and some women of rank were pointed at as the objects of his attention. These intrigues were, however, if not the effect of mere invention, carried on with such caution and address, that they for a long while produced no farther proof than suspicion and calumny.

By the end of 1773 Valentia had fathered four children by his wife, three of whom were still living, the youngest baptized only a few months before Lord Valentia made the acquaintance of Mrs Grace Eliot. Horace Walpole later cuttingly wrote that 'Lord Valentia has preferred Dr Elliot's pretty wife to his own plain one.'

Valentia and Grace carried out their discreet assignations in a bagnio, a type of high-class brothel where a couple could hire a room without being

asked questions or where a gentleman could go to seek the resident prosti-
tutes. As a place for assignations it had merits, as the *Town and Country
Magazine* attested:

> It is well known that a Bagnio (though so alarming to the ear of modesty)
> is certainly the most secret place to carry on an intrigue. It is true, for the
> time, a woman must give up her reputation and class herself with females
> of easy virtue; but this is her security, as the waiters have no curiosity
> excited to discover who she really is. If a comparison may be allowed, it is
> like being concealed in the metropolis, where amongst the multitude,
> nobody thinks of the individual.

Viscount Valentia and Grace tried to act with discretion, to be the individuals that would pass unnoticed among the multitude. They visited different
bagnios in turn, Grace travelling first to her mantua-maker or milliner, then
taking a coach to the playhouse where she simply entered through one door,
walked through the pit avenue and left by a different entrance .[91] Then she
would hire a sedan chair to take her to the bagnio chosen for her rendezvous
and Valentia would meet her there.

On the fateful night, 1 April 1774, the bagnio chosen was one in Berkeley
Row run by Jane Price.[92] They had used this house once before, the first time
just dining together in the parlour. In preparation for her journey, and in the
early evening, Grace ordered a coach to be called for her, letting it be known
that she was visiting a lady who lived in Spring Gardens. With Dr Eliot's suspicions aroused, two of his servants, William Constable and Charles Ryder,
had been sent to watch her and they followed the coach which did indeed set
off down the Strand in the direction of Spring Gardens but, instead of carrying on to its destination, turned instead on to St Martin's Lane. Constable
and Ryder pursued Grace as she got out of the coach opposite to Maiden Lane
and walked down Bulleyn Court back onto the Strand, in effect doubling
back on herself. Another coach was waiting for her on the Strand and
Valentia was inside the coach; William Constable knew him and recognized
him.

With Constable and Ryder still in hot pursuit, the coach, with Grace and
Valentia inside, took a circuitous route to their final destination, Mrs Price's
bagnio in Berkeley Row, Hanover Square. At around nine o'clock the couple,
watched by Eliot's servants, descended from the coach and gave a double
knock on the front door; when this was answered they entered the house.
Constable left Ryder to watch the house and rushed home to tell Dr Eliot
what he had seen. At least, in the trial that followed two years later he testified to rushing home to tell his master but the *Town and Country Magazine*

published just a few months after this tryst tells a different version, one in which Eliot was not at his home in Cecil Street but out on his own nefarious business.

Dr Eliot knew as well as Lord Valentia the benefits of a bagnio as a discreet place to take a mistress and he had arranged to meet with his little milliner, Mrs G___, at the very same house of ill repute to which his wife was heading. In the version printed in the *Town and Country Magazine* Grace arrived at Berkeley Row alone to await the arrival of Lord Valentia. At the same time Mrs G___ had arrived to meet Dr Eliot and so we have both ladies waiting in separate rooms in anticipation of their lovers. The next to arrive was Eliot who, by accident, was shown into the room in which Grace was waiting; Valentia had arrived hot on the heels of Eliot and he was shown into Mrs G___'s room. The *Matrimonial Magazine* had a slightly different version of the events on that evening in which Eliot surprised the two lovers, who were sprawled in 'lullaby attitudes' on a couch. While Eliot flew into a rage and ordered a carriage to take his errant young wife home, Valentia made do with what remained on offer to him:

> [Mrs G___'s] prudence taught her not to expose herself; and whilst the doctor was conducting his wife home in a coach and upbraiding her all the way with the keenest and bitterest reproaches, our hero, like a man of true gallantry, supplied the doctor's place, as he had done often before and was not displeased with the agreeable variety the mistake afforded him.

As amusing as the accidental meeting of the spouses in the bagnio would be, the testimony of Eliot's servants, and of Jane Price and her servant, deny that scenario. In fact, Lord Valentia escorted Grace from the bagnio half an hour before midnight and conducted her into a hackney coach that he had ordered Mrs Price's servant Sarah Race to get for him, seating himself at the side of her. Charles Ryder, who was still keeping watch outside the Berkeley Row house, followed the coach to Charing Cross where it stopped. It is likely that from Charing Cross they planned to return to their homes separately, but had Grace and Valentia been alerted to Ryder spying on them? They certainly suspected they were being followed and, after a brief discussion, ordered the hackney coach driver to return to Berkeley Row but to do so in a roundabout way, not directly, to try to lose anyone who may be in pursuit. Ryder was not to be so easily shaken off his prey though, and he doggedly followed the coach all the way back to the bagnio. There he left them, tired out from chasing round the streets of London in the middle of the night. Both Jane Price and her servant Sarah Race recalled Grace coming back to the house, saying she was 'much frightened, having been watched'. Valentia had not immediately followed Grace into the house and instead had gone in search of a sedan chair in which Grace could return home. Five minutes later she was on her way back to Cecil Street.

There must have been a scene when she returned in the early hours of the morning. She arrived at her house with her clothes 'much tumbled and her hair loose' and instead of charging the fee for the hire of the sedan chair to her husband as she usually did, this time it had already been paid for by another. Eliot would have been in a temper, fully appraised of where his wife had been and with whom, but he had no proof that anything untoward had actually happened in the bagnio. In fact, even at the trial that followed, Jane Price and her servant mentioned nothing more than that the couple had taken a room in their house and dined there. If Eliot was to divorce his wife he needed to find some proof, some hard evidence of her wrongdoing. A further consideration may have been Grace's father. Eliot might have supposed that Hugh Dalrymple would rush to his daughter's rescue and be home in a matter of weeks if Grace needed him, and Hugh certainly had the means to defame Eliot in print through the popular press. Dr Eliot, although consumed with rage, was not about to do anything hasty. As the old adage says, 'revenge is a dish best served cold.'

Had Eliot known at the time, Hugh Dalrymple was an unnecessary consideration having shuffled off his mortal coil in Grenada on 9 March and Grace had lost an influential protector. News broke in England of Hugh's death towards the end of April, and after that Eliot lost no time in putting into action proceedings to divorce his wife.

Grace Eliot was thrown out of her home early in May. She was probably not quite 20 years old, had been married for less than three years, given birth to a son and suffered his death and then, on learning of the death of her own father and being left orphaned, was out on her heels to face the ensuing scandal.

Eliot had found the proof he needed, three letters written by Grace to Valentia, discovered in her bedroom by William Constable, the doctor's loyal servant, and taken from Grace's pocket by Eliot himself. In addition to the letters, another of Eliot's servants, a man named Thomas Sneed, accompanied Grace on a walk in Spring Gardens where she was joined by a gentleman. In Cockspur Street a second gentleman joined the couple and addressed Grace's companion as 'My Lord'. Sneed heard 'My Lord' (the assumption is that this was Lord Valentia), assured the other gentleman that he would take care of Grace, the inference being that Valentia, in saying this, meant if she left her husband. Could the other gentleman have been Grace's brother, Henry Hew Dalrymple? Sneed was unable to shed any light on the rest of the conversation, it being carried on in French. This evidence was given by Sneed at the later divorce trial, the date of the walk given only as one evening in the springtime in 1774; it was likely to have been after the bagnio escapade with John Eliot determined to find out if his wife was still meeting her lover.

Grace was reportedly now sent into the country as a precaution by Dr Eliot in case she was pregnant. As they were still married, any child born would legally be his, even if he knew he was not the father.

Chapter Eight

Divorce from the Cucumber Physician

As Janet had shrewdly known when she entered into legal proceedings to uphold the will of her husband, Peirce A'Court Ashe, a wealthy widow always had a good chance of marrying again and, on 2 September 1773, she did exactly that at the church of St Botolph without Aldgate in the City of London:

> MARRIED. Yesterday, at Aldgate church, William Kelly, of the Crescent, an eminent North-American merchant, to Mrs. A'Court Ashe, (relict of the late Peirce A'Court Ashe, Esq; Member for Heytesbury and sister to the Countess of Peterborough) with a considerable fortune.[93]

Whatever the closeness between Grace and her aunt Janet, in the years when Grace's life and marriage were falling apart and in which she badly needed a trustworthy female confidante and some family support, Janet would certainly have had other matters on her mind and perhaps wasn't able to be there for her niece when she needed her most.

William Kelly, a widower with children from his first marriage, was a native of New York and was in England at that time in connection with the supply of tea. In 1773, with the East India Company (EIC) suffering financial hardship, the British Parliament passed the Tea Act, giving the EIC the right to ship tea directly to America without paying any import duties, while still taxing the American merchants who bought the tea. Although they tried to hide this unpopular tax from the colonists, the details were discovered while the ships containing the first consignment of tea under the new rules were en route. The EIC's monopoly on tea trade was also an issue, as was the fact that they were only selling to a few nominated American merchants, virtually ruining those tea merchants not so nominated. With seven ships sailing for America carrying tea, they were bound for Boston, Charleston, Philadelphia and New York and protest demonstrations occurred at these places. It was believed that William Kelly had encouraged this shipment of tea to America, reputedly informing the British Parliament that

> There was no danger of the resentment of the people of New York, if it should be as high as it was in the time of the stamp act. That, then, they

had an old man [Mr Colden], to deal with, but now they have Governor Tryon [a military man], who had suppressed the insurrection in North Carolina; and he would cram the tea down their throats.[94]

Declared an enemy to his country, an effigy of him with a label on the front saying 'The just reward of that black and horrid crime ingratitude' and one on his back labelling him 'a disgrace to my country' was burnt during the protests in New York.[95] The cargoes were refused at all the ports except Boston, culminating in the Boston Tea Party on 16 December 1773 when the ship was boarded and the tea thrown into the ocean.

Ignorant of the events about to unfold in his native country, just a month after the marriage William Kelly set out to offer himself as a candidate for the vacant parliamentary seat of the City of Worcester; it was generally thought that he would be chosen but he withdrew a few days before the poll, angering his supporters. He gave as his reason the near approach of the general election and, with both requiring a tremendous amount of money to be spent on them, he preferred to wait.

Kelly's opponent at Worcester, Thomas Bates Rous, was rumoured to have spent £20,000 on his campaign; Kelly couldn't or didn't want to match that. The *Worcester Journal* newspaper of 18 November 1773 reported that Kelly had been mobbed in the streets by voters bearing banners and had declared 'I have my friends betrayed'. His wife was reportedly 'sent into fits'.[96]

Now derided on both sides of the Atlantic, it is probably not surprising that William Kelly fell ill shortly after. On 2 August 1774 he drew up his last will and testament: 'I, William Kelly of Percy Street in the Liberty of Westminster, Esquire, being at present in Bath for the recovery of a Numbness that has attacked me in my feet, but enjoying my usual share of understanding.'[97]

He disposed of his estates in Great Britain, North America and the island of St Thomas to his children from his first marriage and his son-in-law, and did not mention Janet at all. It is difficult to know what his motives were; her fortune from her first marriage was protected and knowing that she was financially secure he may have left his wealth to his children with her full blessing but maybe, after she was 'sent into fits' by his withdrawal from the 1773 election, their relationship had become strained for he did not even leave her a token of remembrance.

He died days later, the waters of Bath not being sufficiently curative to aid his recovery, and he was buried in the Abbey Church of Saint Peter and Paul in that city on 14 August 1774, his reputation sufficiently recovered, in England at least, for the following tribute:

On Wednesday died at Bath, where he went for the Recovery of his Health, William Kelly, Esq; well known in the Commercial World for his extensive Connexions, his exact Punctuality, Precision and Integrity. He has left considerable Estates in this Country, the West Indies and North America; and as he lived universally esteemed, his Loss is now as universally lamented.[98]

It was in August 1774 that the *Town and Country Magazine* ran its article on Janet's niece Grace's intrigues with Lord Valentia. Having just buried her second husband, Janet would be of little help to Grace as the newspapers gleefully copied the gossipy article within their pages, word for word, trumpeting Grace's scandalous behaviour to the world at large.

Jacintha too was absent from her sister's side during Grace's unhappy marriage. She and her husband Thomas Hesketh made an extended visit, at the beginning of August 1771, to Carshalton in Surrey to the house of Thomas's sister and her husband, Ann and Henry Byne. Ann Byne was a pretty woman but with a tendency to ill health, while Henry Byne lived far beyond his means and had run through any fortune he had and the couple, who married in 1770, were at each other's throats by the end of 1771, often setting the village of Carshalton in an uproar with their arguments.[99] The Heskeths' first child, a daughter named Harriet Anne, was born in the Bynes' house in December 1771 but towards the end of January the Heskeths quarrelled with their hosts, packed up and left the next day.

On 27 October 1772 Thomas Hesketh was promoted to a captaincy with the 28th Foot, and by February of the following year Jacintha had followed her husband and his regiment to Plymouth where they prepared to sail for Canada. Jacintha gave birth to a son (who died young) while in Plymouth, and in April Thomas Hesketh embarked with his regiment on to a transport vessel lying at Cattewater harbour in Plymouth Sound, awaiting a fair wind to sail for their destination of Quebec.[100] Jacintha and their children sailed with him.

Canada had been held by the British for ten years when Captain Hesketh sailed but, with virtually the entire population speaking French and growing unrest among the Canadians with regard to British rule, the Royal Fusiliers were being sent out there as part of a strong military presence to quell any sign of revolt. Jacintha, with her military family history, followed the example of her namesake grandmother in deciding to gather up her children and follow her husband rather than remain in England without him. The lure of an adventure and travel appealed to her, as indeed it did to other female descendants of the Browns of Blackburn who courageously exhibited a considerable spirit of adventure and a love of travel, not least among whom was Grace herself.

So who would Grace turn to at this time other than Lord Valentia himself? The obvious choice would be her older brother Henry Hew Dalrymple, resident in London and now head of her family. Her aunt Robinaiana might have been induced to step in, but would not have wished to connect herself too publicly with her scandalous niece lest her own less than impeccable past was brought up and paraded for public view. Robinaiana had an unmarried daughter to think of as well, one who was about Grace's age, and so wisely sidestepped the controversy.

So it was probably to Henry Hew that the burden of sorting out Grace's tangled situation fell. Her extended family did try to persuade Eliot to take back his wife but to no avail; he had decided that he was going to petition for divorce.

A divorce, or Criminal Conversation case (Crim. Con. for short), was not an easy process. The law at the time viewed a married woman as part of the property or goods of her husband, hence Crim. Con. saw the husband suing for compensation due to the loss of his 'property' rights. Aside from financial compensation there were then two avenues open to the aggrieved husband: a parliamentary divorce that enabled both parties to remarry if they so wished, or a legal separation. The latter option was the crueller one, for not being able to remarry during the lifetime of the husband was a further vengeance on the adulterous wife, who would remain dependent on whatever pittance she was provided from her cuckolded spouse to prevent her falling into penury. Luckily for Grace her husband preferred the first option, a parliamentary divorce, as Eliot had no legitimate heir and so did not want to deny himself the chance of a future marriage and begetting an heir.

The documentary evidence would suggest that Lord Valentia, if he had promised Grace that he would look after her, did not keep his word, for Grace was just one of his many conquests. The *Town and Country Magazine* ended its report on Grace and Valentia's infidelities thus:

> ... we shall therefore conclude this history with an extraordinary laconic billet, which he [Dr Eliot] received from his wife after their separation.
>
> 'I should be the happiest woman in the world, if you and lord V__ were both dead.'
>
> From which we may conclude that our hero and heroine do not now live upon the most agreeable terms; as his infidelities are, probably, to her as mortifying, after having sacrificed her reputation for his sake, as her perfidy must have been to her husband.

On 14 June 1774 the *Middlesex Journal and Evening Advertiser* reported that Grace, described as the beautiful young wife of the 'Cucumber Physician', had recently made a short excursion with Valentia, but finding she did not much like her new choice had written a penitent letter to her husband, begging him to allow her to return to his house.[101] Eliot, the paper reported, had refused her request and remained bent on a divorce. Seven days later the same papers carried another titbit of gossip; if true, Grace would seem to have been spurned by both men:

> The celebrated Dr. E., has, we hear, received a letter from his *fair penitent*, desiring him to shoot Lord V. for which he will get himself sent to a certain spot, a little way on the Oxford Road, by which method she will get quit of a couple of *rogues* together.[102]

The certain spot on the Oxford Road referred to the gallows at Tyburn where felons would be taken from Newgate prison to meet their end. Would Grace really have been pleased to see her husband swing there? Certainly his status as a society physician would not have saved him from the noose if he had murdered his rival. Laurence Shirley, the 4th Earl of Ferrers, swung at Tyburn in 1760 for murder, even though he was thought to be insane, and the Reverend William Dodd was executed there for forgery in 1777.

Reports suggest that Lord Valentia and Grace did temporarily rekindle their amour towards the end of the year but parted for good early in 1775 while negotiations for the ensuing divorce began to be put into place:

> Yesterday a writ of enquiry of damages was executed at a tavern in Holborn, concerning the matter of crim.con. between the buxom young wife of a little physician at the West end of the town and Lord V. when it was agreed to settle the matter on such terms as to ground an amiable action for a divorce.[103]

Dr John Eliot's Crim. Con. case took almost two years to be heard. Representing Eliot were Dr Buller and William Wynne and for Grace, Dr Harris and Peter Calvert, all four men Doctors of Law.[104] At the trial Eliot's servants William Constable, Charles Ryder and Thomas Sneed all took to the stand to give evidence against their former mistress, with Mrs Jane Price and her servant Sarah Race confirming that Grace and Valentia were at the Berkeley Row bagnio. Two men were called to confirm that Jane Price's house was one of ill repute. The first of these, John Bolton, stated that 'it was looked upon by the Neighbours as a House for the Reception of Ladies and Gentlemen for Gallantry.' The second man, Richard Cosway, gave similar evidence. Richard Cosway was, incidentally, the famous miniature painter who lived at

4 Berkeley Row. A miniature of Grace painted either just before or during the early days of her marriage is attributed to him, so Eliot would have known Cosway as someone who lived close to the bagnio and who could be asked to testify as to the character of the house.

At last, in March 1776, Grace's marriage was finally over. Dr Eliot won the day and secured a full divorce, allowing both he and Grace to marry again if they wished. He had also secured damages against Valentia to the sum of £12,000, with the proviso that Eliot had to pay an allowance of £200 to Grace for the rest of her life but, even allowing for this annuity and the cost to him during their marriage for her bills at her mantua-makers, milliners and jewellers, as well as her gambling debts which he paid, Dr Eliot escaped his marriage with his wealth intact, if not his reputation. Grace escaped with neither.

Grace was asked to nominate two men to act as her trustees in the matter of her annuity from Eliot. She chose her uncle by marriage, Charles Mordaunt 4th Earl of Peterborough, and Stephen Lushington of Henrietta Street in Covent Garden. The Earl of Peterborough was a wise choice: Eliot was being reminded that Grace had influential relatives behind her and he would presumably think twice before baulking on his payments when a peer of the realm was involved. Stephen Lushington as a choice of trustee is a little more puzzling. He had no obvious connection to Grace and perhaps had been recommended by the Earl of Peterborough. However, it is intriguing that Henry Hew Dalrymple, Grace's elder brother, was not named as one of the trustees.

John Eliot did not remarry, although shortly after his divorce there were rumours that he was betrothed to the portly Madame Schwellenberg, one of Queen Charlotte's ladies. His career, however, continued to flourish and in 1774, around the same time that he separated from Grace, he purchased Grove House in Kensington Gore, Knightsbridge from Mrs Ann Pitt, William Pitt the Elder's sister.[105] Ann Pitt had herself purchased Grove House in 1765 and lived there until she left to travel to Italy. Horace Walpole wrote to his friend Horace Mann about the sale, comparing Grove House (which Walpole referred to as Pittsburgh) to the Knightsbridge house of the infamous Elizabeth Chudleigh, Duchess of Kingston, who was accused of bigamy:

> Strawberry Hill, 8th June 1774 … I am sorry to tell Mrs. Pitt that her house in Knightsbridge has been led astray, the moment she turned her back: see what it is to live in a bad neighbourhood! *Pittsburgh*, the Temple of Vesta, is as naughty as Villa Kingstoniana; not that Dr. Elliot's pretty wife has married another husband in his lifetime; but she has eloped with my Lord

Valentia, who has another wife and some half-dozen children. The sages of Doctors' Commons are soon to be applied to.

Grace's journey in her coach to the Berkeley Row bagnio on that disastrous night in April suggested that she departed from Eliot's Cecil Street house; the first stage of her journey was along the Strand in the direction of Spring Gardens which does not fit with her leaving from Grove House. Hence we can say with reasonable certainty that Eliot did not make the move to Kensington until after Grace had visited the Berkeley Row bagnio. Was he hastily making a new beginning for himself or had he been intending to move both himself and his beautiful young wife into this much grander residence, only to discover her infidelities and find himself living there alone? Both scenarios are possible but he did retain his house on Cecil Street, living at Grove House for just a few years before returning to his old address. Most reports agree that Eliot threw his wife out of his house, but perhaps it should be a consideration that Eliot simply bought Grove House shortly after his wife's indiscretions and moved himself and his servants there, temporarily leaving Grace behind in the more modest Cecil Street house, thus effectively illustrating to her just what she had thrown away?

Dr John Eliot was knighted in 1776 and a baronetcy followed two years later. He became physician to the Prince of Wales and, had Grace remained his wife, she would have been entitled to be styled as Lady Eliot and would have had the impressive Grove House as her town residence, from which she could throw grand balls and become a society hostess. Had the divorce never happened, had she become Lady Grace Eliot, mistress of Grove House, then history would have remembered her marriage to Dr Eliot in a very different light. Regardless of the age difference, by the standards of the time he wasn't such a bad catch for her, a girl with good connections, beautiful but lacking any fortune to bring to a marriage.

Sir John Eliot, after his brief sojourn in Knightsbridge, returned to his Cecil Street home and fathered three more illegitimate daughters, each by a different mother.

The first of these was Ann, daughter of Ann Evans who hailed from a small village near Llangadog in Carmarthenshire. Born on 7 April 1779, this daughter was not baptized until 19 April 1781 at St Martin-in-the-Fields, recorded in the baptism register as the daughter of John and Ann Eliot.

Almost two years to the day after this, on 18 April 1783, the second daughter, Marianne, was born. She was probably baptized three weeks later at the Percy Chapel in St Pancras as the daughter of John Edwards and Lucy Thompson.[106] Whether Sir John was aka John Edwards for the day or whether Lucy Thompson passed off her daughter as the child of another man is not known, but Lucy used the surname Edwards latterly. The youngest of the three daughters was born the following year on 10 July 1784 to Martha Stringer and named Mary Davidson Eliot in honour of Sir John's mother.

The details of the last few months of Sir John Eliot's life are given in the letter written by his eldest illegitimate daughter, Elizabeth, to her half-brother John in 1806.[107] She had always been promised a handsome fortune from her father and, in the late spring and early summer of 1786, Sir John wished to bring her out into society. Unwilling to acknowledge her as his bastard offspring, he asked her to change her surname, to leave her mother and to allow him to introduce her as his niece and not his daughter. Regardless of the material benefits this might have brought her, Elizabeth would not agree. Her mother, Jane Jackson, was ill, Elizabeth thought her death not too far off and she told her father that while her mother still lived, she could not do as he wished.

Speaking of her mother in her letter, she said it 'would have been doubly cruel if I had done so, as I must have exposed her to every kind of indignity and have added to the affliction he [Eliot] had already heaped on her.' Eliot was furious with his daughter and told her that she would be severely punished for her determination. In, as Elizabeth describes it, 'a storm of passion and resentment' Eliot sat down on 8 June 1786 to write his last will and testament.

Instead of the handsome fortune she had been promised, Elizabeth was granted the trifling sum of £20 per year for the term of her life and she was not designated in the will as his child, as her half-siblings were, but simply referred to as Elizabeth Jackson, daughter of Jane Jackson, a tea dealer living on Tottenham Court Road Terrace.

It is an intriguing insight into the character of Dr John Eliot, proving him to be a self-important, vindictive and cruel man, interested only in himself with little or no understanding of the feelings and needs of others. He also appears incapable of sustaining a relationship with one woman having, including Grace and their son, sired six children by six different mothers and, with the exception of Grace from whom he must have hoped for a legitimate heir, moving on from each one once he had used them. If he was in 'a storm of passion and resentment' when Elizabeth rebuffed his wishes, then he must have been positively apoplectic when Grace was the one who moved on from him to another. In fairness to him though, it must be noted that his surviving children were all born either well before or after his marriage with Grace: there was no hint of any adultery on Eliot's part other than the mention of his pretty milliner, Mrs G___.

The other illegitimate Eliot children were treated more kindly in his will, as were two of his mistresses, and besides generous bequests he requested that his 'three daughters' take his surname and therefore become entitled to bear his arms, all the while brutally ignoring Elizabeth. His son John was to inherit the bulk of his fortune and instructions were left at the end of the will for a plan by which he might also gain Eliot's Scottish estates. Grace received a brief mention in the will when he asked his executors to ensure that her settlement of £200 per year continued to be paid from his estate as long as she lived. She could expect nothing more from him and nothing more was given.

A boy by the name of William Banks received the sum of £600 in two bequests. Sir John Eliot had been asked to take care of this boy at the request of Captain and Mrs Robert Noble of the cutter *Expedition* and had boarded the boy with a Mrs Pillet in Edgware Road, where his daughter Ann lived, and with a Mr Harrison of St Clements.[108] William Banks was also to be given two suits of Sir John Eliot's clothes 'such as are fit for him' and all of Sir John's 'coarser stockings'. He left enough to cover one year's board at Mr Harrison's and asked that Banks be returned to Captain Noble at the end of this time unless the executors of his will were able to 'dispose of him better'.

The woman in Sir John's life at this point was a Mrs Hotham, an opportunist who 'perpetually tormented' him to leave all his fortune to her daughter rather than to his illegitimate brood, despite the Hotham daughter having no biological connection to Sir John. Perhaps partly to escape this woman, perhaps to put his argument with his daughter Elizabeth from his mind, but also because he was feeling unwell, Sir John Eliot undertook a sea voyage from Gravesend around the southern coast of England to Torbay and from Torbay to the Western Islands, otherwise the Outer Hebrides, off the north-west coast of Scotland.[109] At the end of April 1786 the newspapers were reporting that Sir John was dangerously ill of a 'complaint in the stomach' and he travelled to the Bristol Hot Wells to take the waters; this had such a restorative effect that he quickly regained his appetite and was described as recovering.[110]

He was on the Hebridean islands towards the end of July when Dr William Macleod of Luskentyre on the Isle of Harris wrote to Alexander Gillanders on Lewis, telling him that Sir John Eliot was convalescing in the area and wanted some of Gillanders' honey.[111] Macleod, described by the Reverend John Lane Buchanan, a missionary at Harris, as 'our little tyrannical country Surgeon', said he might call on Sir John at Stornoway on the neighbouring Isle of Lewis. In order to persuade Gillanders to send the honey, Macleod

reminded him of some service that Eliot had performed to Gillanders' kins-
men who went out to India.[112]

The change of scenery also wrought a change in Sir John Eliot for, on his
return, he let Elizabeth know that she was back in his favour and he had
decided to alter his will when he reached London, signalling, as Elizabeth put
it, that Mrs Hotham's reign over Sir John was ended. After disembarking
from his ship, Sir John first went to pay a visit to his friend Peniston Lamb,
Lord Melbourne, at his estate of Brocket Hall in Bishop's Hatfield, Hertfordshire en route to London. The two men had known each other for many
years: in the early 1770s when Melbourne's lover, the actress and courtesan
Sophia Baddeley, was unwell, Melbourne had requested that Dr Eliot be sent
for to attend her. Sir John reached Brocket Hall but he was never to see
London again and so lost the chance to change the will he had written in
anger. He died at Lord Melbourne's estate on 7 November 1786 of a burst
blood vessel and was buried in the Melbourne family vault.

Martha Stringer did not recover from the shock of Sir John Eliot's death
and 'fell a martyr to grief for her indiscretion a few months after Sir John',
leaving her daughter Mary Davidson Eliot an orphan before she was 3 years
old. Elizabeth was a constant friend to her young half-sister until Mary died
in 1804 at the age of only 20 years and 3 days after a six-week consumptive
illness. Mary left a brief will in which she mentioned her sister Elizabeth and
also Elizabeth Penhallow who had been Sir John Eliot's housekeeper, suggesting that the housekeeper, after the death of both Sir John and Martha
Stringer in quick succession, had looked after the little orphaned girl they left
behind.[113]

Elizabeth was sanguine about her fortune, or rather the lack of it. At
St Pancras on 28 March 1790 and under the name of Elizabeth Jackson, she
married John Ogborne, a successful engraver. They owned a house on Great
Portland Street in London and had a long and happy marriage, Elizabeth
living a full ninety years. John Ogborne contributed engravings to *A History
of Essex*, of which Elizabeth was the author. The couple had just one son,
John Fauntleroy Ogborne, who died in 1813 aged only 20 years in a cruel
echo of Mary Davidson Eliot's untimely death nine years earlier.

Although Grace did receive her annuity, the executors of Sir John Eliot's
will and testament, his uncle William Davidson and James Macpherson
Esquires, left the will unadministered and it was not until August 1797 that
administration was finally granted to John Mackenzie Esquire, the executor
of James Macpherson who was then also deceased. Mackenzie had been
appointed by the High Court of Chancery as the guardian of Ann, Mary
Davidson and Marianne Eliot, and upon Mackenzie's own death Ann Eliot

managed the situation so that all Sir John Eliot's affairs fell into her power and she behaved insolently to her sisters. Elizabeth was sure this had contributed to Mary's early death. Ann Eliot died at York Place in Portman Square in November 1827, unmarried.

John Eliot junior became a writer in the East India Company. It is often a case of like father, like son, and the son did indeed follow in the footsteps of the father in terms of his private life. While living in India, John fathered no fewer than eight illegitimate children, some by a woman named Elizabeth (Betsy) O'Brien. On 5 October 1816 at St John's in Calcutta John married Augusta Thackeray, the sister of his late friend Richmond Makepeace Thackeray.[114] The marriage was to be short-lived and childless; John Eliot died at the age of 55 in January 1818 and was buried at Fort William in Bengal.

One wonders how Grace received the news of Sir John Eliot's death. She would have been around 32 years old, still marriageable, still able to bear children and, had she been a wealthy and beautiful widow instead of a divorced woman with a ruined reputation, could have had every expectation of marrying well for a second time, this time perhaps to someone better suited to her. However, she had thrown away any chance of such a future some twelve years earlier at the Berkeley Row bagnio with the worthless Lord Valentia.

Chapter Nine

A Celebrated Courtesan

The preface to Grace's own *Journal of My Life during the French Revolution* states that at around the time of her divorce 'her brother removed her to a convent in France, assigning as a reason for the course which had been adopted, that the lady was about to contract an unsuitable marriage.'

While the preface does contain inaccuracies, it seems odd to totally fabricate such an act on the part of her brother. Therefore Henry Hew – for it had to be him as Grace's other brother, Robert, was in India – played some part in trying to hush the breaking scandal and removed his chastened sister from the scenes of her crime by inducing her into a French convent. For Grace, who had been educated in such a convent, her family would have viewed this as a safe place in which she could temporarily hide and be secluded from the world and her lover, not a long-term arrangement. However, if she was sent there to prevent an unsuitable marriage, it could not have been to Lord Valentia as he was already a married man.

In early 1775 Grace separated for good from Lord Valentia and began her career as a demirep. A shortened form of 'demi-reputation', this denoted a woman of little or no virtue, basically a courtesan or high-class prostitute. Styled as such, Grace now entered into an 'amour with a rich young coxcomb named William Bird, who a year or two later became famous as the paramour of Lady Percy.'

William Bird, only a few years older than Grace and with a family estate at Coventry, must have been the unsuitable match prevented by the actions of Henry Hew.[115] He was small fry, however, compared to Grace's next conquest, one to whom her family would have been only too happy to have sanctioned marriage. It was reported that she met George James, 4th Earl of Cholmondeley, at Hampton Court. From the *Town and Country Magazine*:

> Mrs. E___tt had just been divorced from the Doctor. She had lately had a rupture with lord V___a and was ripe for revenge. Mr B__d fell in her way when she had just come to the pious resolution of being truly benevolent to the first fine fellow that should importune her ... He found her a very agreeable, though a very easy conquest. She bore the belle at the head of female cornuters and Mr. B__d was envied for his good fortune by half the beaux garcons about town.

The article states that the alliance might have continued

> if family affairs had not called him into the country. During his absence she
> for some time bemoaned the absence of her mate; but Mr. B___ having
> remained longer from town than he expected, she began to find that a state
> of widow-hood did not suit her constitution and she thought it was time to
> look out for another paramour. Having come to this determination, being
> on a party at Hampton Court, lord Ch_____y fell into her company; he
> said many civil things to her and threw out several oblique hints, which
> she could not possibly misconstrue; in a word, upon Mr. B___'s return to
> town he found his mistress was in the arms of lord Ch_____y.

If the *Town and Country Magazine* is to be believed, Grace sent a letter to
William Bird, left for him at the St James's Coffee House, alluding to the loss
of the title of Lady Eliot:

> I hope you will not blame me for the step I have taken. I will not blame you
> for your long absence; perhaps business occasioned it, but having lost one
> title by my imprudence, I thought it would be an act of indiscretion to let
> so fair an opportunity slip of sporting a coronet. I acknowledge I have
> ambition and the bait was too tempting. In a word, to afford you some con-
> solation, I was more in love with my new chariot than with his lordship.

John Eliot did not gain his knighthood until after the date of this purported
letter, but the fact remains that Lord Cholmondeley was a much more
attractive catch for Grace than poor Mr Bird.

George James Cholmondeley, born in 1749 and educated at Eton, was only
a few years older than Grace and was her match aesthetically, being tall and
handsome. His father, Viscount Malpas, Colonel of the 65th Regiment, died
at a young age in 1764 five days after returning home from his regiment
in Ireland, so George had succeeded his grandfather to the title of Earl of
Cholmondeley in 1770. His grandfather George, 3rd Earl of Cholmondeley,
was described by Horace Walpole as a 'vain empty man ... fallen into contempt and obscurity by his own extravagance and insufficiency'.[116] The
young earl was everything that Dr Eliot was not and, moreover, was unmarried.

The *Town and Country Magazine*, in yet another of its *tête-à-tête* articles in
1778, described Cholmondeley as 'the Whimsical Lover'. As his father had
devoted his life to dissipation and pleasure, the article claimed that the son,
George James, followed suit in his father's footsteps, although it is a much
jumbled article ascribing to the son events obviously relating to the father.[117]

In some ways, Lord Cholmondeley's childhood experiences had mirrored those of Grace's uncle by marriage, the 4th Earl of Peterborough, for Viscount Malpas had died intestate, leaving his family (George James had one sister, Hester) ill provided for and dependent upon their grandfather, the 3rd Earl of Cholmondeley.

This situation had reversed when George James became the 4th Earl at a young age upon the death of his grandfather and, just into his majority, he suddenly found that he had plenty with which to enjoy himself. The young earl is generally described as a convivial man, with a hearty appetite both for fine women and good food. He was a known gambler but was canny enough to take charge of the faro bank at Brooks's, thereby making a profit out of his peers and never sustaining too great a loss.

Brooks's was a noted gentlemen's club on St James's Street in Westminster; faro (or pharo), a card game popular at the time with good odds of winning, was played with a 'banker' and any number of players. The Honourable Charles James Fox, MP, an inveterate gambler who was a contemporary of Cholmondeley's at Eton and a fellow member of Brooks's, was known to prefer the game of faro to any other card game:

> [Lord Cholmondeley] was one of the four who set up that celebrated faro bank at Brooke's [*sic*] which ruined half the town. They would not trust the waiters to be croupiers, but themselves dealt the cards alternately, being paid three guineas an hour out of the joint fund and at this rate, Lord C___ and other noblemen of the highest rank, were seen slaving like menials till a late hour in the morning. Their gains were enormous, as Mr. Thompson of Grosvenor Square and Lord Cholmondeley realized each between 300,000 and 400,000 pounds. Tom Stepney had a share, but would always punt against his own partners and lost one side what he gained on the other. A Mr. Paul, who brought home a large fortune from India, lost 90,000 in one night, was ruined and went back to the East.[118]

Cholmondeley was, some years later, to make a bet at Brooks's – one of the many eccentric wagers placed in the notorious club – that he would ascend in a hot air balloon to a height of 6,000 feet, with Grace by his side, and 'perform in the aerial regions, the usual ceremonial rites, paid at the shrine of the laughter-loving queen'. The bet of 5,000 guineas was readily accepted by several men who thought the experiment impossible.

The earl attracted a variety of nicknames, playing on his size and physical attributes, 'the Athletic Peer' being one of the least offensive of these jibes. He was also known as 'The Torpedo' and a poem published in 1777 titled

The Torpedo, a poem to the Electrical Eel, addressed to the surgeon John Hunter but dedicated to Cholmondeley, immortalized his manhood in verse:

What tho' Lord CH—LM—D—LY may conceal
A most enormous length of Eel,
Admire'd for size and bone:
This mighty thing when lank, depress'd,
A mere noun adjective at best,
Is useless when alone.

But warm'd by ELL-T'S wanton Wife,
The ponderous body feels new life,
Prepar'd to give the stroke,
Erect in all the pride of Nature,
E'en then to please this beauteous Creature,
It stoops to wear my yoke.

The *Royal Register*, writing in 1780, takes a similar tone, describing him as

the Hero of Debauchery and Prostitution … pursuing such conduct as, to become a bye-word for certain vices, to be the burthen of every dirty song, the theme of every scandalous chronicle, and the boast of every abandoned brothel … a man who has lost the sense of moral rectitude and has no bounds for his sensual indulgence but those which are prescribed by the terrors of the law, or the more yielding pandects of modern honour.

This then was the man who next captivated Grace's attentions, and despite the scurrilous gossip, he was also a man of honour, dependable and reliable. The first public account of Grace being together with Lord Cholmondeley is to be found in an account of a masquerade at the Pantheon, reported in the *Morning Post* newspaper dated 27 January 1776:

ACCOUNT OF THE PANTHEON MASQUERADE
The Masqued Ball on Wednesday evening last at the Pantheon, tho' in point of company it might fall short of the expectations of the managers, was the best conducted of any masquerade that ever was given at that house. The great room was rendered unusually brilliant from the disposition of the lamps, which, being of one colour, gave a delicacy to the general illumination that charmed the eye of every observer: - the dome was remarkably striking.

The company, as usual, was of the mixed kind; composed rather too much of the lower orders, on account of the severity of the weather, which confining many families of distinction at their country seats, prevented their appearance at this Masque. At twelve o'clock there were about 1,200 persons collected together, about two thirds of which were in Dominos and these in reality were the only spirited part of the assembly, for the *characters* were in general as silent and stupid as dullness herself could have desired.

At the top of the *free and easy* were seen the *sentimental* Mrs. *Ell__t* and the pretty Mrs. *M___n*, having each an arm of Lord *Ch____ley*, who was well known, tho' he did not unmask the whole evening, for his lordship by the cautious singularity of his *disguise* and his close attention to a *certain bewitched widow*, rendered himself obviously conspicuous.

Mrs M___n was Gertrude Mahon, also known as 'The Bird of Paradise'. As tiny as Grace was tall, the two became firm friends; Grace, because of her height, revelled in the nickname 'Dally the Tall'. Horace Bleackley called Gertrude a Lilliputian beauty. Her parents were James Tilson, 'a gay and popular Irishman', and the widowed Countess of Kerry. Tilson, upon his marriage to the widowed countess, had built a mansion, Bolesworth Castle, near Malpas in Cheshire.

The Cholmondeley family held an estate in Malpas, and although the Tilson estate was sold in 1763, perhaps it was Gertrude who invited Grace to the Hampton Court party and introduced her to Cholmondeley? Her nickname, 'The Bird of Paradise', came from her love of bright colours: Bleackley said of her that 'her caps and gowns were of the most vivid hues, which few except herself would have ventured to wear.' Gertrude met, and was seduced by, an Irish gamester called Gilbreath Mahon. Knowing that her mother would never allow her to marry a man without wealth or lineage, she eloped with him. The marriage, although happy to begin with, soon unravelled in the face of rejection from Gertrude's relatives and a lack of money, and Gilbreath Mahon ran away with a Miss Russell. Therefore, at about the same time as Grace, Gertrude found herself in a matrimonial limbo and both had the disposition to enjoy their new-found freedom. Gertrude Mahon's mother, Lady Kerry, died in October 1775 and left her fortune to her favoured daughter, so Gertrude, during this period, had money in her pockets and a friend in Grace to help her enjoy spending it.

By the time Lord Cholmondeley (the Athletic Peer) was seen arm-in-arm with the two at the Pantheon, Grace and Gertrude had

for some time ... been inseparable friends, kindred spirits by reason of their matrimonial mishaps and all who observed their close comradeship agreed in thinking that from the standpoint of virtue there was little to choose between them. Further than this 'the Athletic Peer' seemed as devoted to his tiny friend as to his tall one and the journalist did not scruple to hint that he was on equally good terms with both of them.[119]

Another grand masquerade was held at Carlisle House on 19 February; Grace was mentioned in passing in a newspaper report as being in attendance on the night among the 800 guests.[120] The gossip among society was that, once her divorce was finally settled, her lover Lord Cholmondeley would propose marriage to Grace. Six weeks after the Pantheon Masquerade, it was whispered that 'the buz of yesterday amongst the ton was that Lord C____y had actually engaged to marry Mrs E___t, as soon as her husband's divorce bill had received the Royal assent.'[121]

Could Grace really have been expecting marriage? The simple answer is that, yes, she probably did hope for a proposal from Cholmondeley. If her aunt Robinaiana captivated an earl to such an extent that he made her his countess, then why should Grace not hope for a similar ending to her own story? Of course, the difference between the two women was that Robinaiana, while she was prepared to sacrifice her reputation to be kept as a mistress, was not divorced and had not graced the gossip columns of the papers as her wayward niece had done, and Cholmondeley, despite his title, was still to a degree dependent upon relations.

Cholmondeley's grandmother had been Mary Walpole, daughter of Robert Walpole, 1st Earl of Orford. At the time of Cholmondeley's attachment to Grace the 3rd Earl of Orford was unmarried and had only an illegitimate daughter; the next in line, the 3rd Earl's uncle Edward, was also unmarried with three illegitimate daughters; and after him was the renowned correspondent Horace Walpole, a confirmed bachelor. Lord Cholmondeley, although he could not succeed to the Orford earldom, had high hopes of being left their seat of Houghton Hall in Norfolk when the Walpoles ran out of direct and legitimate heirs and the last thing he wanted was to upset his Walpole relations who could easily disinherit him in favour of another. Horace Walpole certainly did not want to see his great-nephew married to Grace and had no difficulty in letting his great-nephew know of his views. In addition, Cholmondeley, a young man-about-town, was disinclined towards marriage at this stage of his life, instead much preferring to keep a mistress.

It was the custom of the day for a wealthy young man to have a mistress or a courtesan and to pay for her dresses, jewels and carriage and provide her with her own establishment. She was an outward sign of his wealth and enhanced his image among his peers. In return, for a time at least while her star waxed high, a courtesan could expect a good lifestyle and a degree of notoriety about town. The newspapers regularly reported on the 'Cyprian Corps' as they were termed, and although some courtesans did indeed manage to make a good marriage to their protector, most did not. Grace's earl provided a house and establishment for her in Dean Street, a quiet road in Mayfair leading to Park Lane and Hyde Park, for Cholmondeley appears in the land tax records for this address in the years 1778 to 1780 in addition to his own address. Now called Deanery Street, it sounds like a desirable address but, at the time when Grace was housed there, it was on the periphery and one gets the impression that Grace was discreetly tucked away in a quiet corner by her earl. Having only seven houses along its length, all on the same side of the street, Cholmondeley's name is listed last for each year, suggesting that Grace occupied No. 7, the furthest from polite view.

A century later Dean Street was described as

> a narrow and winding thoroughfare, leading behind Dorchester House into South Audley Street … It is clearly only an enlargement of a rural bye-road, probably worn by the wheels of carts and wagons proceeding from the market-gardens of Pimlico to the market in the Brook Field … It consists of some half-a-dozen small houses, on one side only of the street, and has few reminiscences, social, literal, or political.[122]

Dean Street does now after all have a social reminiscence, as the residence of Grace Dalrymple Elliott when she was mistress of the Earl of Cholmondeley.

Grace and Cholmondeley, soon after their appearance at the masquerade, also took up residence at his house in Roehampton.[123] Then a village lying close to London, Roehampton is now swallowed up by its urban sprawl but, in the late eighteenth century, there were many grand houses enjoying the rural setting within its environs. The diarist John Baker, barrister and solicitor general of the Caribbean Leeward Islands, recorded an encounter with the couple:

> [7 June 1776] … Came in through Richmond Park and through Roehampton (just before came into which met a Lady walking under a Gentleman's arm – Cousin Jo. told us it was Lord Cholmondeley and Mrs. Elliot (the doctor's wife divorced on account of Lord Valentia) of whom Lord Cholmondeley is exceeding fond and has her with him at his house in Roehampton.[124]

In the summer of 1776 Grace had also been taking the sea air in Kent, staying with her lover at Kingsgate House, owned by the Honourable Charles James Fox.[125] Fox was a fitting companion for Grace and Cholmondeley, a rake and a gamester, but he was also at this time a staunch opponent of the British involvement in the American War of Independence, a war in which Grace's brother-in-law Thomas Hesketh was involved. Jacintha Hesketh was in America with her husband and, even though there had been a rupture between the two sisters since Grace's divorce, she would have known of the dangers and hardships her sister and brother-in-law were facing.

When the Heskeths sailed for Canada in the spring of 1773 their household furniture was left behind but, realizing that they were not coming home any time soon, a year later the decision was made to sell their belongings to raise funds and the sale provides an interesting glimpse into their possessions at the time:

> To be sold by Auction by John Sherrott, on Tuesday next, to begin at eleven precisely. All the genuine Household Furniture of Capt. HESKETH, in Little Hermitage-Street, near the Hermitage, Wapping; consisting of fourpost Bedsteads, with printed Cotton Furniture, Feather-Beds and Bedding, Mahogany-Chairs, Dining, Card and Tea Tables, Pier, Sconce and Chimney-glasses, in carved and gilt Frames, an Eight-Day Clock, neat Brass fronted Stoves, a Parcel of fine useful China and bound Books, Kitchen Furniture, Brass and Pewter.[126]

In Canada, while the regiment was stationed at Quebec and around the same time as the sale, Thomas and Jacintha's daughter Dorothea was born.[127] Also with the Royal Fusiliers in Canada was Lieutenant John Despard, an Irishman born in 1744 in Dublin who travelled to Quebec in 1773, returning home the following year to recruit and going back to rejoin his regiment in May 1775.

Despard was a friend of the family and had been one of the witnesses to the wedding of Jacintha's cousin, Catharina Pitcairn, to the Honourable Charles Cochrane Esquire, younger son of the 8th Earl of Dundonald, at the same church in Rochester where the Heskeths had married with Catharina as their witness.[128] It was another military wedding as Charles Cochrane was also an officer in the army. Did Thomas Hesketh take the opportunity of Despard's return to England in 1774 to instruct him to arrange the sale of the Heskeths' belongings? With Jacintha determined to remain abroad, Grace knew that she had no chance of help from her sister during her separation and subsequent divorce and the two sisters were not to meet again for many years.

The year 1775 marked the commencement of the American War of Independence. Captain Thomas Hesketh's younger brother Robert had followed in his military footsteps and was also present in America with the British army. Robert Hesketh was to see action at the Battle of Bunker Hill during the Siege of Boston, Massachusetts and in the ensuing battle he was fatally wounded:[129] 'At Boston, in America, Robert Hesketh, Esq. Ensign in the

14th Regiment of Foot, Nephew to Sir Thomas Hesketh, Bart. occasioned by the Wounds he received at the Battle of Bunker's Hill, near Boston.'[130]

Jacintha also lost her uncle in the same battle: Major John Pitcairn, in whose family Jacintha had lived at the time of her marriage, had led a force of marines and was killed by a musket shot.

With the realities of war now fully evident to Captain Hesketh and his young wife, September 1775 saw the Royal Fusiliers as part of a British force defending Fort St Jean on the Richelieu River in Quebec, besieged by the American forces led by Brigadier General Richard Montgomery. The wives who had followed their husbands took refuge in nearby Montreal. While the siege was ongoing (and one can only imagine her mindset at the time, fearful for the safety of her husband and still grieving for her brother-in-law and uncle), Jacintha gave birth to another daughter, named Jacinthia-Catherine, on 31 October.[131]

This is the first documented use of the name (or variant thereof) of Jacintha in the Hesketh family and this young Jacinthia-Catherine, perhaps to differentiate her from her mother, was known as Jessy-Catherine to her family.

In Quebec the defenders of Fort St Jean were hopelessly outnumbered and the fall of a nearby fort, coupled with multiple cannon batteries shelling their position, led to their surrender on 3 November, just six weeks after the siege began. Among the many British officers taken prisoner that day were Captain Thomas Hesketh and Lieutenant John Despard. Captain Hesketh appears on the list of the 'Officers of the Royal Fusileers [*sic*] taken at St. John's, November 3, 1775' but with a note against his name saying that he was 'absent with General Montgomery's leave'.[132]

It seems Captain Hesketh was compassionately allowed by General Richard Montgomery, an Irishman who led the Continental Army under General George Washington during the invasion of Canada, to go to his wife and new daughter on his honour to return as a prisoner of war, and he did indeed return to be held in Philadelphia for almost a year, his wife and daughters joining him there. Although a prisoner of war, as an officer and a gentleman Captain Hesketh would have been housed in a style suited to his station and rank but at his own expense; his word would be his bond and, according to the rules of war, he would be trusted not to try to escape. Within certain limits, Captain Hesketh was free to come and go as he pleased and although the family no doubt suffered some discomforts and privations, on the whole Jacintha may have enjoyed having her husband near at hand and not engaged in any combat.

In December 1776 Thomas Hesketh was allowed to leave Philadelphia for New York, upon trust that the British would substitute another prisoner for him. No less a person than General Washington himself reported to the Board of War that

> I met Captain Hesketh on the road and as the situation of his family did not admit of delay, I permitted him to go immediately to New-York, not having the least doubt but General Howe will make a return of any officer of equal rank who shall be required.[133]

A prisoner exchange had already taken place between the American and British forces that included Lieutenant John Despard. Thomas Hesketh had not been included in this list but was subsequently added to it by General Washington, an addition necessitated by the 'situation of his family'. Jacintha was with him and it raises the interesting possibility that she had interceded with the general on behalf of her husband for she had an extremely pressing reason for wanting him released: she was heavily pregnant. So General Washington agreed, compassionately, to exchange her husband and specifically mentioned Jacintha in a letter to the British General Howe:

Brunswick, December 1st, 1776.
Sir,
I am to acknowledge the honour of your favour of the 11th ultimo and to thank you for your polite return of my letter to Mrs. Washington.

Agreeing to the proposition you were pleased to make for the exchange of such prisoners as can be conveniently collected, the gentlemen whose names are specified in the enclosed list, have permission to proceed immediately to New-York. Others, as soon as they arrive, will be allowed the same indulgence. At a proper season I shall require a return of the like number and of equal rank.

Having directions from Congress to propose an exchange of Governour Franklin for Brigadier-General Thompson, I would take the liberty to submit the matter to your determination and to request your answer upon the subject.

Besides the persons included in the enclosed list, Captain Hesketh, of the Seventh Regiment, his lady, three children and two servant maids, were permitted to go in a few days ago.

I am, sir, with due respect, your most obedient servant,
   Go. Washington
   To Lieutenant-General Howe.[134]

Jacintha, with her three young daughters in tow, must have been heartily relieved to reach New York and, just a month after that letter was written, she gave birth there to a son, Thomas Dalrymple Hesketh.[135] It is possible that when General Washington met Captain Hesketh and his family on the road, he passed on a letter for a young American captain in his own army, who was then in New York, asking Captain Hesketh to deliver it for him. For, on 30 November 1776, the same day upon which he met the Heskeths, General Washington wrote to Captain Alexander Graydon's mother, informing her that the letter to her son which she had enclosed to the general had been forwarded to him. Captain Graydon recorded the delivery of this letter in his memoirs:

> Between two and three weeks had elapsed, when I received a letter from my mother. It was brought by a Captain Hesketh, of the British army, who had been a prisoner with us. It acquainted me he had money for me; but a piece of intelligence of still greater consequence, was, that my brother was safe and at home ... I waited upon Captain Hesketh, found him at home and was very politely treated by both him and his lady, to whose notice I had been particularly recommended by Miss Amiel, of Philadelphia, a mutual acquaintance. Among other things, Mrs. Hesketh, who was most communicative, informed me, that they had met General Washington on their road, at the head of his army, which must indeed have been a small one; though this unwelcome truth being spared, I had not the courage to elicit it by any questions.

Another British army officer who had been taken prisoner after the Siege of Fort St Jean in 1775 was John André, a Londoner born to wealthy Franco/Swiss Huguenot parents. He had been held prisoner at Lancaster, Pennsylvania and had also been exchanged in December 1776. On 17 December 1776 he wrote to his mother to assure her that his troubles were over; he was now the 'guest of Captain Thomas Hesketh, an officer in the 7th Foot'. He was 'in perfect health, am in a good house by a good fire'. André's subsequent promotion to the British Secret Intelligence and his espionage work and traitorous correspondence with the American General Benedict Arnold in 1780 led to his execution by hanging later that year after he had been captured by the Americans.[136]

The Royal Fusiliers had established a headquarters at New York in 1777 and the Heskeths seem to have held something of an 'open house' in the city. Jacintha, with her fair share of her ancestral good looks, aristocratic origins and family connections must no doubt have made an admirable and charming hostess.

Back in England, probably unaware of most of her sister's experiences, Grace continued her amour with the Earl of Cholmondeley throughout 1776 and into the following year when she first had her portrait painted by Thomas Gainsborough. Undoubtedly it was the Earl of Cholmondeley who commissioned this painting.

Grace, in the full-length portrait, appears both stately and self-confident. She again wears a simple ribbon choker around her throat, as she did in the *tête-à-tête* image of her with Valentia in the 1774 *Town and Country Magazine*, her only other jewellery being a simple pair of earrings and a bracelet of strung pearls on either wrist, complementing her embellished gown of golden silk. Her eyebrows have been artificially darkened, possibly by rubbing them with burnt cork or cloves, both methods commonly used at the time, and her hair, which was a honey-blonde colour, was fashionably powdered. When the portrait was exhibited at the Royal Academy in Pall Mall during 1778, the *General Evening Post* newspaper called it a 'striking and beautiful likeness' of Grace, quoting some lines from *The Rape of the Lock* by Alexander Pope:[137] 'If to her share some female errors fall, Look on her face, and you'll forget them all.'

More details on the original portrait, lost over time due to its condition, are visible from the engraving made as a copy of it in 1779 by John Dean.[138] On his engraving can be seen a flagstone floor and a burst of light coming over the trees in the background. During treatment of Gainsborough's portrait of Grace, dark paint was visible under the sky suggesting that the picture may originally have been intended to be much narrower, possibly without the landscape in the background. The presence of a small dog that was once in the lower right-hand corner was also revealed.[139]

Around the time she was sitting for Gainsborough, Grace was seen about town sporting her earl's coronet on her carriage. The *Morning Post* reported on 16 July 1777 that

> the female friends of Miss Dal____le give out that she will be Countess of Ch_____y before the next sitting of Parliament: - however far the world may rely on this report, we will not pronounce, but she already sports his Lordship's coronet on her coach, which may be a prelude for aught we know, to something more absurd and ridiculous.

Her carriage was complemented by a pair of fine iron-grey geldings and she was attended by a suite of servants dressed in blue and silver liveries, an eye-catching and lovely sight when combined with her height, beauty and charms.[140]

However, while marriage may have been rumoured, and indeed wished for by Grace and her relatives, a proposal was still not forthcoming and Cholmondeley's relations were aghast at the mere fact that Grace was using his insignia. By early November 1777 the *Morning Post* was reporting that Lord Cholmondeley, probably at the instigation of his great-uncle Horace Walpole, had finally persuaded Grace to relinquish his coronet on her carriage, albeit with 'remonstrances, tears and threats' and with battle lines drawn between the couple. She had only acquiesced, it was hinted, after extracting a promise from her earl that she would be able to legitimately sport his coronet in her own right in the near future, although she must have realized that this was looking increasingly unlikely.[141] Perhaps sensing Cholmondeley's reluctance to marry her, certainly annoyed at his inflexibility over her use of his arms on her carriage, and possibly with a view to scouting for horizons new, Grace attended the first masquerade of the winter season dressed provocatively. The *Public Advertiser* reported on 27 November 1777, under the heading of 'Masquerade Intelligence', that

> On Tuesday Evening Mrs. Cornelys summoned the Votaries of Mirth and Festivity (for the first Time this Season) to an elegant and splendid Entertainment in the tasteful Mansions of Soho ... The *black Dominos* were, as usual, predominant and many assumed the Appearance of the opposite Sex; Men in Female Habits and Ladies in Mens Hats and Dominos, whilst some actually wore the Breeches – Mrs. Elliot was allowed to be a very pretty Boy.

The *Morning Post* of the same day gave additional information:

> Nothing could exceed the magnificence of the decorations on Tuesday night; nothing could be more dull and insipid, than the company ... We were surprised to find few or no persons of distinction in this inanimate assembly; and, what is more remarkable, very few of the fil'es de joye, were to be seen, who are generally deemed the life and soul, of a Masquerade. There were only four of any ton, D____ple, G____son, Benfield and Frederic, the last of whom seemed inconsolable, the whole evening, for the absence of her peer.

While Grace had been enjoying masquerades and sitting for her portrait, the ugly realities of war had once again become all too clear to Jacintha when her husband returned to the battle lines and received an injury, one serious enough to have a devastating and long-term effect on his health and to invalid him from the army. He returned home to his family estates in Lancashire with his wife and four young children, three of whom had never seen

England or their English relatives. Jacintha may have conceived again before her husband suffered his wounds, for upon their return to England a further daughter named Anne-Charlotte was born at Preston in Lancashire.[142]

Captain Hesketh's uncle, Sir Thomas Hesketh, died on 4 March 1778 and Jacintha's father-in-law ascended to the baronetcy, placing Jacintha one step closer to becoming Lady Hesketh. Yet, however close she was to that title, it was to remain out of her reach. Captain Hesketh continued an invalid and eventually succumbed to the wounds he had received, dying at Preston on 5 January 1782, his young son's fifth birthday. He was buried at Rufford eleven days later. The widowed Jacintha had one consolation in the midst of her grief. Possibly the fact had been unknown to her husband before his death but she had one further reminder of him: she was carrying another child and their daughter Lucy was born on 4 September that year.

Chapter Ten

From Maid to Countess

In 1756 Robinaiana, Grace's maternal aunt, had found herself in exactly the position her celebrated niece would covet for herself two decades later. The years of being a mistress had paid dividends, for Robinaiana's earl had made her his countess and, moreover, she was pregnant with her first legitimate child. A male heir would have to wait though, for on 30 June 1756 Robinaiana was once more delivered of a daughter, one she named after herself. In stark contrast with the baptisms of her illegitimate siblings in the clandestine chapel of St George's, this baptism took place in the splendid surroundings of St James's in Piccadilly, Westminster. Sadly, the little girl only survived for three months and was buried later that year in Rickmansworth in Hertfordshire, where there was a tomb containing some of the Earl of Peterborough's ancestors.[143]

Two years later Charles wrote his will, leaving everything to Robinaiana and appointing her as executrix.[144] He did not leave any other bequests or mention any other family members, not even his two daughters by his first wife. Perhaps this was an attempt to safeguard whatever he possessed as, less than two months later, the newspapers were finally able to announce: 'LONDON, Tuesday last the lady of the Right Hon. the Earl of Peterborough, was safely delivered of a son and heir.'[145]

The child had been born a week earlier, on 11 May 1758. He was named Charles Henry (both names having already been bestowed on two of his illegitimate older brothers) and baptized at St James's in Westminster.[146] One more child was to follow, another son named Paulet, the maiden surname of Charles's mother Frances in one of the many varied spellings of it, baptized on 2 August 1759, again at Westminster. A little over three months later Charles drew up a codicil to his will, declaring that, since it had been written, he had had two children born and appointed his wife Robinaiana guardian of these children and any others 'as I shall leave behind me'.

No further children were born to the couple and the last son Paulet was another casualty of the high infant mortality rate of the day, being buried alongside his sister Robinaiana in the family tomb at Rickmansworth on 1 July 1760. Robinaiana therefore was mother to the surviving son and heir,

Charles Henry, and his four illegitimate older siblings Charles, John, Harriat and Henry.

Quite what the Earl of Peterborough was like as a person is something of a mystery. Most writings on his family concentrate on his much more well-known grandfather, often referred to as the *celebrated* Earl of Peterborough and little has been recorded of his less than celebrated grandson. We do know that he wore spectacles, and the only contemporary report of him, apart from in the *Town and Country Magazine*, is to be found in the 1775 edition of the *Complete English Peerage*, which described him as 'Easy and convivial in his disposition, fond of company and the society of the world, perhaps uxorious to excess, this nobleman has some singularities in his temper which cannot fail to mark him as a whimsical character.'

By a 'whimsical character' we can deduce that the 4th Earl was perhaps an unusual person, given to impulsive, unpredictable or odd behaviour, but obviously as he is described as 'easy and convivial' he must have been genial and cheerful company. The *Oxford English Dictionary* defines 'uxorious' as being 'dotingly or submissively fond of a wife; devotedly attached to a wife'. With the lack of any other concrete information regarding how the earl and Robinaiana lived together as man and wife, we have to take this reference at face value and assume that (hopefully) he was devoted to this beautiful Scottish woman who, in her youth, had sacrificed her reputation for his sake.

Two days after the earl's first wife had died, a Privy Seal had been invoked to benefit his two daughters (the assumption is that, after the death of their mother, they had been left totally unprovided for, while their father hastily embarked on his second marriage). This Privy Seal offered to release the Peterborough estate from a debt of £17,000 against their seat at Dauntsey in Wiltshire if £5,000 was paid, or secured, to the two young women, still legally minors. Dauntsey, along with Turvey in Bedfordshire, Durris in Scotland and Clifton Reynes in Northamptonshire formed the estates held by the trustees: under the terms of the 3rd Earl's will this situation would continue until the 4th Earl's eldest legitimate son reached the age of 25. Charles now challenged this, the case being heard in 1760, and the decision was to his immediate benefit. He not only won the right to receive the rents and profits on the estate but also the right to own the Parson's Green estate in Fulham, the mansion that had been given to his brother John, a vast improvement on his previous situation.[147]

George II, the Hanoverian King of Great Britain and Ireland, died suddenly on 25 October 1760, just five days short of his 77th birthday and after reigning for thirty-three years. George II's eldest son, Frederick William, Prince of Wales, had predeceased his father and so, by right of succession, the crown passed to Frederick William's eldest son who became King George III. Just two weeks after the king had married Princess Charlotte of Mecklenburg-Strelitz in the Chapel Royal of St James's Palace, their coronation was held at Westminster Abbey on 22 September 1761 and, as peers of the realm, both the Earl of Peterborough and his countess attended wearing their robes of state and coronets.

Horace Walpole, the future Earl of Orford, is renowned as a man of letters. Writing from his house, Strawberry Hill, situated at Twickenham in London, to his great friend the Honourable Henry Seymour Conway on 25 September 1761 and recounting the events of the coronation, Walpole gives us the only clue we have so far as to how Robinaiana may have become known to the Earl of Peterborough in a wonderful, gossipy, first-hand account of the coronation:

> The Coronation is over: 'tis even a more gorgeous sight than I imagined. I saw the procession and the Hall; but the return was in the dark. In the morning they had forgot the Sword of State, the chairs for King and Queen and their canopies. They used the Lord Mayor's for the first and made the last in the Hall: so they did not set forth till noon; and then, by a childish compliment to the King, reserved the illumination of the Hall till his entry; by which means they arrived like a funeral, nothing being discernible but the plumes of the Knights of the Bath, which seemed the hearse. Lady Kildare, the Duchess of Richmond and Lady Pembroke were the capital beauties. Lady Harrington, the finest figure at a distance; Old Westmoreland, the most majestic. Lady Hertford could not walk and indeed I think is in a way to give us great anxiety. She is going to Ragley to ride. Lord Beauchamp was one of the King's train-bearers. Of all the incidents of the day, the most diverting was what happened to the Queen. She had a retiring-chamber, with *all* conveniences, prepared behind the altar. She went thither – in the *most convenient*, what found she but – the Duke of Newcastle! Lady Hardwicke died three days before the ceremony, which kept away the whole house of Yorke. Some of the peeresses were dressed overnight, slept in armchairs and were waked if they tumbled their heads. Your sister Harris's maid, Lady Peterborough, was a comely figure. My Lady Cowper refused, but was forced to walk with Lady Macclesfield. Lady Falmouth was not there; on which George Selwyn said, 'that those peeresses who were most used to *walk*, did not'. I carried my Lady Townshend, Lady Hertford, Lady Anne Connolly, my Lady Hervey and Mrs Clive, to my deputy's house at the gate of Westminster Hall. My Lady Townshend said she should be very glad to see a Coronation, as she never had seen one.

'Why,' said I, 'Madam, you walked at the last?' 'Yes, child,' said she, 'but I saw nothing of it: I only looked to see who looked at me'. The Duchess of Queensbury walked! Her affectation that day was to do nothing preposterous.

Some nine months before Robinaiana wed her earl, Henry Seymour Conway's sister Anne had married John Harris Esquire of Hayne in Devon, MP for Helston and Ashburton. In referring to Robinaiana as 'your sister Harris's maid' Walpole was being disparaging, but it does raise the question of what was behind his remark. It's not likely that the term 'maid' referred to her being a servant (Robinaiana was too well-born for that), but possibly more a 'lady's companion': a paid position, similar to the role of a lady-in-waiting, which was one way for impoverished daughters of well-to-do or genteel families to make their way in the world.

That the Brown family had many daughters to provide for is a fact and the head of the family, George Cornwallis Brown, Robinaiana's brother, was just a young man in the 1740s trying to make his way in the world, so it is possible that Robinaiana was living in her youth as a lady's companion in the Seymour Conway household, accompanying and chaperoning Anne.

Alternatively, Walpole could mean 'your sister Harris's *bridemaid*', to use the eighteenth-century term. It is entirely feasible that Robinaiana, daughter of a colonel, was moving in military circles: Henry Seymour Conway was also a colonel in the British army so perhaps this was how she became known to Anne Seymour Conway and, sometime prior to 1748, through her she was introduced to the Earl of Peterborough or became known to him?

The earl and his countess lived in genteel obscurity, possibly spending a considerable amount of time abroad. There is little mention of them in the gossip columns of the London newspapers in the years following the coronation and they may have been too short of ready cash to reside long in the capital, although the 4th Earl paid rates and tax against two town houses, both in Soho, 77 Dean Street and 5 Soho Square.[148] Perhaps one house was for his two eldest daughters or perhaps, even though he was such an uxorious husband, the earl maintained a mistress in Soho Square? With or without her husband, Robinaiana lived in the Dean Street house with her children.

The three eldest illegitimate sons, Charles, John and Henry, were all being educated with a view to sending them out to India to make their fortunes, a tried and tested route for disposing of illegitimate offspring. The Earl of Peterborough's finances didn't stretch to establishing sons other than his heir as gentlemen; these three denied the blessings fate had bestowed on their younger sibling had to make their own way. Charles was enrolled in the

French boarding school run by Peter Fargues in Hoxton to learn bookkeeping and was then sent out to Cuddalore in India as a writer for the East India Company's civil service as a 16- or 17-year-old youth. The other two followed in quick succession: John, not very academic but instead athletic and charming, a handsome man and seemingly a male counterpart to his cousin Grace, joined the East India Company's army, and Henry, puny where his brother was strong and probably more suited, like Charles, to the occupation of writer, instead chose to follow John's path.

Did the Countess of Peterborough attend her niece Grace's marriage to Dr John Eliot in October 1771? No records have survived to answer this, but surely a mention would have been made of Grace's connection to this titled family in the newspapers if Robinaiana had appeared at the wedding? The Earl of Peterborough was abroad during 1771 and, if his countess was with him, this would rule Robinaiana out from being the 'faithful monitress' who advised Grace to accept Eliot's proposal.[149]

After the death of her brother George Cornwallis Brown in 1767 and probably around the time of her sister-in-law Susannah's remarriage to Captain Richard King in November 1769, Robinaiana had taken her two young Brown nieces under her wing, bringing them up in her household and under her care. With her elder children leaving for India and the youngest Charles Henry about to be sent away to school, Robinaiana's house was beginning to feel empty and she welcomed the two little girls.[150]

Charles Henry, the baby of the Mordaunt family after the death of his brother Paulet, was favoured as the one and only legitimate heir and as such he received an education at one of the foremost public schools, Westminster, where both his father and great-grandfather had been educated. Styled as Viscount Mordaunt, he entered Westminster in 1772 when he was 14 years of age after spending the two preceding years at Harrow, another noted public school. The 3rd Earl of Peterborough's will had allowed a sum for the maintenance and education of any legitimate children born to his grandson, the 4th Earl. Thus Charles Henry's education was secured, while the schooling of his three elder brothers had to be funded by their father with no help from the trustees and they attended smaller, less prestigious schools. At Westminster Charles Henry met three young boys who were to become his lifelong friends and would also become well-known to Grace.

Joseph Bouchier Smith, George Coventry and Maurice George Bisset had all been at Westminster some years prior to Charles Henry's arrival. All four boys were of a similar age and as they seemed to share very similar tastes in their adult life, we can assume that they also did so as children and quickly became firm schoolfriends. Joseph Bouchier Smith was from an Oxford family of respectability, good standing and breeding, the son of Joseph Smith DD, Rector of St Dionis Backchurch in London and Provost of Queen's College, Oxford, while George Coventry, with the courtesy title of Viscount Deerhurst, was the eldest son and heir of the 6th Earl of Coventry. Maurice George Bisset was the son of the Reverend Alexander Bisset.

It was not until 1773 that the gossip columns recorded the Earl and Countess of Peterborough appearing together in society, attending a masked ball given under the directions of Lord Coventry at the Pantheon. Their absence from the society columns is striking. With an unmarried daughter of marriageable age, one would expect Robinaiana to be on the social merry-go-round and seeking out a husband for her, but instead the countess seems to have been sidelined by her peers or to have preferred a quiet and private life. It is likely that Grace's antics at this time did little to enhance Harriat's marriage prospects and Robinaiana must have despaired. Although illegitimacy was not a bar to a good marriage when the father was an earl, illegitimacy coupled with a cousin fast gaining a high-profile reputation for debauchery was not a good mix.

While the Earl of Peterborough seemed to be little in the company of his wife, he did socialize with other women. The memoirs of the actress and courtesan Mrs Sophia Baddeley, written by her friend Mrs Elizabeth Steele, mentioned a visit made to her by the Earl of Peterborough at Brighthelmstone (Brighton) in the early 1770s: 'On our arrival at Brighthelmstone, before we had been an hour in the house, we had several visitors, Mr. William Hanger, Lord Pigot, Captain Pigot, Lord Peterborough and Captain Crawford. Lord Peterborough stayed for tea and Lord Pigot invited us to Rottendean the next day to dinner.'

William Hanger, the future 3rd Baron Coleraine, was a notorious rake and sometime lover of Sophia Baddeley, so Lord Peterborough was keeping questionable company. From 1775 the house in Dean Street was listed in the Countess of Peterborough's name rather than the earl's, hinting, with no absolute proof, that the couple were living apart at this time.[151]

After so many years of staying out of the society columns in the newspapers, the middle-aged Robinaiana suddenly began to make an appearance. Harriat Mordaunt, although only 22, was still unmarried and an old maid by the standards of the day despite being a beauty and, with Grace's divorce now finalized, Robinaiana no doubt hoped the whole scandalous affair was at an end, allowing her to concentrate on making a suitable match for her daughter.

If Lord Cholmondeley would only propose marriage to Robinaiana's wayward niece then everyone could settle back down into some form of respectability. One wonders if the Earl and Countess of Peterborough did try to influence Cholmondeley in respect to their niece. Possibly with that hope in mind, the earl and his countess appeared publicly as a united family during 1776, their presence reminding Cholmondeley of Grace's family connections. They were among the attendees of a grand subscription masquerade held at Ranelagh Gardens during June of that year, in company with the Duke and Duchess of Cumberland (the Duke was the younger brother of King George III), and the Duke and Duchess of Devonshire (the newly-married Georgiana Cavendish, née Spencer).[152]

Charles Henry Mordaunt and his three friends left their schooldays at Westminster behind and the universities of Oxford beckoned, Joseph Bouchier Smith going to Queen's College where his father had been provost and both Deerhurst and Charles Henry going up to Christ Church in 1776, where Bisset had matriculated a year earlier.

Although they matriculated at Oxford none of them managed to attain a degree, the pursuits of pleasure being of much greater importance than their studies. Viscount Deerhurst stayed at Oxford only a matter of weeks before joining the 64th Regiment of Foot as an ensign and going with his regiment to America to fight in the War of Independence. To further compound things he was sent home with despatches soon after arriving and managed to begin the year of 1777 by eloping with Lady Catherine Henley, daughter of the 1st Earl of Northington. In February he was raised to the rank of lieutenant in his regiment and news of the elopement broke a month later.

Matters were rectified by a hasty marriage under special licence at the house of Lady Catherine's sister, Lady Bridget Tollemache.[153] Within days of the second marriage Deerhurst sailed to rejoin his regiment in America, but upon landing there he sold his commission for £500 and returned to England and his new wife. His father's house was now barred to him; the elopement coupled with the disgrace of quitting the armed services on the opening of a campaign caused an estrangement between them that seemed irreversible. Rumour had it that the quarrel was reinforced by Deerhurst's stepmother (his own mother having died some years before), who wished to promote the interests of her own sons. Despite the problems caused by his rash elopement, Deerhurst very much adored his young wife and was left bereft when both she and the child she was carrying died in childbirth in January 1779 at their house in Ledbury, Hertfordshire.

Joseph Bouchier Smith had also taken a wife, Miss Frances Wilson Cock of Great George Street, Westminster, the goddaughter of a city merchant who had died two years previously and left her a fortune.[154] They married on 12 October 1778 at St Clement Danes, Westminster, the fortune of the bride probably the main consideration for Bouchier Smith who was perpetually in debt.

In the meantime, what of Grace's other aunt, the widowed Mrs Janet Kelly? Janet's Upper Brook Street house had been leased to Stephen Fox, 2nd Baron Holland (elder brother of Charles James Fox) and after his death at the end of 1774 to his widow. With her own house occupied, Janet took over the lease of 36 Old Queen Street in Westminster, not far from Buckingham House (now Buckingham Palace) and close to Birdcage Walk on the edge of Hyde Park, clearly still a wealthy widow despite Kelly leaving her nothing after his death.

Janet was now 50 years of age but not without her admirers, chief among whom was an army officer some sixteen years her junior. Lieutenant Colonel Thomas Edmondes of the 1st Regiment of the Foot Guards was from a Glamorganshire family who had made their money in estate management and the law. A family climbing the social ladder, they added Llandough Castle to their empire late in 1775 (they already owned a house in Cowbridge and an estate at Beaupre, St Hilary). It was John Edmondes, Colonel Edmondes' elder brother, who took out the lease on Llandough Castle.

Perhaps Janet was a beauty like others in her family and was an attractive older woman, or maybe Colonel Edmondes just saw a wealthy older lady and himself shortly to be a wealthy widower free to enjoy his life and her money, but either way Janet fell for his charms and Colonel Edmondes proposed marriage.[155] On 24 May 1776 at St George's Church in Hanover Square, London, the widowed Mrs Janet Kelly, 51 years of age, walked down the aisle for a third time with the 35-year-old Lieutenant Colonel Thomas Edmondes, who no doubt cut a dashing figure in his military uniform. The wedding was witnessed by Janet's brother-in-law, the 4th Earl of Peterborough, and if the earl was a witness then Robinaiana must also have been present at her sister's wedding. Grace may have attended as she was in town at this time: her divorce had just been finalized and she was idling her time away on the arm of her lover Lord Cholmondeley, the town abuzz with rumours of their impending marriage.

Sometime after the wedding, Colonel Edmondes' brother John, in poor health and unable to maintain Llandough Castle, surrendered the lease in favour of his brother and so Thomas Edmondes became tenant for the lives of himself, his brother (who died the following year) and his new wife. He resigned his command of a company in the Coldstream Guards and Janet took the two daughters of John Edmondes' first wife, Charlotte and Anna Maria, to live with them at Llandough Castle.[156]

With Janet settled, attention turned back to Robinaiana's family and the *Morning Post*, never a newspaper to shy away from pointing out the foibles of those who should know better and mocking them purely for the entertainment of their readers, carried the following, very thinly disguised attack on the 4th Earl of Peterborough, suggesting that Robinaiana had been replaced in his affections:

> The *God of Love* has at length kindled a softer passion than *Platonic* admiration, in the breast of the veteran *Earl of P___b___gh*. The agreeable Mrs. D____n, his Lordship's late *conversation favourite*, is declared pregnant and the reality of the above *refinement* once more becomes doubtful.[157]

While the Earl might have tried to explain any attachment he may have had to Mrs D___n as one based purely on friendship, the *Morning Post* obviously thought otherwise! Or was Robinaiana the object of his platonic admiration? If anyone was in any doubt as to the identity of Mrs D___n, she was unmasked a month later when reports of a highway robbery appeared in the papers. The incident took place just before nine o'clock in the evening on the corner of Blacklands Lane on the King's Road in Chelsea, London, at the edge of Chelsea Common, then very rural and obviously a notorious place for such robberies; the same highwayman was believed to have held up a carriage containing a Mrs Hales and other ladies in Chelsea a few nights before.

This second robbery, as the *London Evening Post* reported, was committed 'on the persons of the Earl of Peterborough and Mrs. Dawson, who were going in his Lordship's chariot from Parson's-green to London.'[158] With Mrs D___n unmasked as Mrs Dawson, returning with the earl from his country residence just outside London, the *Morning Chronicle* a few days later couldn't help but remark that the 'silence of the injured parties is noe less astonishing, as it is a point of humanity and justice to apprise society of these events'. The robbery was heard by some 'servants and other persons of two or three families' who had been sitting outside their houses nearby enjoying the late evening summer sunshine; one gets the impression that the earl was perhaps more dismayed by the report getting into the papers than by the actual robbery itself.[159]

Whether to escape the scandal or purely to put some distance between herself and her errant husband, Robinaiana, within days of the highway robbery taking place and the reports appearing in the papers, decamped with her youngest son and daughter to Brighthelmstone.[160] Three years earlier Grace's indiscretions had graced the pages of the *Town and Country Magazine*. Now, with the same publication picking up on the latest gossip, Robinaiana's husband was the subject of one of its notorious *tête-à-tête* articles, the hapless bespectacled earl appearing under the soubriquet of 'Le Comte des Lunettes and Miss D____n'.

Only two years earlier the *Complete English Peerage* had described the earl as 'uxorious'; would they still describe him so? However, the gossip died down and the earl, having learned his lesson, severed all connections with Mrs Dawson and she was not mentioned again.

In 1779 Charles Henry, now of age at 21 and already well established on the social scene, found himself in Brighthelmstone during May, unattached and out to enjoy himself. Fanny Burney, daughter of the musical historian Dr Charles Burney and already at that time becoming well known in her own right as a novelist, kept a diary in which she recorded meeting Charles Henry while she was a guest of the diarist Hester Thrale:[161]

> Brighthelmstone [May 27] ... In the evening we all, adjourned to Major H__'s, where, besides his own family, we found Lord Mordaunt, son to the Earl of Peterborough, – a pretty, languid, tonnish young man; Mr. Fisher, who is said to be a scholar, but is nothing enchanting as a gentleman; young Fitzgerald, as much the thing as ever; and Mr. Lucius Corcannon.[162]

Fanny's description of Charles Henry, although portraying him as a rather indifferent but fashionable gentleman, mentioned his appearance, describing him as 'pretty', and so it's a fair guess that, like so many others in his family, he too had inherited his fair share of good looks. He was therefore already a very eligible young bachelor and about to become even more of a catch when, on the death of his father, he became the 5th Earl of Peterborough and Monmouth.

The 4th Earl of Peterborough died on 1 August 1779 after a short illness and at his house in Soho Square. His last will and testament remained the one written in 1758 soon after his second marriage, together with the codicil added a year later. Perhaps uxorious to the last, he left everything he owned to Robinaiana, her heirs and assigns.

Chapter Eleven

Horizons New

In the summer of 1778 rumours were whispered about town suggesting that Grace had become a mother once again, presenting Lord Cholmondeley with a son. The *Gazetteer* newspaper certainly subscribed to the tale, reporting from the military training camp on Coxheath in Kent that 'Lord Torpedo', who was there as colonel-in-chief of the Cheshire militia, received a letter each day from Grace that threw him into confusion:

> His Lordship was seen to change colour, on reading the letter, which brought him the melancholy account of his *sons* have got the gripes, and *Miss* a violent longing for a *coronet*, with which, it is thought, she will shortly be indulged.[163]

If Grace was kept in London with a newborn, her earl was certainly in his element at Coxheath camp where thousands of soldiers and officers had gathered to muster and train, watched and entertained by a second army of wives, mistresses, whores and hangers-on. Lady Worsley, the bored wife of Sir Richard Worsley, was there with her husband who commanded the South Hampshire militia and she reputedly kept Cholmondeley entertained in Grace's absence.

If there was any truth in the rumours and Cholmondeley and Grace did have a son together, then he can't have survived many months; perhaps this was also the death knell for their relationship.

While the *ton* gossiped over the reputed birth, Henry Hew Dalrymple, despairing of succeeding in any other career, enlisted for service in the British army, joining the newly-raised 75th Regiment of Foot, otherwise known as the Prince of Wales's own regiment, as a lieutenant.[164] By October the regiment was quartered at Chatham, awaiting orders to sail to Africa and the West Indies where they spent the next two years. It is telling that once Grace's brother and protector had left England, Lord Cholmondeley finally renounced any mention of marriage to his lady, just as Dr John Eliot had waited for the news of Hugh Dalrymple's death in Grenada before separating from Grace. It strongly suggests that Henry Hew was fiercely protective of his younger sister and the Dalrymple men seem to have been a force to be reckoned with, both Grace's husband and now her aristocratic lover waiting until such time as the coast was clear before packing her off.

The newspapers charted the end of Grace and Cholmondeley's relationship:

Miss *Dal____ple* has lately embarked for France and it is said parted with her noble gallant in a manner that did not imply an inviolable attachment on either side.[165]

The fatal separation between Lord C____y and his beloved Miss D__le, was occasioned, it seems, by the warmth with which the latter urged the promise of marriage, said to have been made to her by her noble inamorato; – his Lordship hesitating to recognize the *sacred vow*, she flew from him in a paroxysm of rage, ordered posthorses, drove instantly for Dover and crossed the water to seek an asylum from the insults of man within the walls of a *cloyster*; but how long the *flesh* will be sacrificed to *female spirit*, probably a few Calais packets will determine![166]

Quite possibly Henry Hew Dalrymple thought he had left his sister safe in the protection of Lord Cholmondeley but now, out of the country and with no way of easily returning home, in the short term at least he had no way of helping his sister who was left to fend for herself, even more so as her uncle, the 4th Earl of Peterborough, died just weeks later. Although Grace's cousin ascended to the earldom, he was still a young man, bent on pleasure, and so, in quick succession, Grace had lost all her influential protectors.

Henry Hew Dalrymple also had much more important considerations now, other than a wayward sister. He had inherited the plantations their father had bought while established as attorney general on the West Indian island and the management of these estates now fell to the son, although he had not been there since his six-month visit while his father was still alive. Moreover, being the owner of the slaves attached to the plantations weighed heavily on his conscience.

In 1773, and again on later visits, Henry Hew witnessed the cruel treatment of these slaves and it was at this time that he began to stand forth as a free-thinking man, an educated and humane man and, furthermore, one not afraid to stand up for his principles and act on them, even if they went against the accepted customs of the day.

Henry Hew Dalrymple was vehemently opposed to the practice of slavery. He did not agree with the widely-held belief that the African people transported from their homelands to the West Indian islands were content with their situation. Additionally, and for the time controversially, he had found the slaves he encountered to be the equal in temper and disposition of any other person, anywhere. Now posted to the African island of Gorée with his regiment, he made significant efforts to pursue his own agenda and to find out more about the slave trade and confirm his beliefs.

Gorée lies just off the coast of Senegal and was first settled by Europeans in the fifteenth century. In 1779 it was taken from the French and a British garrison installed there to protect this new acquisition. The island was a trading post and had a large port, and it was via the shipping passing through this port that Henry Hew was first able to look more closely into the slave trade for which the island was effectively a 'warehouse'. He was at the garrison in Gorée and at other points along the neighbouring coastline from May until September 1779. He later said that he '. . . was weekly on the continent, with a view of knowing the situation of the country and modes of procuring slaves, because he held slaves himself in the West Indies and wished to ascertain that matter beyond doubt.'

He witnessed the 'caravans' of slaves, sometimes thousands of men, women and children, being brought from inland Africa to the coast to be sold on. Most were presented as prisoners of war and the African people believed that the 'wars' in their country, usually short-lived and of no more than a week or two in duration, were undertaken for the express purpose of procuring slaves under the pretence of them being such prisoners. Henry Hew knew, from talking to the slaves on his own family plantation in Grenada, that their capture had occurred while they were working in their fields or at night from their huts and they had been taken by surprise, not while fighting so-called wars.

On one occasion at Gorée, two men offered a slave for sale to the British garrison there, a free man who had been captured while sent as a messenger from Senegal. The men offering him for sale knew he was a free man and boasted about their capture of him; his fate after this is not recorded. Henry Hew's regiment was stationed there for military reasons, even though he found time to investigate the surrounding area, and there were constant skirmishes with the French in which he bore arms, but the real danger was the illness and disease that was rife among the troops. The *London Chronicle* reported on 19 October 1779 that 'One hundred and six private men of the 75th regiment of foot are dead at Gorée . . . The French at this time have no more than twelve men fit for duty at the garrison of Fort Saint Lewis.'

The difference in the spheres inhabited by Grace and her brother Henry Hew Dalrymple could not, at this juncture, have been wider. While he was defending Gorée, preventing it being retaken by the French, watching his comrades struck down by disease and witnessing first-hand the horrors of slavery, Grace was in Paris looking for a new protector, being courted by the

King of France's brother, the Comte d'Artois, and his cousin Louis Philippe Joseph d'Orléans, Duc de Chartres, both men belonging to the House of Bourbon. Louis Philippe, born in 1747 and the son and heir of the Duc d'Orléans, was married with five young children. He was also a renowned womanizer and a lover of all things British, including a young Scotswoman who had shunned London society for the pleasures to be found in Paris.

Like Cholmondeley, d'Orléans was a tall, well-built man, athletic in his youth, a *bon viveur* and wonderfully convivial company. Known in the more scurrilous quarters of the British press as the 'English Buck' and the 'Gallic Sportsman', he was fond of horses, gambling and women and his easy-going nature predisposed him to republican values and put him at odds with the Queen of France. Considered handsome, despite a receding hairline and a propensity for decorating his waistcoats with pornographic buttons (much to the shock of the Duchess of Devonshire's sister), he was an honourable man whose society was sought by all ranks of the nobility including the Prince of Wales whom he frequently visited. For Grace, who had a knack of choosing men she could rely on, he was an excellent replacement for Cholmondeley and they certainly held one another in a great deal of affection.

While in Paris, Grace rented rooms in the Hôtel de Chartres on the Rue de Richelieu, a fashionable address with both the Palais-Royal and the Comédie-Française theatre in close proximity. Her neighbours in the building included a notorious gambler named Marchioness de Jaucourt who ran a table in the Palais-Royal, and Mrs Gooch, an Englishwoman in a similar situation to Grace. Mrs Gooch (formerly Elizabeth Sarah Villa-Real), well-born and close in age to Grace, had been cruelly treated by her husband who, in their own Crim. Con. case, had obtained merely a separation from bed and board rather than a full divorce, leaving her unable to marry again. She had been banished to France and was, like Grace, pursuing a career as a courtesan. The two women shared the affections of the Duc de Chartres and also of the elderly Duc de Fitz-James, the grandson of the former King James II (his father, the 1st Duke of Berwick, was the illegitimate son of James II and Arabella Churchill). Mrs Gooch and Grace were, for a while, great friends but the Duc de Fitz-James transferred his attention from one to the other creating, as Mrs Gooch put it, 'a shyness between' the two women.

For two years Grace remained in France, first as the mistress of the handsome Comte d'Artois and then the mistress of the Duc de Chartres, all the while making infrequent visits home. It was towards midsummer of 1780 that a very interesting report appeared in the newspapers, mentioning both Lord Peterborough and his notorious cousin Grace: 'Friday Miss Dalrymple set off for Margate, in order to embark for Ostend in her route to Paris; the Earl of

Peterborough and Lord Deerhurst go over in the same vessel, though not immediately in that Lady's suite.'[167]

That the newspapers of the day ignore the familial relationship between Grace and her cousin, Lord Peterborough, when it must surely have been public knowledge to high society, is very odd. Only about four years older than her titled cousin, Grace had been married, divorced and become a permanent fixture in the gossip columns before he had even left school and, as a fascinating and slightly 'dangerous' woman, must have piqued the interest of Lord Peterborough and his friend Deerhurst, who were to go on to exhibit their own debauched and slightly cracked characters to the world. Although the two gentlemen were not in Grace's 'suite', according to the report, to find the three of them planning to travel on the very same boat is a remarkable coincidence and, despite the newspaper declaring the contrary, there is every likelihood that they were in fact travelling companions on their voyage. Grace was absenting herself from the country to escape the gossip surrounding her former lover the Earl of Cholmondeley's rumoured marriage to another woman and to return to her French protectors, with whom she continued until Lord Cholmondeley journeyed to Paris in the spring of 1781.

While Grace had been absent from England her star had been eclipsed by Perdita, the actress Mary Darby Robinson, who was familiarly known by the name of her most famous stage role, one that had captivated the Prince of Wales and earned him the nickname of Florizel to her Perdita. Mary's star waxed and waned though, and the prince eventually moved on from his Perdita; it was rumoured that Lord Cholmondeley temporarily picked up where his royal friend had left off and the courtesan Elizabeth Armistead (who later married Charles James Fox after being his mistress for many years) took over from Perdita in the merry-go-round of the prince's affections.

Lord Cholmondeley set off for Paris and while there rekindled his relationship with Grace and brought her back with him to England a few weeks later (the Duc de Chartres had taken up with a 17-year-old French opera girl and Grace, in a hasty revenge, had alighted on Cholmondeley, so the reports said).[168] George Selwyn wrote to a friend on 13 June 1781 that he had seen the couple riding in Cholmondeley's vis-à-vis (a type of carriage) around the London streets. Perhaps, though, there was an ulterior motive behind her return as Grace now had her sights set higher than an earl or a duke. If Perdita and 'the Armistead' had snared a prince, then why could Grace not do so too?

George Augustus Frederick, Prince of Wales and eldest son and heir apparent of King George III, was but 18 years old when he first made the acquaintance of Grace. We remember him today as the bloated, almost comedic monarch that he became but, back in June 1781, he was young, attractive and clever. He had led a sheltered childhood and, upon being given his own establishment when he turned 18, had run riot, much to the dismay of his parents with whom he did not get along. He had induced his Perdita to leave the stage, promising her £20,000 when he came of age; however, when he tired of her she blackmailed him with the love letters he had written to her and finally settled for £5,000 and an annuity of £500.

The gossip columns of the newspapers fell over themselves in trying to decide whether Grace had indeed bagged herself a prince or whether she was once again with her noble earl. They also revelled in the rivalry between the discarded Perdita and the ascendant Dally the Tall. At the beginning of June the gossip was that Perdita had declared herself to be pregnant and had asked Lord Cholmondeley to inform the prince.[169] Perdita wasn't pregnant but another soon was, for Grace had indeed made a conquest of the Prince of Wales.

Grace must have fallen pregnant towards the end of June or beginning of July 1781. One version suggests that the prince saw the full-length portrait of Grace painted by Gainsborough in 1777 hanging in Cholmondeley's Piccadilly house and desired Cholmondeley to introduce her to him.[170] Could that be the reason for Cholmondeley journeying to Paris and returning with Grace? Did he actually go to her with a request from the prince? Such a scenario would certainly fit with Grace abandoning her aristocratic French duc and returning so swiftly to London, rightly knowing that a liaison with the prince could only be to her benefit. Although nearly a decade older than her royal conquest, she was beautiful and stately and no doubt once she met him she emphasized to the prince that her brother was currently serving in the regiment named in his honour and flattered him to no small degree.

With Grace now once again taking the London scene by storm as a demi-rep, Lord Cholmondeley departed with a small entourage for the European mainland in August to make a tour. Maybe he discreetly left, leaving the way clear for the prince, or possibly he left in anger at Grace dropping him for a greater prize but either way Elizabeth Armistead accompanied him to Spa, Cholmondeley once again collecting up the prince's cast-off mistress. Grace remained in London, the newspapers still undecided as to whether she was awaiting the return of her earl or the further attentions of the prince. The *Morning Herald* ran the following article:[171]

A certain young and beautiful Lady much drew the attention of the Prince last Monday at Windsor and has by the native dignity of virtue so *outréd* the Perdita – the Armistead, &c., &c., that they will no longer shine in any other than a newspaper sphere. The following description will point her out to those personally acquainted with her: Her stature is majestic; her air and demeanour nature itself! The softest roses that every youth and beauty poured out upon modesty, glow on her lips! Her cheeks are the bloom of Hebe and the purity of Diana is in her breast!

It was during this time that Grace sat, once more, to have her portrait painted by Thomas Gainsborough, commissioned by the Prince of Wales, the *Morning Herald* gleefully pointing out that both Perdita and Dally were sitting for Gainsborough for their 'rival portraits'.[172] Grace, knowingly with child, stares seductively from the finished portrait towards the viewer, unusual as very few of Gainsborough's subjects are painted looking so directly forwards and the *Public Advertiser* found this unsettling, saying of the portrait that Grace's eyes were 'too characteristic of her Vocation'.[173]

In this head-and-shoulders portrait Grace once more wears her favourite ribbon choker but this time has attached it to a large sapphire brooch stitched to the bodice of her gown, turning the ornament on her dress into a necklace, a fashion that was popular at the time. She is artfully made up, still sporting darkened eyebrows together with rouged cheeks (she was described as being 'as rosy as Hebe') and a beauty patch or spot. It is a little-known fact that beauty patches had a language of their own, their placement on the face sending out a specific message. To wear a beauty patch on the cheek denoted the wearer as 'gallant'. Grace would have put some thought into how she wished to be presented in this portrait and what message she wished to send through it.

One further aspect should be noted: the gold earrings Grace is wearing appear very similar to those she sported in the engraving of her that appeared in the *Town and Country Magazine* back in 1774 alongside Lord Valentia. They were probably bought for her by John Eliot during their courtship and marriage and retained by Grace after their divorce. To be portrayed wearing the earrings bought by Eliot in the portrait commissioned by her lover the Prince of Wales was possibly an act of revenge by Grace aimed at her former husband, one calculated to annoy and irritate him.

By the end of 1781, even with her rival Perdita having taken off to over-winter on the continent, accompanied only by her young daughter (the product of her marriage to Mr Robinson), Grace, who was still resident in London, knew that she was losing the affection of her prince, notwithstanding her pregnancy. Living in a house on Cumberland Street in St Marylebone, just a short distance from the gallows at Tyburn Turnpike from which she had wished to see her husband swing from the noose a few years earlier, Grace threw a fête anyway to celebrate Perdita's departure.[174] Much as he had provided Grace with a house in the late 1770s when she was his mistress, Lord Cholmondeley had also provided this one for her. His name appears on the land tax records for 1781, with Grace (as Grace Elliott) listed in her own right for the following year. Grace, either to annoy her former husband or maybe just because she preferred it that way, chose to spell her surname differently from his (readers may have noticed several variant spellings of the name within earlier quotes).[175]

It was at Cumberland Street where Grace spent her days towards the end of 1781 and into 1782, noticeably pregnant and no doubt scheming frantically for her future. She let it be widely known that the child she was carrying had been fathered by the Prince of Wales, a fact picked up on and discussed by the newspapers: '*Dally* the *Tall* has certainly been honoured with a *Princely* visit; but it is said to have been only the *how d'ye do* of *indifference*, notwithstanding she is herself pleased to boast, that it terminated in the *kiss amorous*!'[176]

The prince, however, had moved on. One of his next conquests was Elizabeth Lamb, Viscountess Melbourne and wife of Peniston Lamb of Brocket Hall, that great friend of Sir John Eliot's. The Lambs had separated shortly after their marriage and Viscountess Melbourne's son George, born in 1784, was reputed to have the Prince of Wales as his father. Grace's world was a small one! One wonders how bitterly the conversation over the dinner table between Sir John Eliot and his friend Peniston Lamb may have turned to their respective wives, one divorced and one separated but both with a child reputed to have been fathered by the Prince of Wales.

Chapter Twelve

Anglo-Indian Relationships

In 1808 the *Sporting Magazine*, among others, published what they titled 'The Sporting Anecdotes of the Late Col. J. Mordaunt, of the Honourable East-India Company's Madras Establishment.' The author was not named; in other publications the biography was given a slightly different title and one claimed it to have been written by a 'Brother Officer'.[177] The author was possibly William Hickey who had just retired from the civil service in India and was formerly, for a short period, a cadet in the army there and who was certainly well acquainted with both Henry and John Mordaunt, Grace's cousins and two of the three illegitimate sons of the Earl and Countess of Peterborough.[178]

Charles Mordaunt, the eldest son (and not to be confused with his younger brother Charles Henry), was already well established in India as a writer when his brother John enlisted with the East India Company's Madras army, arriving in India in the mid to late 1760s. Henry followed a few years later, joining the Bengal army.

John did not have a happy time in Madras where he suffered ill health, and he managed to travel to Bengal before resigning both his post and his commission as a lieutenant to return home to his family in England.

Although Bengal was considered to be the most advantageous posting for a military man, Madras was, at that time, more likely to provide faster promotion through the ranks as the area was the seat of an active war with Hyder Ali, the Sultan of Mysore. However, the pay was less on the Madras establishment and the military line 'never could be an object for a gentleman'. John, pushed by his father who saw no prospects for his scapegrace son in England, wished to return but hoped to transfer to a captaincy in the Bengal establishment. Sir George Colebrooke, chairman of the East India Company at this date, in writing to the Duke of Portland during August 1770 said he was indisposed to allow a man who 'quit ye service & resign without leave, to obtain leave to go out again, but much more unprecedented for a young man, returned a Lieut. from Madras to go out a Captain to Bengal'.[179] If this was allowed to happen with John, Colebrooke thought that all the 'officers of Madras & Bombay will be inclined hereafter to quit the service & to return to Europe, if ye effects of such resignation is the obtaining increase of rank on ye Bengal establishment.'

We do not know what the earl said on seeing his son reappear in England, but we do know the response of William Hickey's father when he too returned in 1770, neatly mirroring John's own experiences:

> The day after my arrival ... my father addressed me very gravely and truly, representing the enormous expence incurred in equipping me for the East Indies, the whole of which was wantonly thrown away by my hasty and inconsiderate abandonment of the provision made for me in the army ... he would exert all his interest to get me exchanged from the Madras army to that of Bengal, which, should he not succeed in, he saw nothing left for me but to return forthwith to Fort St George [in Madras], as he could not, in justice to the rest of his family, allow me to relinquish the Commission, the attainment of which had cost him so large a sum of money.

The earl's admonition of his own errant son was, we can safely assume, similar in tone to the one Hickey received from his father. Hickey was not to return with either the Bengal or Madras army, instead remaining some years in London until 1775 when he was sent by his despairing father to practise law in Jamaica before again going to Bengal two years later, but in a legal capacity within the civil service rather than as a soldier.

In writing to the Duke of Portland on his son's behalf, the Earl of Peterborough said of John that 'he is very willing to go as you mention and had no other motive to wish for Bengall [sic], but on account of his health, as he was never well at Madras and very well at Bengal.'[180] The earl wrote once more towards the end of January 1771, taking the liberty to trouble the duke once again 'in regard to my Son John Mordaunt, who I find stands no chance to go to India this year without your Graces kind interposition with Sir George Colbrook [sic] who I have reason to think has forgot the affair'. Now merely asking to have John reinstated at the rank he left with rather than a captaincy, he ends the letter by saying 'this affair tho trifling in itself is from circumstance of the utmost consequence to the young man, nothing but my paternal affections which I hope will pleade my excuse cou'd have made me give you so much trouble.'[181]

At some point between January 1771 and 1775 John did indeed return to India, but not as he wished on the Bengal establishment as he returned still assigned to the Madras army. Perhaps encouraged by his brother, Henry also obtained a cadetship in 1772 but with the Bengal army, forewarned by John's experiences in joining the other. At the same time Grace's brother, Robert Cornwallis Dalrymple, had followed the example of his two cousins and also applied for a cadetship in the East India Company's armed forces.

Robert embarked on his cadetship in 1770, the year his cousin John returned, and perhaps influenced by John in the same way as Henry, chose to join the Bengal army and received his commission as a junior officer in the 2nd Bengal European Battalion on 5 November 1771, just a couple of weeks after his sister Grace's marriage to Dr John Eliot.

John Mordaunt was not academically inclined and had reputedly claimed of his schooldays that 'one half of his days were spent in being flogged for playing the other half'. So, on completion of his education, when John was found to be 'about as learned as when he was first sent there', a quarrel ensued between his father and his teachers. John, it is recorded,

> handsomely stept forth to exculpate his master; whose attention he declared to be unparalleled and in slipping off his clothes, exhibited the earnestness of the good man's endeavours; humorously observing, that 'as nothing could be got into his brains, his master had done his best to impress his instructions on the opposite side of learning'.

Despite John leaving school with scant more learning than that with which he had started, he was not unintelligent. His conversation was excellent, according to the 'Sporting Anecdotes', with 'elegance of diction and with a precise appropriation of his words to the particular occasion. He learnt to speak Hindu fluently and was a tolerable Persian scholar though he could not write two lines of English correctly.' The writer recalled that 'Mordaunt surpassed in almost everything he undertook, yet, seeming more by intuition, than by any study or effort to excel.' Naturally clever then, but nearly illiterate despite his schooling! The writer recalled a note John once sent him regarding a horse he had borrowed: 'You may kip the hos as long as you lick.'

In arithmetic also,

> no man could be more ignorant than Mordaunt ... he kept no books, but all his money concerns were on scraps of paper, and under terms and figures intelligible only to himself ... Yet even the most intricate cases never puzzled him; and at settling times he was rarely, if ever in error.

It appears he had no problem with the actual arithmetic, just with the recording of it; possibly he suffered from a form of dyslexia. In truth, he seems to mirror his cousin Grace, surviving on his wit, charm and good looks while making the most of any opportunity offered to him.

On John's return to India he was appointed aide-de-camp to Sir John Clavering and, although he officially remained on the books of the Madras army, he managed to never physically rejoin them, instead enjoying what seems to be a rather gilded existence in the upper echelons of Indian society, his appointment as aide-de-camp almost honorary rather than official. One can only speculate that his father, and perhaps also the Duke of Portland, had pulled a few strings to make the young man's time in India more suited to his attributes and personality.

Charles returned home for a short visit in 1778, having raised himself through the ranks to the position of senior merchant in the East India Company, but this was the last time Robinaiana was to see her eldest child for he died in Madras on 6 April 1780. Not until the following year was the news of his demise received back in England.[182]

William Hickey, who had been in Bengal practising law for some three years, had also travelled home again, arriving during the early summer of 1780. Henry Mordaunt, who had gone out as a cadet in 1772, returned to his mother's house in the same year but on a different ship. A Calcutta merchant named Benjamin Lacam who travelled with Henry let Hickey know that Captain Henry Mordaunt of the Bengal military establishment had been making earnest enquiries for him. Henry and William Hickey met at Mr Lacam's house on Cecil Street, the very street on which his cousin Grace had lived while married to Dr John Eliot just a few years earlier and where Eliot still lived.[183]

> [Henry] entered the room with his usual scowling countenance, but for a minute smiled and shook me by the hand with apparent cordiality. He then began damning the climate, the brutality of the common people and the general stupidity of London, cursing his own folly for being such a blockhead, such an inveterate ass as to quit the paradise of Hindustan to visit the sink of everything despicable by comparison, England, a country no man who had ever enjoyed the blessings and comforts of India could feel comfortable in.

Hickey had an extremely low opinion of Henry Mordaunt, but during this visit home they were to be in competition for the affections of the same woman and this no doubt negatively influenced his attitude towards Henry.

Henry's younger brother Charles Henry, now 22 years of age and established as the 5th Earl of Peterborough, was touring the Continent; an unfortunate circumstance for Henry as otherwise his brother would have been able to introduce him to his society.[184] The difference in situation between Henry and his brother Lord Peterborough was striking: the elder, recently returned from India and knowing no one; the younger, titled, travelling for pleasure and having a wide circle of friends and acquaintances. If Hickey's depiction of Henry as an extremely dissatisfied and disgruntled person is accurate, it is likewise fair to say that Henry must have felt extremely jealous of his younger brother enjoying the position in society that was denied to him.

Hickey and Henry met again later in the day at Colman's theatre, where Hickey promised Henry he would call on him the next day and 'introduce him at a house of fashionable resort where he would find a choice of beautiful girls and might pass his leisure hours agreeable'; a bagnio or brothel, in other words!

> I accordingly called upon him at his mother's, Lady Peterborough, in Dean Street, Soho, from whence I took him first to Mrs. Weston's famous receptacle in Berkeley Row, where having introduced him to the 'Lady Abbess and her Nuns!' we next visited Mrs. Kelly and her bevy of beauties in Arlington Street. Here even the cynical Mordaunt was obliged to confess the women were lovely and he made some efforts to say civil things to the girls, but his common address and manner was so morose and so unpleasant that the Cyprian lasses soon distinguished him by the appellation of the 'Surly Nabob'.[185]

Lord Peterborough had returned to London just before Christmas 1780; Hickey remembered seeing him with his brother Henry at the Opera House, standing in 'Fops' Alley' (the aisles between the benches in the pit where young men would walk and flirt with ladies) and Henry was happier and no longer wanted to return to Bengal, saying of it: 'Oh, damn the place, don't mention it. I should be devilish glad never to be obliged to see it again so long as I live.'

The woman who was to become sought after by both Henry Mordaunt and William Hickey to the detriment of their friendship was Charlotte Barry who, with her younger sister Nancy, was attracting much attention from the nobility. By February 1781 Henry had taken Charlotte 'into [his] keeping', but the duplicitous Charlotte had her eye on Henry's friend Hickey and the threesome seem to have entered into almost a ménage à trois until Henry began to suspect that Charlotte vastly preferred his friend.

False friend that he was, Hickey arranged with Henry to take a trip to Portsmouth to view the English Naval Fleet, then anchored off the coast there, and to breakfast with Henry on the day of their departure. Consequently, Hickey arrived at eight o'clock in the morning at Dean Street, Soho to find waiting outside to take them to Portsmouth a 'smart travelling postchaise, having the family coat-of-arms and coronet handsomely painted upon the panels'.

The journey was a disaster: they were unable to get fresh horses for their carriages and had to halt for the night at Petersfield in Hampshire. The bright spring weather in which they had embarked had turned to snow by the second day but the two men made it to Portsmouth where they stayed for three days, drinking and playing cards, before an argument erupted on the last evening. Henry, in a rage, ordered his carriage and departed instantly for London, paying no heed to the freezing weather or the lateness of the hour.

The roads were little more than a sheet of ice: Hickey took two days to get back to London in the stagecoach, very few people daring to travel in the treacherous conditions. At a coaching inn along the way Hickey was told that only one person had preceded him along the London road, assumed by the staff at the inn to be the Earl of Peterborough, who had left an hour earlier. This was Henry then, in his brother's carriage, pretending to be the earl himself or at least disabusing no one of the notion that he was.

Safely back in London, Hickey called on Charlotte to hear of the events that had befallen Henry during the night:

> Have you not heard of his accident? Tearing along like a madman, as he is, last night in the dark through Wandsworth, his post-boys came in contact with a stage-coach just turning from a stable yard. Mordaunt's chaise was overset and almost demolished, himself and his servant being severely bruised and Mordaunt's ankle sprained. One of his postillions was taken up for dead. Mordaunt in a fainting state was carried into the house, where his impatience and apprehension that his leg was broken and likewise that he had received some internal injury, made him insist upon an immediate removal ... and thus was conveyed to his mother's in Dean Street, where he arrived about eight this morning. Lady Peterborough, frightened out of her wits, instantly sent off for Mr Pott and two or three other eminent surgeons.

Henry suffered not only an injury to his ankle in the accident but also to his pocket as he was compelled to pay for the repairs to his brother's carriage.

With the summer social season in full swing, the young Earl of Peterborough included his brother Henry, Charlotte Barry and William Hickey in his jaunts. With boating excursions along the Thames and trips to the racecourses, while they were embroiled in the social whirl the two young Mordaunt men must on occasion have bumped into their cousin Grace who was dallying with the Prince of Wales. However, the high life in the country began to drain Henry's finances and, by August, his money was fast running out. Henry's

> chief supplies of cash had been from his mother (Lady Peterborough) and Mrs. Brown, a widow of good fortune, sister to her Ladyship, but his

applications to those ladies became so frequent and to such an extent they were at last, though reluctantly, obliged to tell him they could no longer furnish cash to support him in his extravagancies.

A widowed Mrs Brown! Janet was by now the wife of Colonel Edmondes, unless Hickey had mistakenly named her a widow, but if not Janet then the identity of this woman unfortunately remains a mystery. Lord Peterborough was unwilling or unable to help out and, to prevent his admission to a sponging house for debt, Henry was forced to borrow £200 from Hickey. The debt was not repaid by Henry until 1783.

By September of 1781 William Hickey was preparing to return to Bengal and Charlotte informed Henry that she was leaving him to travel to India with Hickey. Henry erupted, making threats to kill Charlotte, and she fled from him to Hickey's lodgings in Portman Square.

Rather than keep a low profile, the errant couple could not miss the closing night of the pleasure gardens at Vauxhall. Henry was there too with his brother Lord Peterborough and a large party of young men of fashion and, to Hickey and Charlotte's amazement, merely ignored them. Over the next few days, drunk, he appeared twice in Portman Square, demanding entrance and ultimately striking Hickey with a stick. Hickey wrenched the stick from Henry's grasp and returned the blows, with Henry yelling for mercy and screaming 'Murder! Murder!' before being arrested and carried off. After being released on bail, Henry promptly fled London, posting first to Margate from where he sailed to Ostend and obtained passage back to India in a Danish ship, leaving his mother and younger brother to sort out the debts he had left behind. They were never to set eyes on him again.

Early in January 1782 it was mooted in the newspapers that Lord Peterborough was expected to marry. The prospective bride was Lady Elizabeth Henley, youngest sister not only to the Earl of Northington but also to Viscount Deerhurst's deceased wife. Since his wife's death, Deerhurst had suffered further tragedy. Reckless as ever, he had attempted an impossible jump while out hunting, resulting in a fall and terrible injuries. The news of his death was initially reported, so severe was the accident. Thanks to the surgeon's skill his life was saved but his sight, in both eyes, was lost and he subsequently wore a green silk eye patch over his right eye which was terribly disfigured.[186] The accident did, however, result in father and son being reconciled.

However, the anticipated marriage did not take place and possibly one factor that might have disinclined the Northington family to agree to it was Lord Peterborough's role alongside his friends Viscount Deerhurst, Joseph

Bouchier Smith and Maurice George Bisset in an extremely high-profile Crim. Con. trial.

Sir Richard Worsley of Appuldurcombe on the Isle of Wight had married Seymour Dorothy Fleming, a very wealthy heiress, in 1775. The marriage was not a happy one and she was reputed to have taken some twenty-seven lovers, one of whom was the Earl of Cholmondeley at Coxheath Camp back in the summer of 1778. Horace Walpole noted that his great-nephew had been 'most talked of for her' and Lady Worsley may again have temporarily replaced Grace in the earl's affections after Grace had left England in high dudgeon for Paris in the early summer of 1779. The lady had also bedded Viscount Deerhurst after his wife had died and before he was blinded, and her final lover was Lord Peterborough's other schoolfellow, Maurice George Bisset, a fellow Isle of Wight landowner and, by the time he tumbled Lady Worsley, a captain in the Hampshire militia regiment of which Sir Richard Worsley was a colonel. Lady Worsley eloped with Bisset towards the end of 1781 and her husband had launched a Crim. Con. case.

Sir Richard Worsley opted for a crueller course than Dr John Eliot had taken with Grace. Lady Worsley had already provided him with a son and heir, he had no immediate need to remarry and so chose to sue for just a legal separation from bed and board, denying Lady Worsley the chance to remarry during his lifetime and forcing her to remain dependent upon him financially, while also suing Maurice George Bisset for a staggering amount of money. With Bisset facing total financial ruin, a plan was quickly put into action.

Lady Worsley and Bisset turned to their friend Viscount Deerhurst for advice. Deerhurst's intrigue with Lady Worsley had occurred in 1779 when he had been a guest of the Worsleys at their mansion on the Isle of Wight. Deerhurst had possibly followed hot on the heels of Lord Cholmondeley into Lady Worsley's bed and escapades with the lady of the house had followed. Upon being caught by Sir Richard in Lady Worsley's dressing room early one morning, he fully expected to be thrown from the house.

In reality though, despite the discovery, Deerhurst continued as a favoured guest for some days. Bisset later also found Sir Richard a very compliant participant during his assignations with Lady Worsley, Sir Richard letting him stand on his shoulders to peer through a bath-house window while the three were at the annual Coxheath military camp to view Lady Worsley as she got out of the bath and dressed.

As the couple had eloped, they could hardly deny the truth of the allegations Sir Richard was making against them. In a wonderful stroke of genius, Deerhurst suggested to them that the best course of action was to portray Sir Richard as an accomplice in his wife's affairs, suggesting that he encouraged them for his own voyeuristic pleasures. In essence, their defence was to totally besmirch Lady Worsley's reputation in order to show her husband's compliance in her affairs.

Lady Worsley had asked many of her lovers to take the stand and give evidence. With Viscount Deerhurst on side, the 'old schoolboy network' pulled together and of course his two friends and co-conspirators, Lord Peterborough and Joseph Bouchier Smith, were drafted into this plan. Although both declined to admit to any carnal knowledge of Lady Worsley (though Lord Peterborough was sometimes alluded to as being one of the twenty-seven lovers and the newspapers did not hesitate to suggest this in their coverage of the case), both testified to the notorious and lewd behaviour of the lady. The Earl of Cholmondeley was abroad and politely but wisely opted to remain there for the duration of the trial.

Did Lord Peterborough think of the Crim. Con. case in which his cousin Grace had taken the starring role just a few years previously? Without doubt his mother the Dowager Countess of Peterborough must have been totally exasperated by her errant son and her family's constant appearances in these affairs. Joseph Bouchier Smith, struggling with debt and awaiting the imminent arrival of his first-born child, while wanting to help his more powerful friends also had good reason for wanting to minimize any damage to his own reputation.[187] Various other noble gentlemen followed Lord Peterborough into the witness box, culminating with Lady Worsley's doctor who testified to treating the lady for a venereal disease.

The outrageous plan worked: Sir Richard Worsley was awarded damages but only the paltry sum of one shilling as a rebuke to him by a jury that was disgusted by his behaviour. However, the reputation of all who had participated was now ruined to varying degrees and the prospective marriage between Lady Elizabeth Henley and the 5th Earl of Peterborough was never mentioned again.[188]

The poet William Cowper, in writing to the Reverend William Unwin on 24 February 1782, mentioned an intended visit by Lady Austen who was to spend the summer near his home at Olney in Buckinghamshire. Lady Austen had been born Ann Richardson and had married Sir Robert Austen, 7th Baronet of Bexley, in 1755, the same year in which Robinaiana had married the Earl of Peterborough. Since then widowed, Lady Austen made the acquaintance of Cowper in the summer of 1781 during a visit to her sister, Mrs Jones, the wife of the curate of the nearby village of Clifton Reynes that formed part of the estate held by the Earls of Peterborough. Following a falling-out over some expressions used by Cowper in his letters to her, their friendship had cooled:

She [Lady Austen] is to spend the summer in our neighbourhood, Lady Peterborough and Miss Mordaunt are to be of the party; the former a dissipated woman of fashion and the latter a haughty beauty. Retirement is our passion and our delight; it is in still life alone we look for that measure of happiness we can rationally expect below. What have we to do therefore with characters like these? Shall we go to the dancing school again? Shall we cast off the simplicity of our plan and artless demeanour, to learn and not in a youthful day neither, the manners of those whose manners at the best are their only recommendation and yet can in reality recommend them to none, but to people like themselves?

Clearly Lady Austen was keeping company that Cowper did not approve of, but his worries were unfounded for his later letters reveal that although Lady Austen did spend the summer as his neighbour, Robinaiana and her daughter did not accompany her. Robinaiana would have been known to Cowper through family connections as Cowper's cousin was Harriet, Lady Hesketh, the widow of Sir Thomas Hesketh of Rufford who had died four years earlier, and uncle to Jacintha's husband Thomas who had died only weeks before Cowper was writing to Unwin. He would therefore have been painfully aware of Robinaiana's previous life as a mistress, of her son's connection with the Worsley scandal and of her niece Grace's shenanigans.

Grace gave birth to a daughter on 30 March 1782, most probably in her Cumberland Street home. Lord Cholmondeley now rushed home from Paris, the newspapers hinting that he did so as soon as he had heard of the birth.[189]

If not the prince, Cholmondeley has always remained the other main candidate as the father of Grace's daughter, her parentage impossible to truly confirm. Along with Cholmondeley and the prince, the Honourable Charles Wyndham, third son of the 2nd Earl of Egremont, was another man who was talked about for the vacant position (he too had testified at Lady Worsley's Crim. Con. trial). Educated, like Grace's cousin Charles Henry Mordaunt, at Westminster School, he was about six years younger than Grace, born in 1760, and probably the most profligate of her admirers. He was a close companion of the Prince of Wales (much to the king and queen's disgust), and therefore also a companion of Cholmondeley. Grace's daughter was thought by some to resemble Charles Wyndham and the Earl of Cholmondeley was the man who stepped forward to look after her but it was the prince who was named as the father on the baptism record.

On 30 July 1782, at the church of St Mary and St Marylebone, Grace baptized her daughter with the feminine form of the prince's names, Georgi[a]na Augusta Frederica; the parents named in the register were His Royal

Highness George, Prince of Wales, and Grace Elliott. Only the Earl of Cholmondeley and one or two other people were present at the baptism.[190]

It will perhaps always remain a mystery as to who was the father. The
prince did not refute the allegation or try to alter his name on the baptism
register, Cholmondeley certainly cared for the little girl as if she were his own
and as for Wyndham, well, if the little girl resembled him then who is to say
that she was not actually his? Little Georgiana, when born, had very dark hair
and the prince, whose family were blond, was reportedly unconvinced on
seeing her for the first time, saying 'to convince me that this is my girl they
must first prove that black is white!'[191]

Letters exchanged between the Prince of Wales and his mother Queen
Charlotte and between the prince and Lord Cholmondeley some years later
in 1799 while discussing the propriety of Georgiana being presented at court
strongly suggest that, despite the darkness of her hair, both the prince and his
mother firmly believed the little girl to have royal blood. Cholmondeley also
seemed to accept this view. The king, kept firmly in the dark, had nonethe-
less somehow been told that Georgiana was Cholmondeley's natural daughter
and, following this revelation, the prince wrote to his mother, the queen,
suggesting how Georgiana might still be presented: 'There is one mode . . . by
which I think still it might be effected by, which is, Cholmondeley's saying
what is *perfectly true*, that she is *no daughter of his*, but *his ward*, & contradict
by that means what she has been by some people supposed to be.'

The queen responded negatively to this idea, saying:

> As to the proposal you make about the manner in which the K[in]g might
> be undeceived about the suspicion of M.S. [Miss Seymour as Georgiana
> was known] being Lord C's daughter, I will fairly own, as you wish me to
> speak the truth, that you will act more kindly towards her by giving it up
> entirely, for you know how difficult it is to deceive the K[in]g, & should by
> any accident which cannot now be foreseen (but yet may happen) the real
> truth ever come to light, I am convinced the dear K[in]g never would
> forgive it.

Cholmondeley replied to the prince's letter on the subject of the impropriety
of Georgiana being presented at court, saying 'I am sure your Royal Highness,
with your usual goodness, will at all times honor her [Georgiana] with your
protection.'

The question then of whether the prince believed himself to be the father
seems to be settled in the affirmative; what cannot be deduced is whether
Cholmondeley thought his friend the prince was duped and believed he was

the natural father or whether he was simply behaving honourably in providing a home for the innocent daughter of his friend and his ex-mistress, possibly at the request of the prince. Grace's views on handing over her infant child to her former lover, still a bachelor, have not been recorded, but it undoubtedly would have been a wrench for her although she was probably given little choice in the matter. However, for Grace, the important point was that her daughter was recognized by the prince as his and Cholmondeley was someone she knew she could trust implicitly and so she acquiesced.

Chapter Thirteen

The 5th Earl of Peterborough and Criminal Conversation

In April 1782 a masquerade ball was held at the Pantheon, attended by his Royal Highness the Prince of Wales and several of the Worsley Crim. Con. participants. Lady Worsley herself was there in fancy dress but unmasked, conducting the blind Viscount Deerhurst around the ballroom; Lord Peterborough who 'distinguished himself by wearing the only black domino in the rooms'; the Marquess of Graham and Mr Wyndham.[192] Revelling in her notoriety, Lady Worsley being there unmasked was a challenge to Sir Richard. Grace was not listed as being in attendance (she had given birth only three weeks earlier), but she was back on the social scene less than a month later when, at another masquerade graced by the presence of the Prince of Wales, 'Lady Worsley and Miss Dalrymple in dominos, were arm in arm the whole evening', the reporter scathingly adding that 'not a woman of rank was to be seen'.[193]

Grace Dalrymple Elliott and Lady Seymour Dorothy Worsley were two of a kind. Not only did they have the Earl of Cholmondeley in common, they were a similar age, both of good birth and well connected, and both with their reputation and character ruined; they could perhaps rely on each other to a much greater degree than they could rely on any man and a friendship grew between them that would survive many trials and a great many years. Among the demireps of the Cyprian Corps they stood apart as two of only a select few who were well-born as opposed to those with a background in the bawdy houses or on the London stage.

The previous year, in August 1781, Lady Worsley had given birth to a daughter fathered by Bisset, and who was baptized at St Mary and St Marylebone as Jane Seymour Worsley, daughter of Richard and Seymour Dorothy Worsley. Even though Lord Worsley was patently not the father, the child was legally his, his name appeared on the baptism register as her father and he cruelly took the babe from his wife and her lover. The little girl died six months later and was buried in Paddington churchyard on 10 February 1782. Lady Worsley and Grace therefore had a further connection as they had both recently given birth to a daughter. One wonders whether Lady Worsley, now openly living with Maurice George Bisset, was one of the few people who attended the baptism of Grace's daughter.

The summer months of 1782 were probably heady ones for Grace; although she had lost the prince's favours, she had a hold on him through her child and hoped this would secure her future. The portrait of Grace painted by Thomas Gainsborough and commissioned by the Prince of Wales was exhibited to great acclaim in London. Her infamy continued into the following year. The *Rambler's Magazine* of January 1783 published a pretended conversation between Dally the Tall, Perdita and the Bird of Paradise, in which they discussed which of their latest *puffs* should appear in the newspaper (Grace's concerned a duel in Hyde Park fought on Grace's behalf between an English baronet and an Irish nobleman, after which the two men got drunk and auctioned her with the English baronet the highest bidder). The article came complete with an engraving of the three women getting dressed to receive company, in which Grace was pictured at her mirror applying her trademark rouge to her cheeks. She appeared in public with Charles Wyndham in the absence of Lord Cholmondeley who had taken himself off to mainland Europe, and the two were an acknowledged couple at the Pantheon masquerade.

PANTHEON

Never, perhaps, was seen, on a similar occasion, a more numerous company than assembled here on Thursday evening. ... Besides the usual groups of characters that exhibit at a masquerade, the most singular were, a half parson half a soldier, a half Englishman half Frenchman, a droll, a curious figure of Fortune pouring out gold from the Cornucopia, and moving all-round the room on a transparent wheel; a groupe of Indians stunned the ear of every one with their horrid war-hoops and death-hollos! – A few of the Cyprian Corps in elevated life were present – Mrs Elliott's dress, the *chemise de la reine*, and Miss Sheppard's were the most elegant of the whole group. The Perdita and the T__le__n paired off very early. Mrs B__nw__ll, and Col. F___tz__ck were in close Tête-à-Tête all the evening, also Mr W___nd__m and Mrs Elliot, Lady Gr__v__r likewise perambulated the circle for a considerable time.

The company were very sociable, and the dances continued till past seven in the morning.[194]

While Perdita was squired by her new love, the handsome Colonel Banastre Tarleton, Grace was clearly the star of the show. Her dress, the *chemise de la reine* or, more properly *chemise à la reine*, was the height of fashion. A diaphanous white muslin gown with a coloured sash ribbon tied high on the waist, the wearer appeared fashionably *déshabillé* or undressed; the chemise had, until this time, been used as an undergarment but now it was worn as a dress in its own right with no corset underneath. It was popularized in France during the summer of 1780 by Queen Marie Antoinette, hence its name, who was painted wearing such a dress by Élisabeth Vigée Le Brun to the outrage of her subjects who were scandalized to see their queen dressed in such a simple and romantic way.[195]

Marie Antoinette had sent a few of these chemises to her aristocratic friends in England, in particular to Georgiana, Duchess of Devonshire. The duchess and Mary Robinson are usually credited with introducing the fashion to England but Grace was also an early devotee of the style. She had spent time at the French court as the mistress of the Duc de Chartres; had she too been sent a *chemise à la reine* from friends in France?

Despairing of rekindling her relationship with either the prince or Cholmondeley, Grace returned to France to renew her relationship with the Duc de Chartres.[196] This time, though, Grace had competition. The beautiful and 'celebrated' Mrs Mary Benwell was in Paris too and had caught the eye of the duc. Mary Benwell, or Moll, at least a decade younger than Grace, is one of those people who have dropped through the cracks in the floorboards of history. In her day she was every bit as well-known as her fellow courtesans; now she is all but forgotten.

Purportedly born in Wapping and starting her career as one of the girls to be found at Mrs Weston's bagnio in Berkeley Row (visited by Henry Mordaunt and Hickey during their residence in London), by the summer of 1783 Moll had already been the mistress of at least two titled men before moving on to Colonel Richard FitzPatrick, who was to prove a more long-term association.

A handsome man, the Honourable Colonel Richard FitzPatrick, second son of the Earl of Upper Ossory (an Irish peer), was part of Grace's inner circle; he was a close and loyal friend of Charles James Fox (the two men had known each other since their schooldays and Fox implicitly relied on FitzPatrick) and one of the intimate group that included the Earl of Cholmondeley, the Prince of Wales and Charles Wyndham.[197] An officer with the 1st Regiment of Foot Guards, FitzPatrick had recently been promoted to the rank of colonel in recognition of his service during the American War of Independence, even though his principles meant he had been opposed to that war. The dashing colonel was also an inveterate gambler, a solo balloonist, bon viveur and wit.[198]

As befitted such a great friend of Charles James Fox, FitzPatrick had stood as a Member of Parliament, holding the borough of Tavistock from 1774, but gave as little time as he could to matters of business, preferring to devote himself to pleasure instead. He boasted that 'he had thrown the dice more frequently than any man in England' and was no doubt a regular at the faro tables run by Cholmondeley at Brooks's.[199] He lived on his credit and trades-men were always denied access to his house when they called to press their bills. Because of her own debts, Moll had left the colonel in the spring of 1783; she couldn't pay them and neither could he, and so she journeyed to Paris at the same time as Grace:

> If we may credit our intelligence from France, English beauties are not less admired in Paris, than in their native kingdom – the reigning toasts there at present are, the Benwell, and the Elliot; the former is allowed to be by far the most elegant woman that has appeared there these many years, they term her the Kitty Fisher of her time, from her likeness to that beautiful woman. The Duc de Chartres has made himself extremely ridiculous on her account, following her to all public places; to the contempt with which she treats him and his promises (which that nobleman is but too apt to make) she may attribute his constant attendance on her.[200]

Colonel FitzPatrick read the above report in the *Morning Post* and sat down the same day to write to his 'dearest Moll'. She had been continuously corre-sponding with her former lover and was in Paris hopefully awaiting his arrival or his instructions to return to England. FitzPatrick gave her the news that he was once more a secretary of state and, while it didn't bring any immediate financial gains to him, it did improve his credit. He wrote:

> The comfort is, at least, that you need no longer stay at Paris against your inclination; for though <u>we</u> shall not be much richer, our credit will be much greater, while we [referring to the Ministry] are in place ... Drabs delight not me, nor ladies neither, as Hamlet says, I know but one woman worth looking at, speaking to, kissing, touching, &c., and she is a little Brimstone that is diverting herself at Paris. Pray give my love to her, and tell her that unless she comes home soon, I shall think her a good for nothing monkey, since it is now impossible for me to come to Paris.[201]

Quite possibly the promise of renewed credit did the job and FitzPatrick's 'little Brimstone' returned to England; Grace must have been pleased to see the back of her and the way to the Duc de Chartres left clear once more. Once her rival was removed Grace quickly regained the duc's attention; she was back in England by the middle of May, appearing at Ranelagh Gardens, with the newspapers reporting that she had come over in the suite of the duc and had passed unsearched at Dover as his 'secret baggage'.[202] Shortly after-wards gossip began to surface suggesting that both Grace and Lady Worsley were pregnant.[203] Lady Worsley did indeed have a child in 1783 whose father was almost certainly Maurice George Bisset, but nothing remains to suggest that Grace was with child.

The winter of 1783 found the tables turned and Grace in London with Mary Benwell back in Paris; King George III was on the verge of dismissing the government and so FitzPatrick's credit would once more be on hold. In a letter from Paris, an extract of which was printed in the *Morning Post* of 16 December 1783, Mary Benwell was again praised for her beauty:

> By the bye, the Benwell (as they call her here) is, in my opinion, by far the most beautiful woman and the most admired. The French Nobility seem frantic after her, in all the first circles the Benwell and the air balloon engross the conversation … It is my firm opinion she will do more by example towards the abolition of that cursed custom of disguising nature with loads of filthy cosmetics than all that has ever been done or said against it. The stile she lives in here is amazing; and entre nous, I fancy she will surprise you in the spring, by introducing to your country a visitor that will not a little astonish the great world; to my certain knowledge he has asked leave for that purpose, and will most assuredly obtain it. You will ask how came I so much in the secret? It is no secret here that he is devoted to her, and his asking leave I had from an intimate of his, therefore it is no great stretch of conjecture that she will company him.

FitzPatrick, in London, saw the above piece and immediately cut it from his newspaper to send with a letter to his Moll:

> Dearest Moll, I write you a short line to tell you the news, and inclose you a paragraph about yourself. Notwithstanding our victories in the House of Commons, we have been beat in the House of Peers, and shall all be out in a few days, but I am afraid we shall be all in again too soon to let me make the best use of my idleness by coming to see you at Paris; the world is all in astonishment, and very busy times are coming on. If we go to the length of hanging our opponents, or being hanged ourselves, I will give you notice that you may come to the spectacle. Why do not you write you idle monkey – pray do immediately; adieu, dearest Moll, in or out you know,
>   I am yours for ever,
>   R.F.[204]

With her rival once more stealing her thunder in Paris, Grace, in London, exacted her tit-for-tat revenge and found herself a new protector, snaring for herself the Honourable Colonel Richard FitzPatrick. Did he also want to make a point to his dearest Moll who had not returned to him?

The clues that he was Grace's lover are twofold. Firstly, a newspaper report described Grace being 'azurized' towards the end of April 1784 or, in other words, she was wearing the 'true blue' favours of Charles James Fox's political party; King George III had indeed dismissed the Fox-North coalition government, which he was opposed to, and instead appointed William Pitt the Younger as prime minister. Pitt had little support in the house and, after action by Fox, in March of the following year Parliament was dissolved and an election campaign began.

The supporters of Charles James Fox took to wearing 'true blue' colours and favours on the streets, denoting their support of American Independents and their hostility to Pitt and his ministers. At a rout held by 'the celebrated beautiful and witty Mrs Crewe', blue and buff (the colours of the uniform of Washington and his troops) were worn by both men and women. The Prince of Wales attended and toasted Mrs Crewe, saying 'True Blue and Mrs Crewe' to which the lady responded without missing a beat, 'True Blue and all of you'.

The election ran for six weeks from 30 March with the Duchess of Devonshire famously canvassing on the streets of Westminster for Charles James Fox who was reputed to be her lover. For this the duchess was attacked in the press, depicted in satirical prints as selling kisses in exchange for votes and never ventured again into politics in the public arena. How else to view the following newspaper report of Grace then, other than in the vein of emulating the political fervour shown by the Duchess of Devonshire and showing her support for Fox and his cohorts but in a more modest way?

> Miss Dalrymple is so *azurized*, that nothing under the *blue* sky can exceed her; she wears a *blue* hat; her eyes are *blue*, her breast-bows and ribbons are the same colour; her carriage is also *blue*; and she is called by way of distinction the '*Blue Belle of Scotland, &c. &c*'.[205]

Pitt did win the day and was returned to the house as prime minister, but Colonel Richard FitzPatrick was returned in his seat of Tavistock for the Whigs and Charles James Fox for Westminster. So, with Grace proclaiming her allegiance to the 'Foxites', the second clue comes from her address during 1784 and 1785. Many years later, when creditors were catching up with her, a newspaper advertisement appeared, referring back to the period around 1785 and giving her address as New Norfolk Street near Hyde Park.[206] New Norfolk Street, often referred to simply as Norfolk Street and now known as Dunraven Street, ran parallel with Park Lane and was opposite Hyde Park; not too far away from the Dean Street house in which Lord Cholmondeley had tucked Grace away a few years earlier, it was also just minutes away from her aunt Janet's town house in Upper Brook Street. One noted inhabitant of New Norfolk Street at the time when Grace lived there was none other than Colonel FitzPatrick himself.

If Grace was living with FitzPatrick before and during the election she could expect little of benefit from him financially; once more he was temporarily without funds or the means of credit but it would seem that, in the April of 1784, Grace was dressing herself in blue to proclaim to the world her support for both her lover and his politics. There has been little suggestion in the past of any interest in the political world from Grace but her father voiced his opinions on the matters of the day and her brother, Henry Hew Dalrymple, was to steadfastly declare and act on his own principles in the future. It is not surprising that Grace, as daughter and sister of these men and an educated and clever woman in her own right, would actively take part in the political world she inhabited.

Once the election fervour was over, and in contrast with the turmoil of those few months, Grace spent the summer months attending the races in Brighton in the company of several French nobles – the Duc de Chartres, the Duc de Lauzun, the Marquis de Conflans, the Comte de Seguir and others – who had come over from France via Dover especially for this event.[207] The newspapers were still speculating on the paternity of her daughter, the *Morning Post* reporting that 'Great disputes have recently happened about Mrs. E___t's child, L__d C____y saying it must be the P___'s, from its mouth and eyes, while the latter affirms it to be C___y's, from its nose.'[208]

Meanwhile, Grace's brother, Henry Hew Dalrymple, was returned from his posting to Africa and the West Indies and was resident in Paris. He wrote from there on 4 June 1784 to the editor of the *Rambler's Magazine*, a publication that regularly featured his sister in their gossip columns:

> We were never in a greater dearth for news or even scandal than at present: the latter indeed is more unaccountable than the former … If it were not for the *Rambler's Magazine*, half our tea-table chat would be exhausted, and we should become as silent as Englishmen, bringing out some wise sentence once in half an hour.

Signing the letter simply as 'H.H.D.' and with a flourish of '*Adieu! Tres cher amie! Vive l'amour et la bagatelle!*' he despaired of the French press, who confined themselves to romance and fiction instead of the amours of 'the Duc de C___rs, or Monseigneur le D___n__as'. Given that his sister was the on/off mistress of the Duc de Chartres, Henry Hew, it would appear, was entirely accepting of the fact that he was the brother of a celebrated courtesan. Were brother and sister really so dissimilar?

The Earl of Cholmondeley, while cooling his relationship with Grace, had stepped forward to provide for her young daughter Georgiana, housing her within his own establishment and bringing her up as if she were his own child. Cholmondeley behaved with great kindness and love towards the girl and treated her in every way as if she was his own daughter. In fact Grace could hardly have found a better home for Georgiana than the Earl of Cholmondeley's nursery. It was in March 1784 that Sir Joshua Reynolds painted the 2-year-old girl, then known as Miss Elliott.

In the original of this painting Georgiana was wearing a cloak and a wide-brimmed hat, tied under her chin, with the lace of a cap peeping out from underneath. At some point these have disappeared from the portrait, the mob cap alone remaining perched upon the little girl's head.[209]

William Cowper, having escaped the intended visit of the Dowager Countess of Peterborough in 1782, three or four years later found his Buckinghamshire neighbourhood intruded upon by her son and he wrote to his friend, the Reverend John Newton, saying

> We have new neighbours; with whom, however, we should be very sorry to live as such; but there is no danger. Lord Peterborough and his Lady Anne Foley have hired a house at Weston and a young man of the name of Smith, who they say finds it convenient to be at a distance from his creditors, is of the party.[210]

This, then, was Lord Peterborough and his friend Joseph Bouchier Smith, visiting the area of the earl's estate at Clifton Reynes, but the presence of Lady Anne Foley at Weston Underwood with these two men is the result of a scandal that had preoccupied the *ton* and provided much gossip and entertainment in the preceding months.

Lady Anne Foley was the younger sister of Lord Peterborough's friend, Viscount Deerhurst. Born Lady Anne Margaret Coventry, she had married the Honourable Edward Foley, MP, of Stoke Edith Park in Herefordshire some years earlier but, true to her Coventry blood, indulged in a few extra-marital indiscretions.

There were unconfirmed rumours of her dalliances with various gentlemen: a Mr Lloyd, Mr Storer, Captain FitzPatrick, prior to his promotion to colonel and Grace's bed, and Lord Melbourne (Sir John Eliot's old friend), most of these conducted under the very nose of her trusting husband. Indeed, Lady Foley reputedly sent a letter to FitzPatrick after the birth of her short-lived son: 'Dear Richard, I give you joy. I have made you the father of a beautiful boy ... P.S. This is not a circular.' Matters came to a conclusion, however, in September of 1784 when she was discovered *in flagrante delicto* in a shrubbery at Stoke Edith with Lord Peterborough. John Davies, a mason employed by Lord Foley, saw them: 'his [Lord Peterborough's] hands were about her middle and her hands about his neck. The rest is too indelicate to be mentioned. He [Davies] further said that he was about twenty-five yards from them.'[211]

One could have supposed that the 5th Earl of Peterborough, aware of his cousin Grace's Crim. Con. trial in 1774 and a participant in the trial of his friend Maurice George Bisset only two years earlier, might have paid more heed to his reputation and position in society rather than plunging headlong into a scandal. It was a licentious age and men more than women were able to get away with bestowing their favours where they chose, but it is very tempting to draw parallels between his behaviour and Grace's antics a decade or so earlier and to conclude that the morals in this family were sufficiently lax as to permit this disregard of personal reputations, both for themselves and others, the pursuit of their own pleasure being always first and foremost. Certainly the *Town and Country Magazine* of April 1785 that published the tale of the amours of the 5th Earl and Lady Foley in its 'Histories of the *Tête-à-Tête* annexed' column, titled 'Memoirs of the Incautious Lothario and the Honourable Mrs F___' thought so, for they said he was 'Descended from an amorous as well as a noble family' and continued by repeating the story of his father's affair with Miss Dawson that had appeared in the same magazine some eight years earlier, conveniently ignoring the fact that the same charge might also be laid against his mother.

Before becoming enamoured with Lady Foley, Lord Peterborough's 'intrigues in the Green-room at both theatres were pretty much talked of and he was particularly happy in possessing the affections of a certain Opera dancer;' an Italian, her identity remains a mystery. Lord Peterborough was 'for a considerable time her voluntary captive and his chains were so rivetted, that it was thought by his friends that nothing but death could sever them.' However, Lord Peterborough entertained suspicions (according to the article, ones that were not ill-grounded) that his Italian opera dancer was seeing a foreign ambassador behind his back and Lord Peterborough rushed from her arms 'at a time when he was thought to be irrevocably her slave'. Furthermore, shortly after rushing from the opera dancer's arms, he fell headlong into those of Lady Anne Foley while spending the summer and autumn of 1784 at Cheltenham where a great concourse of society was gathering for the races and festivities.

It was no surprise to anyone when, early the next year, Edward Foley brought an action for Criminal Conversation, publically accusing Lord Peterborough of an affair with his wife and seeking damages of some £2,500. What is more surprising is that with Grace's notoriety still at its peak, no contemporary paper even hinted at the family connection between Lord Peterborough and his notorious demirep cousin.

As recounted in the trial, held at the beginning of May 1785, Lord Peterborough came to the Foleys' home of Stoke Edith Park, not too far distant from Cheltenham, in company with his partner in crime Joseph Bouchier Smith during the month of June to stay with the couple. The Reverend John Napleton, questioned as a witness during the trial, declared he gave Edward Foley warning that 'Lord Peterborough's visit to Stoke was not upon an honourable intent'.

Unsure of leaving his wife with Lord Peterborough but declining to dismiss him from Stoke Edith in accordance with the wishes of Napleton, Edward Foley assured him that 'From the bottom of my soul, I do not believe Lord Peterborough means anything dishonourable; but I have desired Lady Ann not to go out with him, for the reasons you have mentioned; and shall desire her again.' There were suggestions that Foley, a spendthrift, had run through the fortune his wife had brought to the marriage; was he now looking for a way out? Lord Peterborough had possibly presented himself as a timely and unwitting dupe as it was hinted that Foley had already looked into the possibility of divorcing his wife. Reports of her affair with Mr Lloyd had reached his ears but he could do little without proof of his wife's infidelities. If the *Town and Country Magazine* is to be believed, an attachment had already formed between Lord Peterborough and Lady Anne Foley, the two having met at a rout that saw Lord Peterborough losing his money to the lady 'with an excellent grace ... so enveloped in contemplating the beauty of her brilliant eyes, that all his judgement at play was obliterated'.

Lord Peterborough, taking a leaf out of his friend Bisset's book, decided to try the same defence to the Crim. Con. charge, suggesting that Edward Foley had known about his wife's many affairs and, in declining to prevent them, had acquiesced and signalled his acceptance of them. Accordingly witnesses were paraded through the court, all of whom had some knowledge of the various gentlemen who had been entertained in Lady Anne's boudoir with, they said, the full knowledge of her husband. With yet further echoes of the Worsley vs. Bisset trial, that faithful old friend Joseph Bouchier Smith appeared to support his friend Lord Peterborough's arguments.

At the beginning of the trial a letter from Lord Peterborough to Anne Foley was read to the court, written after Foley's suspicions had been aroused, and with Lady Foley under the watchful eye of William Maull, the master of the Crown Inn at Worcester. Maull had sent one of his own servants, Benjamin Smith, to Stoke Edith with a pair of horses and Smith remained there while the master of the house was absent, driving Lady Foley and Lord Peterborough's carriage and phaeton, and voyeuristically peering through the carriage window when the couple quite clearly thought themselves un-observed. From Lord Peterborough's letter, it would seem that he had no idea he had been spied upon in his intimacies with the lady on the back seat of the carriage and that Smith was reporting back to Maull and Maull to Edward Foley:

> Cheltenham, Saturday Morning.
> My dear ANNE!
> I had not left you two minutes last night before I repented of having fixed on Sunday for our meeting. A thousand reasons (of which few will be necessary to convince you) occur to me now, which did not at the time, owing to the total privation of my senses at the sight of you when I almost despaired of it. I think Mr. Foley's coming to-morrow a certainty, as the Hereford election is to be on Monday, which will be a much better day, as you are sure of his not being with you. Maull's guardianship will also expire on Mr. F.'s return, without the possibility of his having anything to say against you. You had better air on the London road to meet him, as your apparent impatience to see him will certainly please him; and by that means you will have also an opportunity of giving the first account of yourself, which, when he finds it corresponds exactly with Maull's, will not only remove all suspicion of our having met intentionally, but will restore you to a greater confidence than ever. I hope that you will pardon me for having advised you what to do, who can judge so much better for yourself; by my anxiety about everything that interest you and the impossibility of communicating your sentiments to me, which I think on this subject must agree with mine, will justify me.
>
> Adieu, My Dear Anne! Until Monday, when I will be at the three-mile stone from Ledbury, at half after five.
>
> My ride yesterday has quite destroyed the good effects of the waters.

Further witnesses were examined who swore that Edward Foley was besotted by his beautiful wife, his supposed acceptance of her affairs due to not being able to believe any ill of her and simply being far too trusting in his care of her. Lord Peterborough's case failed; Edward Foley was believed. The jury found in favour of the aggrieved husband and Lord Peterborough was ordered to pay damages in the sum of £2,500 plus costs.

Perhaps, as suggested by the *Morning Herald* newspaper, if Lord Peter-borough was going to pay, then he was going to have a return for his money and he continued in his relationship with the fallen lady.[212] Their subsequent movements are recorded in the Foley's Divorce Bill heard in the House of Lords on 29 March 1787 before a goodly number of the earl's noteworthy peers; Lady Anne Foley had been personally served with the order for the first reading of the bill at the Earl of Peterborough's house at Brompton in Middlesex, although they also resided on his estate at Dauntsey in Wiltshire.[213]

The divorce was granted, Lady Anne was now free to remarry and plans were afoot for her to become the next Countess of Peterborough. The Peterborough estate of Clifton Reynes was sold in February 1787, no doubt to pay the damages awarded to Edward Foley and to provide for the forthcoming nuptials. The *Public Advertiser* intimated that the sale had been at the 'particular instance' of Lady Anne and others and had yielded some £72,000.[214] William Cowper must have been delighted by the news. However, there was one further twist in the story to come. Just weeks after the sale of Clifton Reynes, Lady Anne had told Lord Foley 'That notwithstanding she was in a few days to be a Countess, she had rather live with him on any terms, than be united to Lord Peterborough – whom she hated.'[215] Lord Peterborough behaved very justly to his inconstant lady who, after providing him with two years of trouble, a tarnished reputation and costing him a considerable amount of money, had now professed her desire to return to her husband, should he want her (he didn't!). He allowed Lady Anne to remain in his Brompton house, to be attended by his servants and have the occasional use of his carriage for another month before she finally packed her belongings and left.[216] By summer Lord Peterborough was consoling himself with the attractions on offer at Margate and Lady Anne was at Lowestoft.[217]

Joseph Bouchier Smith was in France, avoiding his creditors and unable to return home due to the debts that had mounted up behind him. Their friend Maurice George Bisset, having long since abandoned Lady Worsley, finally made it up the aisle, becoming Lord Peterborough's brother-in-law when he married the earl's sister Harriat, that haughty beauty having eventually, at the age of 34, consented to become his wife.

Charles Henry stood as bondsman on the marriage allegation for the soon-to-be-wed couple. With Bisset's departure from her side, Lady Worsley had been left to fend for herself with only the pin money she was allotted from her hated husband on which to survive. Grace, much better placed than her friend, had returned to Paris, still high in favour with her wealthy and influential French duc.

Chapter Fourteen

French Affairs

On 3 September 1783 peace treaties were signed in Paris between the United States of America, Great Britain, France, Spain and The Netherlands, signalling an end to the hostilities of the American War of Independence. Three of the founding fathers of America were in Paris to sign the treaty: Benjamin Franklin, John Adams and John Jay.

A year later as part of the ongoing peace negotiations a British commission was sent to Paris to establish a treaty of commerce and to settle disputes over African boundaries. The man chosen to head the British commission was the Scottish diplomat George Craufurd, a man opposed to liberal trade and one whom the British government could rely on to be stubbornly obtuse and do little to further the negotiations. Another Scotsman was appointed as Craufurd's secretary, an army officer now out of service due to the disbandment of his regiment earlier in the year and already in Paris in the early summer of 1784: Henry Hew Dalrymple.

Was he chosen because of his knowledge of the African coastline gained while stationed there with the 75th Regiment of Foot? King George III ratified the appointment and officially granted it to Henry Hew, and with Grace's contacts within the political world and especially via the Earl of Cholmondeley to the Prince of Wales, it is tempting to think that she may have whispered in a few ears and sent out a few letters to anyone of her acquaintance with some influence in these matters, recommending her brother to them. However it came about, in the autumn of 1784 George Craufurd and Henry Hew Dalrymple were both in Paris engaged upon the commission's business, staying in the Hôtel d'Orléans on the Rue des Petits Augustins.

Thomas Jefferson arrived in Paris and replaced Benjamin Franklin on the American delegation discussing the treaty of commerce. While Craufurd, as expected, prevaricated and left the American gentlemen with no great impression of him, Jefferson and John Adams found in Henry Hew Dalrymple a kindred spirit, someone who shared their ideals and values.

John Adams' son, John Quincy Adams, had travelled with his father to Paris. In his diary he noted meeting Henry Hew a couple of times during the month of March 1785 at the lodgings occupied by Benjamin Franklin, and wryly noting of Craufurd that the treaty of commerce was said to be about as far advanced as when Craufurd had left England nine months previously.

The Duc de Chartres had for some time been insistent in his requests to Grace, asking her to return to France and to his side. There was little left for her in England: the Prince of Wales had lost interest in her, as had Lord Cholmondeley, and her daughter was being well cared for. With her brother in Paris and seeing greater prospects for herself in France, Grace relented and returned to her former lover.

Did brother and sister move in the same social circles? Henry Hew Dalrymple certainly mixed with the Scottish nobility resident in Paris, particularly some of the ladies of the Stewart family from Traquair in the Scottish borders. These ladies introduced Henry Hew to Madame de Villette, otherwise Reine Philiberte Rouph de Varicourt, a young, beautiful and married French noblewoman in her late twenties known as 'La Belle et Bonne' ('the Beautiful and Good'). The young woman had been the adopted daughter of the writer and philosopher Voltaire, who had visited her father's house and found her as a young 14-year-old crying because she had been told that her father's finances would not stretch to a dowry for her and she was to be placed in a convent to devote her life to God. Enchanted by her and pitying her situation, he took her with him, securing a marriage for her to the young Marquis de Villette which proved unhappy. La Belle et Bonne therefore found herself in Paris and in the company of Henry Hew.

It was another Scotsman and friend of Henry Hew, Sylvester Douglas, the future Baron Glenbervie, who left behind the record of Henry Hew's amour with the young Frenchwoman and, in doing so, added a little character to Henry Hew, proving him to be a true Dalrymple in the mould of his father and sister.

Madame de Villette, as Sylvester Douglas pointed out, had long ago lost any pretensions to the use of the word 'bonne' in connection with her name regarding female virtue. Indeed, she had obviously thrown that away by 1785 if Douglas is to be believed, although he did not go into details, merely noting the 'Tête-à-Tête incidents of [Henry Hew's] intercourse' with the lady that were told to him by Henry Hew himself. The lady employed a confidential maid at the time of her relationship with Henry Hew who had formerly worked for the actress Mademoiselle Dubois. This maid had told her mistress, who in turn told Henry Hew, about his friend Sylvester's own indiscretions with Mlle Dubois in the year 1770 when, as a young man, he had undertaken a continental tour. As he had heard Sylvester's secrets, Henry Hew chose as repayment to reveal his own secret, describing his liaison with Madame de Villette to his friend.

Many years later in 1818 when Madame de Villette was an old lady – the 'belle' then gone along with the 'bonne' – Sylvester Douglas himself met her and the two reminisced about the days before the French Revolution, Madame remembering Henry Hew as 'an amiable young Scotchman whom she had known'.

So, during the latter part of 1784 and into 1785, while Grace reclaimed her position as mistress of the Duc de Chartres, Henry Hew was in the same city, romancing Madame de Villette on the one hand and engaging future presidents of America in political and moral discussion on the other, impressing in equal measure in both activities.

On 10 May 1785, in Paris, Thomas Jefferson had 200 copies of a pamphlet privately printed. This pamphlet, 'Notes on the State of Virginia; written in the year 1781, somewhat corrected and enlarged in the winter of 1782, for the use of a foreigner of distinction, in answer to certain queries proposed by him' had been written by Jefferson in response to a series of questions posed by the French politician François de Barbé Marbois, seeking familiarization with the thirteen states. Jefferson's notes grew to become a complete description of Virginia; of its history, land and people as well as presenting his views on the future of the state. They also revealed his view of the practice of slavery, confirming his attitudes more explicitly recorded than elsewhere other than his first draft of the Declaration of Independence. By early 1784 people were asking for copies of this manuscript.

He did not go ahead with the publication until he arrived in Paris where the cost of printing was so much cheaper and 200 copies were printed. Most of these went back to America to be distributed there; just a few were withheld to be personally given to friends in Europe, and it is a measure of the friendship that had grown up between Thomas Jefferson and Henry Hew Dalrymple that one was given to Henry Hew, personally inscribed to him on the frontispiece.[218]

The inscription, in Jefferson's own hand, reads:

Th. Jefferson having had a few copies of these notes printed to offer to some of his friends & to some other estimable characters beyond the line, begs the favor of Mr Dalrymple to accept of one. Unwilling to expose them to the public eye, he asks the favour of Mr Dalrymple to put them into the hands of no person on whose fidelity he cannot rely to guard them against publication.

However, copies did fall into other hands and such was the demand for the manuscript that unauthorized copies began to be printed, badly translated from the original. To counter this, Jefferson amended his work and, in 1787, a

London publisher was allowed to begin wholesale production. Henry Hew's copy though, one of the original 200, was the edition Jefferson was most happy with and the inscription written within it proves that Jefferson considered him a worthy and trusted friend.

Further proof of Jefferson's regard for Henry Hew comes from a letter he sent to John Adams, dated 27 December 1785:

> ... This will be delivered you by Mr. Dalrymple, secretary to the legation of Mr. Craufurd. I do not know whether you were acquainted with him here. He is a young man of learning and candor, and exhibits a phenomenon I never before met with, that is, a republican born on the North side of the Tweed.

If a true republican, then Henry Hew Dalrymple was of an opposing point of view to his sister, for Grace had an inherent interest in the survival of the monarchy and aristocracy, both in France and in Britain. However, Grace's lover, the Duc de Chartres, now the new Duc d'Orléans since the death of his father in November 1785, shared her brother's republican values.

Grace had been resident in France for a year by this time, the debts she had accumulated and was unable to pay while she lived on New Norfolk Street forcing her to flee abroad, and the Duc d'Orléans provided a home for her on the Rue de Valois in Paris adjacent to the Palais-Royal which was one of his properties. This was a time of contentment and pleasure for Grace, housed in comfort at the centre of d'Orléans' circle and with her elder brother close by.

In January the British press reported on a hunt that took place in the environs of Paris, probably at Meudon where the château was used as a hunting lodge. The Duc d'Orléans was

> accompanied by most of the English gentlemen resident in Paris, who shewed themselves by far the best horsemen. Seven of the Parisians were dismounted in leaping over very easy ditches; but his favourite, the celebrated Mrs. E. our countrywoman, after running many miles close by the Prince, had the satisfaction of being in at the death. Her noble figure, superb Amazonian dress, and velvet cap, with a fox made of feathers on the top of it, in the form of a crest, gave the beholders an idea of Tasso's description of the warlike Clorinda.[219]

Grace favoured the fashion of the day, wearing masculine-style riding habits, not only for the hunt but also for more everyday activities and, with her tall, willowy frame, must have known what a dramatic figure she cut in this dress. Ladies traditionally obtained their habits from a tailor rather than a mantua-

maker and Grace used Louis Bazalgette, a Frenchman who had set up in business in London and was also the Prince of Wales's tailor.[220]

She sometimes had her young daughter with her and Queen Marie
Antoinette had allegedly praised the beauty of the little girl. Grace later
recalled in her journal that, when Georgiana was about 3 years old, at the
French royal residence of St Cloud the queen had kept the little girl sat upon
her knee all the time they were at dinner. St Cloud, a palace on the banks of
the river Seine a few miles outside Paris, was owned by the father of Grace's
lover, Louis Philippe I, Duc d'Orléans, having been in his family for generations.

The old duc had not visited St Cloud for some years and in 1785 he sold
it to his cousin, King Louis XVI, who wished to buy the palace for Marie
Antoinette. If Grace's daughter was 3 years old at this time then, if true,
the meeting at St Cloud must have been around the time of the sale of the
palace. Grace was still newsworthy, appearing as a fashion icon of the period,
and in the spring of 1786 the British papers were reporting on the new head-
wear she had been seen sporting in Paris, a cap of her own design modelled on
the helmet worn by the Roman goddess of war, Bellona:

> Bellona's helmet is the fashionable ornament at present in Paris for the mode
> comme il faut. The vizor is of tiger spotted sattin, bordered with a narrow
> black ribbon, the cawl, very high and puffed, of blue sattin, tied round with
> a broad nakara-coloured [bright poppy-red] ribbon, edged with black. This
> ribbon forms a large bow before, and another behind, and joins two wide
> lappets of Italian gauze, descending below the waist. Five feathers, two of
> which are green, two nakara, and one black, form the crest of this beautiful
> helmet: The hair flowing behind, and two large buckles falling on the
> bosom, complete the tout ensemble. The honour of this invention is intirely
> due to our handsome countrywoman Mrs. E____, still the favourite of the
> D. of O.[221]

Why pick Bellona's helmet as an inspiration for a cap? It actually raises
the interesting possibility that Grace was presenting herself as an advisor to
her lover, the Duc d'Orléans, in maintaining diplomatic relationships with
Britain. Ceremonies regarding matters of foreign treaty, and of both war and
peace, were held in the Temple of Bellona (Templum Bellonæ) at Rome
conducted by the fetiales or priestly advisors. By recreating herself in the guise
of Bellona, Grace might have had a deeper intention rather than just design-
ing herself an outlandish but very fashionable new cap.

Maybe she pushed her luck a little too far in trying to meddle in d'Orléans'
affairs for, just months later, Grace reputedly received £500 as 'the last mark

of the Duke of O___s' generosity' and decamped to Strasbourg with Prince Louis, Duc d'Arenberg who, like Viscount Deerhurst, had been left blind following a hunting accident when he was still only a young man (although d'Arenberg's blindness had been caused by a badly-aimed shotgun and not by a fall):

> It is remarkable that this lady always disdained the sighs of vulgar swains. Her pride is to have Princes in her chains, and, from the arms of the Lords V___a and C___y, she has shared the bed of the presumptive heir of a Crown, that of the first Prince of the blood in France, and now that of a Prince of the empire.[222]

Despite her romantic ups and downs, there was still one man who was an ever-constant presence in times of need. Lord Cholmondeley, reliable as always even though they were no longer a couple, was continuing to provide financially for Grace, perhaps in agreement to her leaving her daughter in his charge. On 23 February 1787, and no doubt in response to a begging letter from Grace, he wrote from his Piccadilly mansion to his agent and his letter was then forwarded on to Paris:[223]

> Sir,
> If you have not pay'd Mrs Elliot any thing on my account since I last saw you I shall be obliged to you to pay her seventy five pounds & to draw upon me for it.

Meanwhile travel on the Continent again beckoned for Grace's cousin, Lord Peterborough; on 26 April 1788 *The World* newspaper reported that he had visited Paris. Did he visit his cousin Grace? We have no way of knowing but privately he could hardly object to her morals or behaviour when his own were no better, and even if he publicly wished to keep his distance, she would have been an introduction to entertainment at various parties, salons and ballrooms. Grace remained a close of friend of Lady Worsley and both ladies were living in Paris, so it is probably more inconceivable to think that he did not make use of this acquaintance rather than the opposite.

Although he continued to provide for her, Grace had been replaced in the affections of the Earl of Cholmondeley by a French lady, Madame Saint-Albin (known in England as Madame St Albans). She was Marie-Françoise Henriette Laché, supposedly born around 1767 (although probably a little earlier) in Saint-Malo, a bustling port in Brittany on the north-western coast of France, and renowned both for her beauty and her intelligence. Before Cholmondeley she was the long-term mistress of Charles-Pierre Maximilien Radix de Sainte-Foix, a man around thirty years her senior but one who could place her within the prestigious environment of the French court. Radix de Sainte-Foix was superintendent of finance to the Comte d'Artois, the French king's younger brother, to whom he had made himself indispensable and his home, where Marie-Françoise Henriette reigned supreme, was the superb and picturesque Château de Neuilly on the outskirts of Paris.

Disaster befell Radix de Sainte-Foix in 1780 when he was accused by Jacques Necker, the French minister of finance, of embezzling money entrusted to him by the Comte d'Artois, although many thought it a scheme by d'Artois to avoid repaying the money he had borrowed. Radix de Sainte-Foix was nevertheless made the scapegoat and on 6 September 1782 was told of his imminent arrest; he immediately took flight to London, taking Marie-Françoise Henriette with him. While Radix de Sainte-Foix remained in exile in England, his mistress seems to have crossed the Channel, travelling back and forth while acting as his courier.

Although they had been a couple for some months, the earliest report of Madame Saint-Albin with Lord Cholmondeley is in the *Morning Post* newspaper in early April 1785:

> Lord Cholmondeley is become a *Benedick*, in everything but the ceremony, a sedate, domesticated man. He does not wander, he does not roam, as in former days; but confines himself to one snug little place of residence: he has made over his old spacious *tenement* to the *Duc de Chartres*, and now resides entirely in *St. Albans*.[224]

Cholmondeley was once again besotted and devoted himself to his new mistress in much the same way as he had with Grace. The two women had probably known each other in France; was Grace the one who introduced Cholmondeley to 'the prettiest woman in England'?[225] The earl had a monstrously elegant vis-à-vis built for Marie-Françoise Henriette, a purple and gold stripe on the bodywork with a bright yellow silk interior complete with purple and gold trimmings. On the door panels were a silver cypher and a French coronet, the cypher denoting that she belonged to Cholmondeley while the French coronet hinted at her aristocratic French origins. Madame Saint-Albin dressed in the latest fashions and sparkled with the jewels bought for her by her earl.[226]

During the summer of 1786 Cholmondeley and Madame Saint-Albin went to Kingsgate at Margate, the same house in which he had spent a summer of pleasure with Grace almost a decade earlier.

Radix de Sainte-Foix maintained contact with his former mistress Marie-Françoise Henriette, using her as a 'go-between' by which he was able to exchange letters with Lord Cholmondeley. Cholmondeley had the ear of the Prince of Wales and the government while all the time maintaining the aura of not being overtly political; he was probably, then, a very good choice as a discreet intermediary. France was suffering upheavals; in July 1789 the Storming of the Bastille signalled the beginning of the French Revolutionary period. With armed soldiers on the streets of Paris and the people openly rioting and looting, many French *émigrés* began to flee to England. Radix de Sainte-Foix was among those 'foreigners of distinction, who have been forced, by the perils of the times, to abandon their native country' for whom Cholmondeley and Madame Saint-Albin gave a grand dinner at their country villa, Trent Farm near Barnet.[227]

Grace did not flee and remained in France, still protected for the time being by the Duc d'Orléans. She moved from her house overlooking the Palais-Royal to a new address on the Grande Rue du Faubourg du Roule, now an extension of the Rue Saint-Honoré, not too far away from another of the duc's Paris estates at Monceau, a fine château with elaborate pleasure gardens. D'Orléans promoted the ideals of a more democratic government in France and made himself popular among the people, opening the Palais-Royal to them, allowing shops to open in its precincts and providing food for the poorest in times of famine. While distancing himself from politics as much as he was able, he walked a tightrope between the French monarchy to which he belonged and his belief in equality for all.

In England, Madame Saint-Albin was 'breeding', as Horace Walpole so delicately put it in a letter to his close friend Mary Berry, written on 2 August 1790. The child was born in January 1791, initially reported to be a son but in reality a girl who was named Harriet. Maybe giving the earl a child was a last attempt to keep his interest in her but if so it failed. Lord Cholmondeley, with perfect good sense and mindful of his position, was about to announce his engagement and it was to be to a totally respectable heiress. His choice fell on the 30-year-old Lady Georgina Charlotte Bertie, daughter and wealthy joint heiress of the late 3rd Duke of Ancaster and Kesteven. Little Harriet was ensconced in the Cholmondeley nursery alongside Georgiana and her mother was handsomely paid off and banished from his side. Marie-Françoise Henriette duly departed for Brussels in company with Colonel Keppel, a cash lump sum, an annuity of £800 a year and her jewels as compensation.[228]

By now a confirmed bachelor, Lord Peterborough passed his days much more quietly than previously, living at his mother's Dean Street house in Soho when in London. The *Stuart's Star and Evening Advertiser* newspaper of

1 April 1789 published an extract of a letter received in London containing news from Bath stating that 'Lord Peterborough's health mends but slowly; Mr and Mrs Bisset are his constant companions' and by August he was once again at Cheltenham but this time, far from being in the company of Lady Foley, he was there with his mother, Robinaiana, the Dowager Countess of Peterborough.[229]

Robinaiana saw out the twilight years of her life in Bath where she died on 6 December 1794, having outlived all but two of her children. Her son, Lord Peterborough, took her remains back to his estate at Dauntsey in Wiltshire, where she was buried in the family vault. Her will had been written less than a month before her death and in it she appointed her son, Lord Peterborough, and her sister Janet (who in 1793 was living in Chiswick) as executors of her estate and asked for £1,500 to be invested, the interest gained thereon to be paid to her daughter Harriat and then to her little granddaughter, Jane Harriet Bisset.

Robinaiana made no further provisions for any future children born to Harriat, who was now aged over 40, in her will. However, Harriat was not past her childbearing days and was in fact to have one further daughter, Ann, born in 1798, who inherited nothing from her grandmother.

Maurice George Bisset settled down into comfortable family life and there is every indication that he and Harriat were perfectly happy together. The *Morning Post* newspaper certainly thought so, for they opined: 'Were Lord Peterborough to contemplate the happiness of his relation, Mr. Bissett, he would not be so squeamish about the matrimonial pill.'[230]

Owning estates at Knighton Gorges on the Isle of Wight, Shepton Mallet in Somerset and at Lessendrum in Aberdeenshire, Scotland, Bisset was very much the landed gentleman and had suffered but little loss to his reputation over his affair with Lady Worsley.

The house at Knighton Gorges, a picturesque Elizabethan mansion, had been demolished by 1820, and many sources say that Bisset had it pulled down in a fit of temper to stop his eldest daughter inheriting after she married her cousin against his wishes. As Bisset died three years before his eldest daughter married, this is quite clearly an implausible theory; instead the estate, which he had inherited from his grandfather, was entailed upon the male heirs only and would pass to his brother William upon his death.

After trying and failing to bar the entail, it is quite probable that he had the building demolished out of spite but to his brother not his daughter, to prevent his sibling being the beneficiary of it. Bisset passed the end of his life in Bath and at his Scottish estate of Lessendrum, where he died on

16 December 1821. His daughters were treated equally in his will, written three years earlier, both getting £100 a year until their mother died or they were married, and each to have £3,000 as a marriage portion. After his wife's death he willed that his estate be divided between his two daughters and for the youngest, Ann, to have £1,000 more than her elder sister to balance out Jane Harriet's inheritance from her grandmother Robinaiana. His will proved Bisset to be a devoted husband and father.

Chapter Fifteen

Cock-fighting in Calcutta

While Grace had been capturing the attention of the Prince of Wales, across the world, in India, the newly-promoted Captain John Mordaunt was in attendance at the court of the Nawab of Oudh, playing fast and loose. Warren Hastings, Governor General of India, writing to John Macpherson on 12 December 1781 from Benares in Bengal said that 'Capt. Mordaunt had a princely fortune yesterday: God knows what to-day: he is not in the service, therefore absolutely adrift and particularly recommended to me by Mr. Barwell.'[231]

Captain John Mordaunt was the aide-de-camp who attended the wife of Warren Hastings when she travelled hastily to her husband's sick bed. Travelling rapidly by ship along the River Ganges (she covered some 400 miles in three days), Marian Hastings was nearly drowned during a monsoon storm in rapids by the Rocks of Conglong in Bihar. Luckily her arrival brought about a turn in the condition of her ailing husband, who began to recover almost as soon as he set eyes on her. Warren Hastings sent for Captain Mordaunt and, while still in his sick bed, took him by the hand and proffered his grateful thanks for his care of Mrs Hastings, promising to never forget him.[232]

John was often to be found at Lucknow where the British Residency was in the process of being built by the nawab, but frequently needed to address queries to the presidency town of Calcutta.[233] Communication between the two locations was, for John, problematic: he would rather not put pen to paper and demonstrate his lack of command over the written word if he could help it, even if it meant going to extreme lengths to avoid this simple task. George Nesbitt Thompson, Hastings' private secretary, said of Captain Mordaunt that he would rather travel from Lucknow to Calcutta in the hottest weather to ask a question than write a few lines about it.[234]

William Hickey, Henry's old protagonist, arrived in Calcutta in 1783 with Charlotte accompanying him, living as his wife in name, if not by law, until her early death on Christmas Day of that year. Hickey threw himself into his legal work, but also drank heavily to try to assuage his grief. When not at the nawab's court, John Mordaunt was also resident in Calcutta and in the habit of dining at Hickey's house upon the esplanade. Henry Mordaunt was an absent friend: for most of 1784 both he and Robert Cornwallis Dalrymple had been on duty with the Bengal army in the Upper Provinces (Agra and Oudh) during the 1st Rohilla War but, by December and with the campaign concluded, Henry too was in Calcutta, once more welcome at Hickey's house.

John was gaining minor celebrity at the court of the Nawab Vizier Asaf-ud-Daula, ruler or governor of the Oudh region of the Mughal Empire who presided over an extravagant court at Lucknow, attended by many Europeans who were seduced by the exotic way of life and the opportunity for financial advancement. Indian and European alike shared equal status at the court. John Mordaunt was a particular favourite of the nawab's and acted as the commander of his bodyguard; they apparently shared similar low tastes and a passion for cock-fighting, long considered an ungentlemanly sport but still indulged behind the scenes. John had imported his own game-cocks to India from England and they were the envy of the nawab. Johann Joseph Zoffany (1733–1810), a German-born artist, had travelled to India to make his fortune by painting portraits of his wealthy East India Company patrons and of the Indian princes, and he immortalized John and his game-cocks at the nawab's court in a portrait known as 'Colonel Mordaunt's Cock Match'.[235]

The portrait was commissioned by Warren Hastings, the first governor general of Bengal in 1784, who was present at the cock-fight on 5 April 1784 although he is not shown in the painting.[236] Almost a year after the cock-fight, Warren Hastings wrote to John Macpherson: 'Let me entreat you to be kind to Capt. Mordaunt: allow him to return to Lucknow; the Nabob Vizier will be able to pay part of his private debts in the next year and Mordaunt has an equal claim to any.'[237] It has been suggested, and indeed is possible, that John acted as a spy for Hastings at the vizier's court. He was still there years later when, in a letter to Ozias Humphry on 11 March 1789, the Frenchman Claude Martin wrote to say that John was

> now at the Vizier's Court, hunting, fighting cocks and doing all he can to please the Nabob in expectation of being paid the large sum due to him by that Prince, but I fear much of his success, as the Vizier is not much willing to pay his debt particularly to Europeans, for what I know of his character I think it such, that if one could read in his heart he would perceive it loaded with many dark sinister intentions and as you know those who compose his Court, you then ought to know what man he is. A man that delights in elephant and cocks fighting would delight in something worse if he feared nothing.[238]

Again demonstrating the 'easy and convivial disposition' he seems to have inherited from his father, John entertained his way around India, flattering the Indian rulers in order to promote the interests of the East India Company:

As a bon vivant, as master of the revels, or at the head of his own table, few could give greater variety or more satisfaction than Mordaunt. He had the best of wines and spared no expence, though he would take little personal trouble in providing what was choice and rare. He stood on little ceremony, especially at his own house.

Military duties took a back seat but John was an excellent shot, except on one important occasion. A quarrel over a game of cards led to a duel and although John was shot and injured by his adversary he missed his target, perhaps deliberately.

Now, somewhat surprisingly, both daughters of George Cornwallis Brown travelled out to India. With no great fortune of their own, their aunt and guardian, Robinaiana, Countess of Peterborough, decided to send them out to join their elder cousins. So Janet and Susannah Brown, exhibiting the same pluck for which their cousin Grace was renowned, took their future happiness into their own hands and embarked on a far-flung overseas husband-hunting expedition.[239]

It was a tried and tested method of securing a wealthy spouse. Eligible young girls were encouraged to travel to India by the directors of the East India Company who were aghast at their men taking local girls as their wives and adopting Indian custom and practices, in effect 'going native' even though the practice did ensure a certain level of influence for the British officials with the rulers of the territories. If enough British girls could be sent out there, then it was hoped that the company men would settle with them instead. The two Brown sisters had enough male relatives already in India to look after them, and they could expect their Mordaunt and Dalrymple cousins to introduce them to their fellow officers and to the best society that India had to offer.

They resided in Calcutta with Colonel John Mordaunt at his house on the esplanade in the Chowringhee area, formerly a tiger-infested jungle but, since the construction of Fort William thirty years earlier, abounding with magnificent houses built by the British residents.[240]

Their scheme worked. On 24 May 1788 in the church at Fort William, Calcutta, consecrated only the year before, Janet Lawrence Brown married John Kinloch (at the consecration of the church in 1787 John Mordaunt had been one of a party who arrived drunk as lords after spending the previous evening in 'Bacchanalian rioting').[241] The *Calcutta Chronicle* reported the marriage five days later and revealed the nickname by which Janet was known to her family: 'MARRIAGES: On Saturday evening last, at the New Church, John Kinloch, Esq. to Miss Jessy Brown.'

The name Jessy was regularly used in the extended Brown of Blackburn family as a nickname for Janet. It was also used for one of the daughters of Jacintha (herself also really a Janet) whose daughter Jacinthia-Catherine Hesketh went by the name of Jessy-Catherine.

John Kinloch, one of the younger sons of Sir David Kinloch, 5th Baronet of Gilmerton situated in Athelstaneford in North Berwickshire (close to the area formerly inhabited by the Brown family when they owned Blackburn House), was employed by the East India Company's Civil Service and, at the time of his marriage, was Collector of the Customs of Burdwan in western Bengal. Between 1784 and 1788 John Kinloch commissioned a portrait of himself by the rising London painter, Arthur William Devis, who had arrived in India looking for rich patrons.[242]

Around the same time, and probably to mark her forthcoming marriage, Jessy Brown had her own full-length portrait painted by Thomas Hickey (no relation to William Hickey).[243] It's an interesting counterpart to the full-length portrait of Jessy's cousin Grace painted just a few years earlier by Thomas Gainsborough. Whereas Grace appears worldly and sophisticated, Jessy appears as an artless and innocent girl, wearing no jewellery and a simple dress. In tone it is more reminiscent of the Cosway miniature of Grace painted shortly before her own marriage.

On 29 February 1788, three months before his marriage, John Kinloch had written out his will and testament, leaving everything he owned to 'Jessy Brown of Calcutta ... spinster' for 'the great regard, love and affection I have for [her]' and making her sole executrix. After the marriage he had crossed out the name, writing 'my wife Jennet Lawrence Kinloch of Burdwan in the Province [of Bengal]' above it. The marriage, however, was short-lived: John Kinloch was in bad health and, hoping that a change of air would cure him, he journeyed to Serampore on the banks of the Hoogli River but this did not prevent his death which occurred less than four months after his marriage.[244]

The day before he died he had altered his will, rewriting it to include a bequest of one of his gold watches to Mr Kegan, Surgeon of Bheerbhoom (Birbhum) who had attended him during his illness (noting that he was weak and sickly, although of sound mind). His wife was again named sole executrix and to inherit everything except a bequest to his 'much valued friend' Thomas Brooke of Burdwan who was to receive the sum of 20,000 sicca rupees. Regrettably, the inventory of John Kinloch's estate revealed an unfortunate fact: he was in debt to the sum of 14,000 sicca rupees. Several huge sales of Kinloch's effects and properties followed; an attempt by Janet to clear his debts and leave herself with a tidy lump sum. Interestingly though, the first item listed in the inventory was 'J. Mordaunt's bond', dated 15 March

1788 and for 10,000 sicca rupees, none other than Janet's cousin John Mordaunt, the illegitimate son of the Earl of Peterborough and his wife Robinaiana.

Six months later, at the same church in which her now widowed sister had married, on 3 March 1789 Susannah Robiniana Brown married Major Samuel Farmer, an officer in the Bengal army. Samuel Farmer was considered one of the three best officers in the company's service and he moved in the same social circles as her cousins Colonel John and Captain Henry Mordaunt. At the sale of John Kinloch's effects Major Farmer was listed as the buyer of many of the household items, perhaps purely setting up his own home prior to his marriage or maybe purchasing as a favour to Susannah Robiniana to help out her sister.

Major Farmer had already fathered at least one illegitimate child, a daughter named Eliza Cheap Farmer, born in 1781 and sent home to reside with a guardian in England. Following his marriage another daughter was born on 27 January 1791 at Fort William in Bengal and named Jesse Hyde Farmer. She was baptized the day after her birth but died shortly thereafter.

Colonel John Mordaunt never fully recovered from the pistol shot he received in his breast during the duel and this, coupled with 'one or two serious attacks on his liver' (the result of the drinking and 'Bacchanalian rioting' in which he indulged), hastened his death at the early age of only 40 on 26 October 1790. He died of a fever on board his budgerow (a large boat similar in shape to a gondola, with several cabins) near Chunar.[245]

According to an inventory made after his death, John was possessed of a fortune of over £12,500 pounds, held in England at his bankers Samuel Smith & Co. and in India, plus wearing apparel and possessions estimated at around £600.[246] The end of 'The Sporting Anecdotes' magazine article would form a fitting tribute to him:

> His heart was formed for friendship; he was warm in his attachments, which were however very select; and, notwithstanding the peculiar blunt-ness of his manner, I cannot say I ever hear him utter a rude thing, or do an uncharitable act.
>
> Such are the outlines of a man who, had he been bred in courts, would probably have been the Rochester of his day; for he was inordinately fond of women and seemed, when ill, to regret his situation chiefly as depriving him of their society.

It would be a fair consideration that John and his cousin Grace Dalrymple seem to have been cut from the same cloth; had John lived out his life in Europe he would undoubtedly have made a good playmate for the demirep

Grace. Both lived life primarily for pleasure but were fondly remembered by those who had lifelong attachments to them, despite their behaviour. Henry did not long survive his brother, dying on 8 February 1791 at Buxar. Again, Hickey gives us more information:

My London antagonist and ci-devant rival, Captain Henry Mordaunt, fell a martyr to the climate this season. He had been some time in possession of the lucrative appointment of Commandant of the Fortress of Buxar, where he died but not before he had amassed a fortune of full ten thousand pounds, the whole of which his mother, Lady Peterborough, received, the Crown having very liberally relinquished all claim to the property of the deceased who, by reason of his illegitimacy, could have no legal heir.

Henry had not amassed as great a fortune as accredited to him by Hickey, but still not far off. The inventory of his goods, chattels and credits, dated 1792 (which declared him to be both a 'bastard' and a bachelor), including bills due to him by the East India Company, amounted to £7,151 19s 2d.[247] Most of this was in the hands of his agents, Messrs Raikes & Co. of Bishopgate (this was the banking house that the dandy Thomas Raikes, friend of Beau Brummell, belonged to, although in 1792 his namesake father was in charge, Raikes junior being still at Eton).

On 30 June 1792 Grace's brother, Robert Cornwallis Dalrymple, who had attained a captaincy in the 2nd Bengal European Battalion, was buried in the cemetery at Dinapur. Within such a short space of time all three men lay in their graves in the same region of Bengal.

Jessy and Susannah, who had gone out to India with such hopes for their future had, in the five years they had lived there, seen most of the people closest to them die. However, amidst the sorrow there was some joy, for Susannah gave birth to a son who did survive the heat and disease. He was born at Chunar in Bengal on 6 October 1794 and named John Charles Farmer.

Samuel Farmer wrote out his last will and testament before the birth of this son. He mentioned no legitimate children of his own (so his daughter, Jesse Hyde Farmer, was deceased by this date), but provided for his wife and any children that they may have together. He also left bequests to his illegitimate daughter living in England and to her guardians. The executors were his wife and his brother-in-law John Bebb.

Janet remained a widow for over four years before accepting the proposal of John Bebb Esquire, a wealthy East India Company director. Their marriage settlement was drawn up on 12 January 1793 and John Bebb promised to pay 100,000 Indian rupees or £10,000 sterling into a trust to be administered by several trustees including the Honourable Charles Stuart of Calcutta, a Member of the Supreme Council of the East India Company on their Bengal establishment, and Janet's brother-in-law Samuel Farmer. This trust would be for his wife's benefit in the event of her becoming a widow. A short time later, at the same church in which she had married her first husband, Janet, widow of John Kinloch, walked up the aisle for a second time to become Mrs John Bebb. Although this marriage was to prove childless, it was a long and happy union. Sadly, this was not to be her sister's fate.

Samuel Farmer had been serving in the Bengal army in India for a great many years, joining as a cadet in 1768 when he was 18 years old and rising to the rank of major. On 27 November 1794, just weeks after the birth of his son, he died at Cawnpore (now Kanpur) in Northern India. He was buried in the Kacheri Cemetery there, recorded as a major of infantry aged 44 years. An inventory of Major Farmer's effects after his death revealed that, among other more mundane possessions and his bungalow at Chunar, he owned two boats, five tents, several bullocks, three camels and an elephant. By 16 June 1795 much of his estate had been sold.

Unbeknown to Susannah and Janet, at the time that they were simultaneously celebrating the birth of John Charles and mourning the death of Samuel Farmer, back home in England their mother had also passed away, unaware of the birth of her grandson. The *Gentleman's Magazine* paid tribute to her, recording her death on 18 October: 'At Southampton, Lady King, wife of Vice-admiral Sir Richard K. bart.; a most amiable and truly virtuous woman.'[248]

Chapter Sixteen

Prisoner in France

In 1793 the Traitorous Correspondence Act was passed, a direct result of the revolution in France, which not only suspended correspondence deemed to be traitorous but barred any aid or assistance whatsoever being sent to France. Following this, any British citizens who found themselves stranded in France, whether or not they were prisoners of the revolution, were unable to receive any financial help from their friends and families. During April the bill received its third reading and was passed by a majority vote. Among the names of the minority who voted against it were 'Marquis Lansdowne, Lord Guildford, Lord Lauderdale, Lord Stanhope, Lord Derby, Lord Hay and Lord Peterborough'.

It is heartening to think that Lord Peterborough possibly voted against this bill out of concern for the plight of his cousin, for Grace was one of those who had left it too late to leave France and, along with her friend Lady Seymour Worsley, was forced to remain there at the mercy of the revolutionaries.

Grace had been replaced in the affections of the Duc d'Orléans some years earlier but, if her own account is accepted, she still enjoyed his protection, patronage and companionship. Her life still remained a gilded one.

Just about all that is known of Grace's life in France during this time comes from her very own pen. She wrote down her experiences and they were published many years after her death under the title *Journal of my Life during the French Revolution*. While this journal contains much that is true, it is also a highly-embellished account of Grace's experiences.[249]

Grace recalled that on Sunday, 12 July 1789, she left Paris for the day in company with d'Orléans, Prince Louis D'Arenberg and others to spend the sunny afternoon fishing at d'Orléans' château of Raincy in the Forest of Bondy, dining there in the early evening. The party arrived back in Paris at eight o'clock in the evening, intending to finish the day with a visit to the Comédie-Italienne theatre. Instead they found their carriages halted by reports of a mob abroad on the streets and hastened to d'Orléans' house at Monceau just outside the city walls. Prince Louis wished to visit the Duc de Biron, a nobleman and French military hero who had fought against the British in the American Revolutionary War, to seek his counsel. Armand Louis de Gontaut, Duc de Biron (formerly Duc de Lauzun), lived nearby and, as Prince Louis was blind, Grace walked with him to guide his way. On her return to Monceau she found d'Orléans with Madame de Buffon, the woman who had replaced her in the duc's affections.

Madame de Buffon, formerly Marguerite Françoise Bouvier de la Mothe de Cepoy, was only 22 years old, still in the first flush of youth compared to Grace who was now in her mid-thirties. When aged only 17 she had married the Count de Buffon but shortly afterwards had captivated d'Orléans instead, leading to a separation from her husband. Grace accused the younger woman of having revolutionary sympathies and would later blame her for instilling her ideals into the head of d'Orléans. Persuading d'Orléans to come outside with her, Grace walked with him in Monceau's ornate gardens, trying to give him advice for his actions on the coming day. The summer evening being warm, they promenaded until two o'clock in the morning when Grace left to walk the short distance to her house on the Rue du Faubourg du Roule.

All was panic the next day. The Duc d'Orléans, soon after Grace had left him, went to Versailles to speak with the king but with little benefit to either of them. The Comte d'Artois, younger brother of the French king, the Prince of Condé who was brother-in-law to d'Orléans, and Condé's father, the Duc de Bourbon, all fled Paris, heading for exile in Britain.[250] Amid scenes of riot and horror, in the evening Grace decided to go to her jeweller in the Rue Saint-Honoré: perhaps she was taking stock of her gems with the idea of following the exiles and returning to the safety of London? Sitting next to Grace in her carriage was an unnamed English lady, just possibly her friend Lady Worsley, but before they could reach the jeweller's the mob surrounded their carriage, shouting, haranguing and among them the French guards holding aloft the severed head of Joseph-François Foulon de Doué (Grace calls him simply Monsieur de Foulon) who had been in charge of the finances of the king's household. Foulon de Doué had become disliked by all sides and lost his life to the mob who, having two or three times tried to hang him from a lamppost (he was too fat and the rope kept breaking), instead beheaded him. The guards thrust the head, which was affixed to a pike, into Grace's carriage, her English companion having enough courage to berate the mob in return. Here though we have the first inaccuracy in Grace's account: Foulon de Doué fled Paris after the Storming of the Bastille on 14 July 1789 and was killed just over a week later on the 22nd, not on the 13th as Grace avers. Had she simply misremembered the date and events when writing her account some years later?

Grace heard the taking of the Bastille prison while partaking of breakfast at a fashionably late hour with d'Orléans and two of his friends at his château of Monceau, from where they could clearly hear the cannon shots. Grace saw little of d'Orléans for some time after this and, to escape the troubles, left Paris to spend the rest of the summer pleasurably with a friend who had a château at Ivry-sur-Seine just outside Paris. The troubles in the city worsened as the prelude to revolution took hold; Louis XVI and his family were forced from their palace at Versailles to the Tuileries where they were held under house arrest.

Perhaps acting on behalf of her former lover, in the spring of 1790 while d'Orléans was on an extended visit to England, Grace journeyed to Brussels which was then under Austrian control. Belgium, like France, was in a state of turmoil with fighting between the Austrians and Brabant rebels who wanted independence, but this seems not to have deterred the intrepid Mrs Elliott. In the Belgian capital she spoke with several of the duc's agents, including his banker Edouard Walquiers, and remained in the country until July when she returned to Paris and dined with d'Orléans, who had himself just arrived from England.[251] She claimed to have left Brussels the day after the Austrian troops moved out of the city where they had spent the night camped near her home in the Parc de Bruxelles, the location of the Royal Palace (home to the Dukes of Brabant), charitably passing food and drink from her window to the soldiers.

Why go to Brussels at a time when it was in a state of unrest? Why return to Paris when this too was fraught with danger and she could so easily have taken a boat for England? D'Orléans had seen Grace's daughter, Georgiana, now 8 years old, and had brought letters from her to her mother and Grace must have longed not only to see these but Georgiana herself. Perhaps England was barred to her, in a similar way that it was to her friend Lady Worsley who forfeited her annuity if she returned home, or maybe Grace was acting on behalf of d'Orléans, either hoping to regain his full affection or because she was his spy and he could unobtrusively communicate with his friends back in England through her.

Rumours have persisted that Grace was involved in the murky world of espionage during this period of her life and she was certainly plucky enough for this. With her myriad contacts both at home and on mainland Europe she would have been able to pass messages and information on to those who needed them, and it was not unknown for women, even of Grace's station in life, to operate in this way. It is entirely possible that, by writing to England, she was able, in relative secrecy, to get messages from the Duc d'Orléans, via Madame Saint-Albin and Lord Cholmondeley, to the Prince of Wales and vice versa, and was maintained by both Cholmondeley and d'Orléans for this very reason, even if it did put her in a dangerous position.

Grace didn't stay long in Paris but instead, during the summer months of 1790, took a house at Issy in the countryside surrounding the capital, a fine château that had formerly belonged to the Duchesse de l'Infantado and where d'Orléans often came to dine. Issy had been a favourite retreat of Marie Antoinette and Grace's journal recounts visits made by the queen, still forced to reside with her husband and children in the Tuileries Palace but who was allowed twice to walk, uninterrupted by Grace, in the gardens at Issy. Marie Antoinette, believing that Grace meant to return to Brussels, sent a lady in her service to Grace's house at Issy with a letter for her sister, the Arch-duchess Maria Christina (Mimi), at Brussels and a small box that she wished Grace to take to her. Although returning to Brussels had not been Grace's plan, she acquired a passport and travelled there, arriving just after the arch-duchess had left.

In March of 1791 Queen Marie Antoinette had begun to plot her escape from the Tuileries, assisted by her lady-in-waiting, Madame Campan. Her plan was to escape to Brussels but, as befitting a queen (and completely ignor-ing the practicalities of the situation she found herself in) she wished to have a complete wardrobe there for herself and her children. So Madame Campan had to arrange for clothes and linen to be made up and sent, via a network of sympathizers, to the widow of the mayor of Arras who was one of the queen's women, ready to be taken from there to Brussels at a moment's notice.

However, the transportation of Marie Antoinette's dressing-case was a little more difficult to arrange. This case held jars of ointment and perfumes and Marie Antoinette could not do without it. Being persuaded that if she sent it ostensibly as a gift to her sister in Brussels her intended escape would be revealed to all, Marie Antoinette instead arranged an elaborate plan whereby her sister's envoy asked publicly for her to arrange an identical one to be made and sent to the archduchess. However, by the time the escape was imminent, the dressing-case was still some six weeks from completion and in the hands of the ivory-turner. The queen then announced that, as she had promised her sister the dressing-case, there was nothing to be done but empty her own and send it, hoping that her ruse would fool all those around her. At no point does the more sensible plan of travelling without the case seem to have been contemplated, at least by the queen, and it was Marie Antoinette's attachment to this indispensable item that uncovered her plan as the ward-robe woman knew she would never be parted from it and told the authorities of her suspicions.

Was Grace then entrusted by Madame Campan with a small box of Marie Antoinette's necessities to take to Brussels in readiness for the escape? The escape attempt was ultimately doomed: Louis XVI and Marie Antoinette, their children and some attendants fled from Paris (the royal family disguised as servants to a Russian baroness who was played by the children's governess), but were stopped at Varennes and taken back under armed guard to Paris. It seems that Grace just might have been so employed, for she left for Spa in Belgium on the very evening that the royal family arrived back in Paris, 25 June 1791, and if she did indeed have anything to hide in connection with the escape attempt then this was a wise precaution. The box that she had been unable to deliver to the archduchess she had instead given to General Johann Peter de Beaulieu at Mons, commander of the Austrian army, in accordance with Marie Antoinette's instructions and suggesting that Marie Antoinette was in fact, as she was later accused, plotting an alliance with the army of her homeland.[252] Grace subsequently placed herself in further danger when she visited La Merci, a male convent in Marais in which two of the colonels of the French army accused of plotting to help the escape were imprisoned, Comte Charles Damas and Claude Antoine Gabriel, Duc de Choiseul-Stainville. She visited at the request of Comte Roger Damas, who was serving in the counter-revolutionary Army of the Émigrés under the Comte d'Artois, to deliver a letter to his brother and, fearing that the letter enclosed details of the escape which might incriminate the receiver of it, she visited to deliver it into his own hands and met with both men at no inconsiderable risk to herself. This very contact with counter-revolutionaries and émigrés who were mustering on the borders of France put Grace in mortal danger, and she wisely kept her head down and attracted as little attention as possible.

Grace now saw little of the Duc d'Orléans. He was fully occupied with politics and Madame de Buffon who, towards the end of 1791, found herself pregnant with his son. Around July 1792 Grace, having tired of the château at Issy (she found the locale 'too Jacobin'), instead took a cottage in Meudon, a small and charming hilltop village surrounded by wild woods in the countryside some miles to the south of Paris. This cottage was much smaller but very pretty with a thatched roof and it became known as 'la Chaumière anglaise' ('the English thatched cottage'). Situated on what is now known as L'Avenue Jacqueminot, a road leading to the royal Château de Meudon, it stood quite alone with no near neighbours apart from an elderly couple who were staunch royalists and was therefore very private. When Grace lived in Meudon, the fine royal château for some time only used as a hunting lodge was beginning to fall into disrepair, as eventually did her thatched cottage which sadly no longer exists.[253]

Grace still retained her Paris house though and it was there on 10 August, shortly after she had seen Marie Antoinette at her last public appearance at the Comédie-Italienne, that she was awoken by the sound of cannonades. The National Guard, followed by a mob, had stormed the Tuileries and, in terror, the king and queen had fled to the dubious safety of the National Assembly. The king's Swiss Guard put up a stout defence but could not hold out for long and many people died in the ensuing chaos; soldiers, commoners and courtiers alike.

With the barriers to the city closed Grace could not escape and was forced to remain in her house on the Rue du Faubourg, but once again was able to muster her courage in the face of adversity. Her garden backed on to that of Major Karl Josef von Bachmann, a Swiss aristocrat with his own company of Swiss Guards, who lived on the adjacent Rue Verte. He had been the man who had escorted the king and queen to safety from the Tuileries earlier in the day and three or four of Bachmann's soldiers had taken refuge in his house and, during the morning, had clambered over the wall into Grace's garden. She hid them in her house till the darkness of evening had fallen and they then left to an uncertain fate. Major Bachmann himself had been arrested and faced the guillotine less than a month later.

Grace now desperately needed to leave Paris. She was aided in her escape from the city by her maid; this clever woman took her to a man formerly in the employ of Grace as a porter and gardener and who knew of a breach made by smugglers in the city walls, close to his house behind the Invalides military hospital. Grace and her maid walked to this man's house at nine o'clock in the evening, taking care to be discreet, and he, although apprehensive, showed Grace the breach and she crossed safely over, sending her plucky maid back home.

In the darkness Grace walked alone across the plains of Vaurigard, a flat open landscape, until she reached the base of the steep hill that led to Meudon and the safety of her cottage there. The hill was bordered with vines and Grace hid among these when she thought she heard someone following her, exhausted and with her feet sore and bleeding from the stony path she had traversed: she had only delicate shoes of white silk on her feet and no stockings. Eventually she reached her house and allowed her servants to put her to bed. Her thatched cottage provided a safe haven and Grace kept out of sight until a note was brought to her door from a friend in Paris, Mrs Meyler.

The latter was an English lady, a confidante of Grace who was also trapped in the turmoil, unable or unwilling to return to England. It is a distinct possibility that the name was a subterfuge to hide the identity of Grace's great friend and fellow courtesan, Lady Seymour Worsley. Lady Worsley's name was still notorious in 1859 when the journal was published and Grace's granddaughter's Victorian sensibilities may have been repulsed by seeing such a name writ bold as her grandmother's confidante. If true, it is also the first hint that Grace's own words may have been edited, after her death, in the journal we see today. Alternatively, given the lackadaisical spelling mistakes in names in the journal, Mrs Meyler could also possibly be a misspelt Mrs Naylor, a woman who was to figure in Grace's later life.

Whatever Mrs Meyler's real identity, upon receiving her note Grace immediately went to the mayor of Meudon and, as requested by her friend, obtained a passport for herself and a servant to allow them to travel into Paris and return to Meudon before midnight. She travelled alone in a cabriolet, the pass for the servant designed to smuggle someone out of the city. Her papers were inspected at the Vaurigard barrier and she explained the lack of a servant by saying she had sent him back to collect some papers. Few people were trying to enter the city that day as there were rumours that the Prussians and Austrians were marching towards Paris and the astonished guards tried to deter Grace, telling her the streets already ran with blood, but she lied and said that her mother was dying and they let her through with no further argument.

Mrs Meyler lived on Rue Saint-Fiacre, adjacent to one of the relatively new boulevards.[254] Her small apartment was up four flights of stairs at the top of the building and, when Grace entered, she found to her surprise that her friend was harbouring a fugitive.

Louis-Pierre Quentin de Richebourg, Marquis de Champcenetz, had been an influential figure. The same age as Grace, he had served as valet of the king's chamber and governor of the Tuileries (as had his father before him), captain of the hunt at Meudon, Bellevue and Chaville and an officer in the king's army. He was also greatly disliked by Grace's protector, the Duc d'Orléans.

Grace had thought him dead as he had been by the king's side on the morning of the 10 August insurrection. When the king had made his escape to the National Assembly, Champcenetz had bid the royal family adieu and leaped from a window into the garden where he lay hidden in the heat of the midday sun among the corpses of the Swiss Guard. Aided in his escape by one of the National Guard, who had recognized Champcenetz and given him his coat to wear to disguise his uniform, he managed to get away and made for the house of the English ambassador in Paris, Lord Gower, on one of the new boulevards in the Faubourg Saint-Germain. Lord Gower would not receive Champcenetz, although his secretary William Huskisson did do so and was kind to him: Huskisson could do little more as a proclamation had been cried through the streets prohibiting, on pain of death, any assistance being given to those who had escaped the Tuileries. Champcenetz was given some clothes and shown to the door. Afraid of going to any of his friends, he remembered meeting Mrs Meyler at Grace's house and knew her to be a good-natured lady, moreover a royalist who lived very quietly in a private part of Paris with just the one maid. In desperation he made for her house. He was in luck as Mrs Meyler, with the support of her maid, bravely agreed to hide him and there he remained until Grace came to the rescue on the night of 2 September.

The royal family had been imprisoned in the Temple since the insurrection and nightly domiciliary visits had begun to be made throughout the streets of Paris. Ostensibly they were searching for arms but really searching for fugitives and everyone dreaded the knock on their door. Suspicion and the fear of being informed against by other citizens reigned supreme across the city; against this backdrop Mrs Meyler had intrepidly hidden Champcenetz but she could do so no longer. Hearing that the searches were to become more severe, she had begged Grace to return to the city.

Paris was in uproar. Princesse de Lamballe, part of the extended French royal family and trusted confidante of the queen, had been separated from the royal family and taken to La Force Prison. On 3 September, after standing trial and being found guilty, she was thrown to the mob that ended her life, probably by stabbing her, and was decapitated. Although rumours have persisted of atrocities carried out on her body, including her breasts being bitten off, these have been exaggerated and her headless body was still clothed when it was handed over to officials, a clerk noting the contents of her pocket. Her head was stuck on a pike, however, and paraded through the streets before the idea of taking it to the Temple and Marie Antoinette's window took hold. The Temple was no great distance from Rue Saint-Fiacre and Grace recalled meeting with the mob and the shocking sight of the disembodied head on the boulevard adjacent to her friend's home. However, the dates do not quite match. They are only a day out and Grace was writing a decade after the events had taken place: has she simply got the date wrong and Mrs Meyler summoned her to Paris on the 3rd and not the 2nd of September?

Grace decided to get Champcenetz out of Paris using the second passport she had obtained, so as soon as it was dark the two of them entered Grace's cabriolet and made for the Vaurigard barrier. Alas for them, after the troubles of the day the barriers were closed and no one was allowed in or out of the city. Grace now had only an hour or so before the domiciliary visits began for the evening and, if she was found abroad in her carriage, she would certainly be taken up for questioning. While she could return to her house in the city, she could not take Champcenetz with her for she had too many inquisitive servants and her cook in particular was a great Jacobin. The danger of betrayal was too great.

rait of Grace Dalrymple Elliott by Thomas Gainsborough, 1778. (*Metropolitan Museum of Art*)

South view of St Pancras Church as it would have looked when Grace Dalrymple married Dr John Eliot. (*Wellcome Library, London*)

Parish Register entry for the marriage between Dr John Eliot and Grace Dalrymple. (*London Metropolitan Archive*

M,ᵐˢ E___t

Lord V___entia

Mrs E___ and Lord V___ (Mrs Elliott and Lord Valentia) from the 'Histories of the *tête-à-tête* annexed' in *Town and Country Magazine*, 1774. (*Lewis Walpole Library, Yale University*)

'The Indiscretions of noble blood cured medicinally': a depiction of Grace and Valentia being surprised in the bagnio by Dr Eliot, from *Matrimonial Magazine*, February 1775. (*The Franklin Collection, Yale University Library*)

Portrait of George, Prince of Wales (later George IV) by Thomas Gainsborough, c.1781.

rtrait of George James, 4th Earl and later 1st Marquess of Cholmondeley, by Sir Joshua Reynolds, 1780.
oughton Hall Estates)

(*Left*) Grace admires herself in the mirror while Perdita adjusts her corset and the 'Bird of Paradise' puts on her stockings, from *Rambler's Magazine*, January 1783. (*Beinecke Rare Book and Manuscript Library, Yale University*)

(*Right*) Georgiana Seymour, Grace's daughter, depicted as an infant by Sir Joshua Reynolds, c.1784. (*Metropolitan Museum of Art*)

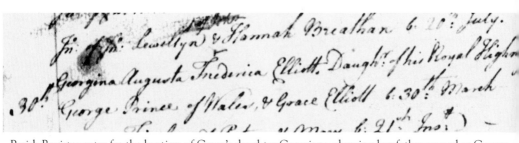

Parish Register entry for the baptism of Grace's daughter Georgiana, showing her father named as George, Prince of Wales. (*London Metropolitan Archives*)

The Aerostatick Stage Balloon, December 1783: Grace sits on the top gallery of the balloon (which is filled by the vanity of its passengers), in the centre between Perdita (left) and Lady Worsley (right). On the second gallery, left to right, are the 3rd Duke of Portland, Lord North, Charles James Fox and the Pope. The lower gallery contains various celebrated quacks and London celebrities. (© Science Museum/Science & Society Picture Library)

Miss D___n and Le Comte des Lunettes (Miss Dawson and the 4th Earl of Peterborough) from the 'Histories of the *tête-à-tête* annexed' in *Town and Country Magazine*, 1777. (Lewis Walpole Library, Yale University)

N.º XXII.   N.º XXIII.

Miss D___n.   *Le Comte des Lunettes.*

'A Bath of the Moderns', March 1782: Lady Worsley is depicted adjusting her stockings while Maurice George Bisset watches from atop the shoulders of Sir Richard Worsley. (*Library of Congress*)

Hon. Mrs F___ and the Incautious Lothario (Lady Anne Foley and Charles Henry, 5th Earl of Peterboroug from the 'Histories of the *tête-à-tête* annexed' in *Town and Country Magazine*, 1785. (*Lewis Walpole Library, Yale University*)

'The Battle of Bunker Hill, 17 June 1775' by John Trumbull, 1786: Grace's uncle, Major John Pitcairn, is depicted in the centre falling back, mortally wounded, into the arms of his son, Lieutenant Thomas Pitcairn. (Yale University Art Gallery)

'Colonel Mordaunt's Cock Match at Lucknow': Grace's cousin, Colonel John Mordaunt, is shown at a cock match at the court of the Nawab of Oudh; John is dressed in white standing to the left with his hands outstretched. (Yale Centre for British Art, Paul Mellon Collection)

Louis Philippe Joseph, Duc d'Orléans, engraving by John Raphael Smith after Sir Joshua Reynolds, 1786. (*Rijksmuseum*)

'View of Paris from the Pont Neuf' by Jean-Baptiste Raguenet, 1763; Paris as Grace would have known it before the Revolutionary years. (*Digital image courtesy of the Getty's Open Content Program*)

The arrest of Louis XVI and his family at the house of the registrar of passports at Varennes in June 1791, by Thomas Falcon Marshall. (*Carolus/Wikimedia Commons/CC-BY-SA-3.0*)

View of the Château de Meudon, engraved by Jacques Rigaud, 1733; Grace's cottage lay just beyond.
(*Photograph © Ec.Domnowall/Wikimedia Commons/CC-BY-SA-3.0*)

Brompton Park House, pencil drawing by Thomas Hosmer Shepherd. Grace occupied the middle house with her companion Sophia Seneschall in the early nineteenth century, while her friend Lady Worsley occupied one of the wings. (*Kensington Central Library*)

Portrait of Georgiana Charlotte, Marchioness of Cholmondeley, with her eldest son Henry, by John Hoppner, 1805.
(*Houghton Hall Estates*)

Miniature of Georgiana Seymour as a child.
(*Private collection*)

Double miniature of Lord Charles Bentinck and Georgiana Seymour, possibly dating to around the time of their marriage. (*Private collection*)

Portrait of Lady Charles Bentinck (Georgiana Seymour), painted in 1813 by Anne Mee for the Prince Regent. (*Royal Collection Trust/© Her Majesty Queen Elizabeth II, 2015*)

Portrait of Georgiana Seymour by George Sanders, 1806, possibly painted while she was visiting her friend Lady Jersey. (*The Earldom of Jersey Trust*/© *Peter Trenchard*)

George IV when Prince Regent, miniature by Henry Bone after Lawrence, 1816. (*Metropolitan Museum of Art*)

(*Above left*) Portrait of John Kinloch by Thomas Arthur William Devis, painted while in India. (*Gilmerton House*)

(*Above right*) Portrait of Grace's cousin Janet Lawrence Brown at around the time of her marriage to John Kinloch, by Thomas Hickey. (*Gilmerton House*)

(*Right*) Photograph of the head and shoulders portrait of Grace Dalrymple Elliott by Thomas Gainsborough, probably commissioned by the Prince of Wales, c.1782. (*Private collection*)

Heading once again for the porter who had previously helped her to breach the wall, she asked the driver of the cabriolet to take them to the Allées des Invalides where he left them, no carriages being allowed on the streets after ten o'clock at night. Grace and her companion sank to the ground beneath a tree, both now fearful for their lives: she recalled that her knees were knocking together, such was her fright, and nightfall had done little to dispel the summer heat which did not help her state of mind. After a few minutes they made for the porter's house, but found their way blocked by patrols. Grace, now at her wits' end, burst into tears and Champcenetz begged her to give him up but despite her fear Grace was made of sterner stuff. Determined to see him to safety, she insisted on crossing the Seine, ending up in the Champs-Élysées from where they could see her house.

Grace no longer lived on the Rue du Faubourg, her household having moved to a newly-built residence on an adjoining street, Rue de Miromesnil, leading at one end onto the Champs-Élysées and at the other opening onto fields leading to Monceau and the château belonging to the Duc d'Orléans. (Grace's house on the Rue de Miromesnil is listed in later documents as No. 1107, suggesting it is possible that she had an apartment in the building rather than the whole house.)

Champcenetz now suggested he hide in the grounds at Monceau and Grace, while not liking this idea (she had seen little of the duc for some time), reluctantly agreed but there was no way to get there and avoid the patrols without walking along Rue de Miromesnil. As they reached the end of the street Grace spotted her servants, sitting outside taking advantage of the warm summer night. A nearby house was still under construction and Champcenetz hastily hid within its half-built walls while Grace boldly approached her own gate, explaining her sudden and unexpected arrival to her servants by saying that news of the day's events had reached her in Meudon, whereupon she had come directly to Paris. While she was trying to persuade her Jacobin cook to break the curfew and leave the house to get her some food (and allow her to smuggle Champcenetz inside) he pre-empted matters by turning up at her front door, flushed from his hiding-place by the sound of an approaching patrol. The cook recognized him but was placated and persuaded to leave for a while, giving Grace and the few servants she trusted time to hide the poor man, who was by now close to collapsing, before the cook returned to believe Grace's lie about turning Champcenetz away from her door.

With the domiciliary patrol in the street, no time could be lost in securing a hiding-place. Grace's bed was in an alcove and had many thick mattresses and, with the help of her porter, she pulled two of the mattresses to one side, creating a space against the wall in which Champcenetz could hide. As the bed now looked tumbled, Grace got into it to prevent any suspicions being raised.

One or more of the servants remained in the room for most of the time, the cook abusing Champcenetz and saying he would end on the guillotine, and Grace could do nothing for the fugitive except surreptitiously pass him a spoonful of her warm negus (spiced port wine) when the room was clear. Just before four o'clock in the morning the patrol arrived at Grace's door.

They searched throughout the house, telling the servants that they were seeking Champcenetz (he had been seen entering the house), eventually ending in the bedrooms. They began to tear apart the beds belonging to the servants, stabbing their bayonets into the mattresses, and at last they entered Grace's suite where, from her bed, she calmly and courageously confronted the forty or so men who piled into the room. Illuminated by candelabra and the light of the breaking day, Grace just had time to think that the scene in front of her now resembled a ballroom rather than a bedroom before she fell back on the recourse she knew best and sweet-talked the men, using all the charms she had become known for when flirting in the ballrooms and drawing rooms of Paris and London. She offered to conduct them around her house and to provide some wine and cold pies for them and her ruse worked. They allowed her to remain in her bed rather than getting out and dressing in front of them, merely patting the top of the bed and peering underneath rather than stripping it and running their bayonets through as they had with the others.

They spent around an hour searching everywhere in Grace's room except where Champcenetz was hidden, while the Jacobin cook strenuously asserted that she knew her mistress had turned Champcenetz away and would never harbour a man who was so disliked by the Duc d'Orléans. At last they left and once Grace was sure they were far enough away she leaped out of bed and, with the help of her very surprised maid who had known nothing about the presence of the fugitive in the room, pulled Champcenetz, half-suffocated, on to the floor.

They made up a bed for him in the small boudoir leading off Grace's bedroom and locked the door. On returning to him in the evening of the next day Grace found him feverish and delirious and was in the anguished throes of wondering how she would dispose of his body, should he die, when the Duc d'Orléans noticed she was at home and so entered her suite of rooms. Grace told him the tale of the previous night's search, omitting any mention of his enemy, knowing that d'Orléans would be furious to realize Champcenetz had been concealed in her room. D'Orléans, who had recently accepted a place on the National Convention, renounced any succession to the French crown and had adopted the name of Philippe Égalité, choosing to highlight his support of the people, wished that she had remained at Meudon but still thought Grace would be safe. He too had seen the head of the Princesse de Lamballe, sister-in-law to his wife: it had been paraded beneath the windows of the Palais-Royal where he had been dining and he assured Grace he had done everything he could to try to save the unfortunate woman, although to no avail. D'Orléans, stunned and disheartened by the recent events, told Grace he would give everything he had in return for a small estate and a quiet life in England but he was now 'in the torrent, and must rise or fall with it'.

D'Orléans returned the next day, on his way to the National Convention. Over the breakfast table in her suite, Grace admitted to him that Champcenetz was in her house and appealed to him for help. D'Orléans berated Grace for risking herself to save such a man, for he could see no way of assisting either her or him; his own house at Monceau was filled with servants who were Jacobin spies and he knew no way of negotiating the barriers. Angrily wishing that she was safe in England, he left Grace's house but with a promise to return the next day. When Grace asked if he would see Champcenetz, he replied '*Nous verrons cela*', leaving her with a glimmer of hope.

However, any hope of help was dashed when d'Orléans called the next day to find Champcenetz waiting for him in Grace's room. Although he expressed sympathy as the fugitive was clearly ill, his concern was all for Grace, made worse as he could do nothing to help. To Champcenetz he declared:

> We will neither talk of the past, nor on any other subject; but the situation of this good person who is trying to save your life at the expense of her own. She is ill, and I fear both you and she are in a scrape. I would be of use to you on her account if I could, but I fear that it is impossible … I am sorry that you cannot get away, as I shall not be at peace till I see you out of her house.

With nothing else for it, Champcenetz remained hidden in Grace's boudoir until the barriers to the city were reopened and then Grace took him in her cabriolet to Meudon. D'Orléans sent a trusted servant to say that Champcenetz could get passage in the mail-cart from St Denis which, for a sum of money, would take him to Boulogne to sail for England and safety. Accordingly Grace and Champcenetz, accompanied by her elderly royalist neighbour, left Meudon in the early hours of the next morning and Grace saw him safely delivered on to the mail-cart, bound for freedom.

In Paris the king, now known merely as Louis Capet, had been brought to trial. D'Orléans, although he had promised Grace he would not do so, was one of those who voted for his cousin's execution and Grace, shocked and deeply disappointed in him, could find no excuses for his behaviour.

She had arranged for the Duc de Biron, now a general in the French army, to bring d'Orléans to her house on the Rue de Miromesnil on 17 January 1793, giving the two men a chance to talk for Biron could have no conversation with d'Orléans at Madame de Buffon's abode. D'Orléans had become something of a stranger to Grace since the Champcenetz episode but, still concerned for her welfare, he came to her house that evening. Grace and Biron implored d'Orléans to remember that the king was his cousin but he knew if he voted for the king's deliverance he would, by default, more than likely be voting for his own death. Biron suggested that the duc should feign illness and not appear on the day of the vote.

With matters so arranged, Biron invited Grace to come to the hotel where he was staying in Paris on the night that the vote was to take place, to pass the evening with him and two ladies, Madame Dumouriez and Madame Laurent, the latter his mistress. Grace arrived to find the threesome very dismal. Every half-hour a list arrived with the votes and they could see that an increasing majority had voted for the death of the king and then, shortly after Grace had arrived, came the news they had dreaded but probably expected: the Duc d'Orléans had entered the Convention. Two hours later the king had been sentenced to die and d'Orléans had been one of those who had voted in favour of this act, saying 'My conscience tells me that Louis deserves death.'

Grace, in tears like the others, was aghast to think that the man she had once loved could betray his cousin in this way. She returned home and threw out of sight everything given to her by d'Orléans, anything that reminded her of him. The king's execution was set to be held two days later on Monday, 21 January 1793 and the day before, unable to bring herself to remain in Paris, Grace got a passport to return to Meudon from where she heard the distant commotion and cannon fire that attended the dreadful event.

In truth, although Grace might have wished her former lover to play the hero, d'Orléans' vote, made so late in the evening that it could not have been said to influence others, made no difference to the eventual outcome. He was mindful that he had not only his own head to think of but those of his sons too and knew the people with the power to take these would judge his action, or inaction, on the fateful evening. He also had his estates and property in France that he needed to safeguard for the future security of his family; indeed, a few men had voted for the death of the king but only after the expulsion of the entire Bourbon family from France. However, another view took hold and people began to suggest that d'Orléans had voted for the death of his cousin as he wanted the throne for himself, as damning in the eyes of the Republic as if he had voted against the execution of the king.

Grace, now under suspicion from the authorities, received many worrying nightly visits from officials wishing to question her and she became unwell. The Duc d'Orléans, hearing that she was ill, sent her a letter begging her forgiveness and daily began to ask about her health. Grace planned to make use of his continued support for her to obtain a passport that would allow her to travel back to England. She consequently arrived to see him at the Palais-Royal and the pair had an awkward reunion during which he offered her money to buy a passport if she could, but made it clear that his influence was all but ended and he could offer no other help than his best wishes.

His best wishes were of little help to Grace now. D'Orléans and the remaining members of the Bourbon dynasty were rounded up and arrested, first held in Paris and then taken to the prison of Fort Saint-Jean in Marseilles. His eldest son had been his downfall; he had joined with General Dumouriez (possibly the estranged husband of the Madame Dumouriez with whom Grace spent the evening at the Duc de Biron's Paris hotel on the night that Louis XVI was sentenced to death) in a plot to march on Paris and overthrow the Republic. The son escaped with his life, making for Switzerland, while his family was left to suffer the consequences of his actions. With Grace's benefactor and protector imprisoned she was left exposed and vulnerable.

Just before d'Orléans' arrest Grace had received a letter from Madame la Comtesse de Talleyrand-Perigord (formerly Madeleine Henriette Sabine Olivier Senozan de Viriville), pleading for help and hoping that Grace could use her influence with the duc. Madame de Perigord's husband, Archambaud de Perigord, had been in hiding for some time with their eldest child before managing to flee France. His wife, with two younger children, was left on her own in Paris and feared for her life as the authorities suspected she had helped to conceal her husband.

Grace met with this desperate woman at her Paris house on the Rue de Miromesnil, even though she knew that d'Orléans could do nothing to help. The next day Madame de Comtesse de Jarnac, an Irish heiress, formerly Elizabeth Smyth of Tinny Park in County Wicklow, came to see Grace. Madame de Jarnac was of a similar age to Grace and a neighbour on the Rue de Miromesnil. Madame de Perigord was at Madame de Jarnac's house, determined not to spend another night inside the city, even if she had to sleep in the fields. Grace agreed to help and took Madame de Perigord and her two children, a girl named Melanie around 8 years old and a little boy named Alexandre-Edmond who was a couple of years younger, to her cottage at

Meudon and left them there while she returned to Paris. Another domiciliary visit was scheduled for that night and she did not want to arouse any suspicion.

They must have decided that Meudon was no safer than Paris, for the next day Grace brought her new house guests back to the Rue de Miromesnil and housed them there for ten days or more while Madame de Jarnac tried to arrange a false passport and passage from Calais for Madame de Perigord. Amid the panic, on 4 April 1793 Grace received what was to be her last visit from the Duc d'Orléans.

His son had recently fled to Switzerland with Dumouriez and the duc, under suspicion, was now accompanied by two gendarmes. He showed Grace a letter his son had sent him, upbraiding him for the king's death, and d'Orléans burned it in Grace's room. Discussion then turned to money: Grace had placed her money on his estates and d'Orléans hoped, if he knew his death was imminent, to secure the annuities he paid her. Also, he told her, if they paid his creditors after his death, many of which were owed money on Grace's account, she would be so much the richer. D'Orléans left, saying he would return for a breakfast with Grace on the Sunday.

That evening Grace and Madame de Perigord had been sitting quietly together when panic erupted through the house; a sudden and unanticipated inspection was taking place. Grace just had time to hide her friend in a concealed closet before the men entered her room. They didn't find Madame de Perigord but in Grace's secretaire they did find a sealed letter addressed to Charles James Fox in London. Grace was indeed acting as a go-between and the letter had been given to her by a French courier who had come to Paris from Sir Godfrey Webster in Naples, via Admiral Latouche Tréville, a decorated French naval officer and an aide to the Duc d'Orléans, but Grace had yet to forward it to London. Sir Godfrey was travelling with his wife, Elizabeth, and a party of friends including the Duchess of Devonshire's mother and sister. Lady Webster had been brought to bed of a son in Naples two months earlier, shortly after the French fleet had bombarded the Naples harbour.[255]

Grace was arrested and taken from the house, leaving Madame de Perigord behind, still in the closet. As no seals had been placed on Grace's doors (to break one carried a sentence of death), she made for Madame de Jarnac's house as soon as she was able. Charles James Fox, the intended recipient of the letter and that old friend of Grace's from her days back in London when she had 'azurized' herself in support of his Whig party, was sympathetic to the revolutionary principles and it was perhaps this fact alone that kept up Grace's spirits and nerve when she was about to be questioned. She spent the night in the Section House close to her home and was taken to the Mairie the next morning, a Friday, but she was not finally seen until lunchtime on the Saturday and then her case was sent to the Comité de Surveillance. As she entered the building she passed the Duc d'Orléans on his way out, who exclaimed '*Mon Dieu!* Are you here? I am very sorry indeed.' It was the last time she would ever set eyes on him.

After much debate, while Grace professed her ignorance as to its contents, the letter was opened and, as it was written in English, Grace was called to the table at which the Comité was sitting to translate it for them. Relief must have flooded through Grace as she did so for the letter, as she had hoped, was nothing but complimentary to the French and the Comité declared her free to return to her home. However, her ordeal was not over yet: she had been seen speaking to d'Orléans and one member of the Comité wanted to question her on their conversation, suggesting she knew that d'Orléans wished to be king and had information that would betray him. In tears Grace managed to negotiate their questions and even the appearance of the dreaded Robespierre in the room and was finally allowed to leave.

She went straight to her bed, determined to go to Meudon the next day despite d'Orléans being due to breakfast with her. D'Orléans never got to know that Grace intended to cancel their appointment: he was arrested in his bed at the Palais-Royal during the early hours of the morning and taken with his 11-year-old son to the prison de l'Abbaye. On the same day Madame de Perigord came to Grace begging her to adopt her two young children while she risked her escape, helped by Madame de Jarnac. Perhaps the distraught mother thought they would be in more danger in the escape attempt than they would be by remaining in Paris, perhaps they would be an unwanted hindrance in the attempt, but whatever the reason Grace agreed to her request and took the children under her care. They were safe from the guillotine for victims had to be at least 16 years of age; their mother was terribly in danger, although her only crime was to be the wife of an émigré and she needed to act quickly to save her life.

For six weeks Grace looked after the children before being once again arrested. The authorities were going through the papers of the Duc d'Orléans, now being held in Marseilles, and suspected Grace of being his agent in passing information to England. Her house was sealed and she was taken to the prison of Sainte-Pélagie but, before leaving, managed to instruct her maid to take the children to the house of Madame Jarnac. To her dismay, on her arrival at Sainte-Pélagie she discovered her old friend the Duc de Biron was also a prisoner. Sainte-Pélagie had been a house of refuge for 'sinful women' before the Revolution, named in memory of a courtesan of Antioch; one wonders whether Grace appreciated the irony.

It's quite likely that Grace was guilty as accused but nothing could be found to incriminate her and a short time later she was once again free. She returned to her home but found it now dismal. The only friends she saw were her neighbour Madame de Jarnac and Mrs Meyler who had moved to be closer to Grace.

Grace's journal has so far fairly truthfully recorded her experiences at this period in her life with just the odd mistake in dates, but it is at this point where the inaccuracies begin to creep into her narrative and this has led to her journal being discredited instead of viewed as an excellent first-hand resource and eyewitness account. Whether these embellishments sprang from Grace's pen or whether they were later additions, perhaps added by Richard Bentley when he acquired the rights to the manuscript, is open to debate, although the only change Bentley said he had made was to divide the document into chapters and paragraphs.[256] It has been suggested that Grace had taken the experiences of a friend, perhaps the mysterious Mrs Meyler, and written them as her own. While writing of her imprisonment in Sainte-Pélagie she recalled Madame du Barry, the former courtesan and mistress of Louis XV, arriving in the gaol and sitting on Grace's bed talking of England and the court there. However, Grace said she was released from that gaol in June 1793 and Madame du Barry did not enter until September, three months later.

Instead, on 6 September 1793 Grace spent the evening at Mrs Meyler's house with three other French ladies. Although Mrs Meyler was ill, Grace came home happier than she had been for some time, although she should not have been. The trial of the Widow Capet, the unfortunate former Queen Marie Antoinette, was under way and the day before there had been riots in the city culminating in the National Convention being invaded and the decision to declare that 'Terror is the order of the day', marking the start of the Reign of Terror under which anyone suspected of being an enemy of the republic could be arrested. However, Grace was in good spirits and, because of this, her maid delayed telling her of the danger she was in. Instead she woke her mistress at six o'clock in the morning and gently told her the news, impressing upon Grace the need to quit Paris immediately.

Orders had gone out for every English person who had not been resident in France before 1789 to be arrested (Grace should have complied with a law passed shortly before that required her to provide two witnesses who could attest to her *civisme* (citizenship) but it's likely she hadn't done so). These arrests were in retaliation for the burning of ships belonging to the French fleet that lay in the harbour at Toulon where the British had been laying siege to the town together with French royalist forces before being driven off by the French revolutionary army that included a young Captain Napoléon Bonaparte. Grace was now seen to be more English than Scottish and her birthplace would not save her. The maid had heard from a man who was both a grocer and a member of the Section, but who knew Grace and wished her well, that her arrest was imminent. With no time to lose Grace leaped from her bed and hastily dressed, stuffing her pockets with diamonds and trinkets before she ran from the house. She wandered the streets and the fields behind Monceau before approaching Louis-Jacques-Jessé Milon, a ballet master, and his new wife, the former Mademoiselle Marie-Catherine Bigottini, who were connected with the opera and who she knew were staunch royalists. Monsieur Milon accompanied Grace to Meudon where she threw herself upon the mercy of the mayor.[257]

In Meudon Grace now fell between the jurisdiction of two departments (Versailles and Sèvres) but outside that of Paris. Although she didn't want to be arrested at all, she was determined not to be arrested by the Paris authorities as she was sure a detention made by them would not lead to any desirable resolution. The mayor could do little though, even when Grace pleaded with him to arrest her and throw her into the castle prison; instead she had to go home and wait for the Versailles authorities, for whom the mayor promised to send, to come for her.

It seemed in the morning that Grace's worst fears had come true, for at her gate was the Section from Paris who had come for her accompanied by the men from Sèvres and Grace believed Sèvres to be every bit as bad as the Paris Section. While they were ransacking her house and telling her that they would all go to watch her execution, the Versailles men arrived, furious to find the others there, and Grace found herself in the middle of a bizarre tug-of-war while they argued about who should take her. Versailles won the day and shortly afterwards she found herself in the Récollets prison there.

Grace was indeed questioned, as she claims in her journal, on 8 and 9 September 1793, for documents exist in the Archives Nationales in Paris to confirm this. What is not so clear is the veracity of Grace's version for the address on the documents, and one assumes the place in which she was interrogated, was Rue Nicaise in the 1st arrondissement of Paris, not Versailles. The documents suggest that seals were being put on Grace's house in the Rue de Miromesnil, denying her access to her belongings, no matter how desperately she needed them.

Whatever the true circumstances of Grace's arrest, certainly she was now no longer a free woman. News did not take long to spread back to England, the newspapers reporting at the end of September that 'Mrs. ELLIOT, the former favourite of Lord CHOLMONDELEY, is in the most deplorable state of poverty in FRANCE. She has had FREEDOM *to the full*, and now feels the consequences.'[258]

Possibly the authorities had been looking for an excuse to arrest Grace for some time and the Duc d'Orléans had unwittingly provided the means. His words to Grace on his last visit to her house suggest that some of his debts were for goods bought by her on his credit and on his account. There exists in the Paris archives, connected to the papers detailing Grace's arrest, a list of money owed against a vast array of hats ordered by Grace from a Paris milliner. With d'Orléans in prison was Grace arrested for debt, then to be questioned further to see if she was really an enemy of the republic? Although the authorities needed little excuse to interrogate anyone, it certainly could be a reason for Grace's exaggerated version of events and it is certain that she would rather be viewed as a prisoner for her royalist sympathies than for her inability to settle her bills.

While in the Récollets she shared a room for a time with the elderly Doctor Richard Gem, a gruff old physician who had lived in Paris for thirty years, attached to the British embassy, and whose staunch republican views had not prevented his arrest. His great-nephew was William Huskisson, secretary to Lord Gower who had initially helped Champcenetz in his escape. Henry Swinburne, writing in 1796, confirmed that Dr Gem was imprisoned for three or four months, locked up for at least some of the time in a cell with Grace and her dogs.[259] His information came from James Harris, Earl of Malmesbury, a man who was on the most convivial and intimate terms with both Grace and the doctor, and who told Swinburne that Gem had 'cried the whole time, was terrified to death – no candles even allowed them, or fire after it was dark'. Grace, who knew Gem well as he too had a house in Meudon, made the doctor's bed and darned his stockings while they were together, although she contradicts Malmesbury's repetition of her story to him as, in her journal, the two prisoners had both candles and a fire that Gem used to light each morning.

While Gem was soon released, Grace, in her own account, remained in the Récollets. She was there when Marie Antoinette followed her husband to the guillotine and, with her situation worsened, Grace was actually in a dungeon when she heard that her former lover and protector, Louis Philippe, Duc d'Orléans, had suffered the same fate.

Grace's servant had seen the tumbrel containing d'Orléans in the Rue du Roule near the Pont Neuf and followed it to its destination. The procession cruelly paused for some ten minutes outside the Palais-Royal, under d'Orléans' own window. With his light grey coat with a black collar slung over his shoulders, his hair powdered and his hands tied behind his back, he stood still and grave with his head held high, although Grace's servant said that he paled as they entered the Place Louis Quinze and the guillotine came into view.

Grace, repeating in her journal the information given to her by her servant, gets both the date of the execution and one of the occupants of the tumbrel wrong. Citizen Philippe Égalité lost his head on 6 November and Grace places a beautiful woman in the tumbrel with him, Madame de Kolly, but she had made her own journey to the scaffold a day earlier, listed under her maiden name of Marie Françoise Joséphine Derabec. The other two occupants of the tumbrel Grace lists as a man by the name of [Pierre] Coustard and a blacksmith who Grace calls Brouce but who was actually a locksmith, Antoine Brousse. With darkness falling by the time they reached the scaffold, d'Orléans was the first to be executed while the assembled mob still had enough light to view his end; in haste to get it over with, he made no last speech and within minutes the executioner held aloft his head.

Was Grace really still in prison at this time? She worsens her own situation in her account, recalling her confinement in a dungeon and then her transportation via two further prisons to the notorious Carmes. With her usual inaccuracy in dates, she mentions that her old friend the Duc de Biron was executed at the beginning of December (and showed less courage than d'Orléans) and claims that she heard the news while she was a prisoner. However, Biron, who penned a last letter with only hours left to live to 'Citoyenne Laurent' (the same Madame Laurent with whom Grace had dined on the night they heard that the king was to die), did not make his journey to the scaffold until 31 December, the last day of that terrible year of 1793, and Grace, despite what she wrote in her journal, had tasted freedom again before then. Far from being in prison, she was back in her cottage and free, at least within the liberty of Meudon, to come and go as she pleased, for on 9 December 1793 Grace took a newborn girl to the Meudon town clerk to register her birth.

The babe was named Georgina Frances Giguet (named for Grace as she used the name Georgina to sign all documents in France), the daughter of her servant Nicolas Giguet and his wife Elizabeth, née Dourdant. The birth had taken place under Grace's roof and the entry of the birth in the Meudon archives mentions that the father was ill and so Grace and the midwife, Agathe Tuffer, had registered the event.

It is tempting to view this girl as Grace's own daughter, nefariously listed as the daughter of her servant to conceal her illegitimacy and, while it may be a possibility for rumours to have swirled through time that Grace had at least one more child, the official paperwork does not suggest anything other than Grace helping out a loyal servant. The girl grew up in Meudon and nothing further connects her to Grace.

However, Georgina Frances Giguet was not the only child to appear in Grace's life in France. She revealed another just three weeks later when she was arrested once more and questioned, this time by the Meudon authorities who she could at least trust to be fair. This interrogation does not appear in her journal but on 30 December 1793, the day before Biron's execution, Grace was questioned in the Meudon *maison d'arrêt* (house of detention) as the authorities executed the new law ordering the arrest of all foreigners.[260] The Comité referred back to her interrogation in April and the letter to Charles James Fox, and then Grace confirmed her residence in Paris for many years, listing her addresses there, and told the men questioning her that she had drawn all her money out of England and invested it in France. While in her journal she was feisty, sticking up for her principles, in reality (and very sensibly) she presented herself as a good republican who sympathized with and supported their values. She also gave the surprising information that she had cared for a child for the past five years, for no such child is mentioned in her journal. We are not told whether this child was a boy or a girl, nor their age, but the mother had been widowed and left with five children to care for. Grace had stepped in to unofficially adopt one of them and the mother was prepared to make a statement swearing to the truth of this. At the end of the interrogation Grace was asked to provide the Comité with three things: a certificate proving her residency in France for a period of ten years; a similar document proving her adoption of the child; and she would need to swear the Oath of Liberty and Equality. Grace was ready and willing to do all of these. However, despite the fact that she had fellow citizens there to attest to her residence and also the mother of the child ready to make a statement, she did not have the necessary certificate and on this technicality her friends were dismissed without being heard.

Was Grace now once again held prisoner? If so it was for no longer than a couple of months, for on 20 March 1794 she signed papers to formally adopt a young girl, the daughter of one Guillaume Staunton, a former groom of the Duc d'Orléans.[261] It is almost certain that this was the same child she had previously been caring for, having finally managed to get the official documentation, and with it the necessary paperwork to safeguard her freedom and allow her to remain at liberty as a citizen of France.

However, in Grace's journal she places herself in the Carmes prison in Paris from around the first day of the New Year, 1794. Her friends Madame de

Jarnac and Mrs Meyler were, she says, also prisoners there. Among the misinformation, Grace claimed that one of the first people she met in Carmes was General Hoche, who in reality did not enter until April, and she witnessed the touching farewell between Madame de Custine and her young husband who had been condemned to the guillotine, except that he was imprisoned in the Conciergerie and their final meeting took place there. She also described herself as a confidante of Josephine de Beauharnais, the future wife of Napoléon Bonaparte, and amid these claims her manuscript abruptly terminates, leaving her inaccurately imprisoned in Carmes in the summer months of 1794.

While Grace escaped the worst atrocities of the French Revolution, others were not so lucky. Her friend Madame de Perigord failed in her attempt to escape to England. She had been arrested and held in the prison of Saint-Lazare and, even though she had divorced her émigré husband, was sentenced to death on 26 July 1794. In order to delay it she claimed that she was pregnant, that she had slept with a man named Charles while imprisoned in Saint-Lazare. Three other women – Louise-Cécile Quévrin, maid to the elderly and infirm Comtesse de Narbonne-Pelet, Madame Marie-Alexandrine-Renée de Jassaud, a West Indian by birth and the wife of the Comte de Butler, and Françoise-Thérèse de Choiseul, otherwise the Princesse de Monaco, wife of Joseph Grimaldi – also claimed to be pregnant.

All four gained but one more night; they were examined and with no signs of pregnancy being evident they all climbed into the tumbrel to be taken to the dreaded guillotine. The Princesse de Monaco claimed she had only lied about being pregnant to give her time to cut off her own hair, which she did with a piece of broken glass having first plaited it and which she asked to be given to her two young daughters so they would have something to remember her by. Calm in the face of such violent suffering, she comforted the Comtesse de Narbonne's maid who was in a state of total distress, saying 'Courage, dear friend, courage. It's only crime that gives way to weakness.'

A day later and they might have survived. Maximilien Robespierre, lawyer, politician and republican, was a merciless driving force behind 'The Terror'. He had recently established the 'Cult of the Supreme Being', which he envisaged as becoming the French state religion, a radical move indeed in the predominantly Catholic country. This, together with the suspicion and fear felt by the populace who suspected everyone of being an informer and the atrocities being carried out daily, eventually led to his downfall. On the day that Madame de Perigord was convicted he knew the game was up; on the day that she was taken in the tumbrel to the guillotine he was arrested. The riots and throngs of people in the streets of Paris, when news of his arrest began to spread, made the authorities wonder if the executions planned for that day should be postponed but the decision was taken to press on with them regardless, and so Madame de Perigord went to her death.

Grace, both in her journal and in the newspapers, was reported as being the *intimate* of Josephine de Beauharnais, later the wife of Napoléon Bonaparte, and Thérésa Cabarrus, the divorced wife of the émigré aristocrat the Marquis de Fontenay, two women who managed to effect a different outcome to their imprisonment from Madame de Perigord.[262] Thérésa, perhaps to save her own neck, became first the mistress and then the wife of Jean Lambert Tallien, a republican who signed the king's death warrant and who was instrumental in spreading The Terror in 1794. She was known to have used her influence with Tallien to save many other prisoners (he was instrumental in securing the release of Josephine) and also to moderate his views.

Had Grace found herself in a similar position to those poor souls herded into the tumbrels to be taken to the guillotine, undoubtedly she too would have carried herself with dignity and courage, for courage was something she never lacked. However, while the game was in full play, she did what she could to avoid attention and detention, whether by cajoling influential friends to help or by using every ounce of her natural charm, wit and intelligence, and if this meant, like Thérésa Cabarrus, flirting with or even bedding men to achieve her aim, then so be it for Grace was, after all, a courtesan. However she managed it, she survived.

Chapter Seventeen

The Further Adventures of
Henry Hew Dalrymple

While Grace had been in the midst of revolutionary France her brother, Henry Hew Dalrymple, had been embarking on his own daring adventures.

During 1788 and 1789, unemployed and seeking a new role, he travelled back to the Caribbean, visiting St Vincent, Tobago, Carriacou and Grenada where he owned a plantation.[263] Perhaps for a while he fancied himself as a colonial planter but, appalled at the treatment of the slaves on the islands he visited, upon reaching Grenada he took the decision to free all the slaves on his own land and close down his plantation.

While Henry Hew was settling his affairs in Grenada, back in London, William Wilberforce, MP for the county of Yorkshire and an ardent slavery abolitionist, stood before the House to deliver a speech on the subject, his first major speech and the first step towards bringing in a bill to abolish the repugnant trade.

Opposition towards this was great, many men being dependent upon the trade for their fortunes, not least of whom was Banastre Tarleton, lover of Mary Robinson, who opposed the bill in support of his Liverpudlian relations who were directly concerned. With those opposed to abolishing the trade thinking they were losing the day, they moved that evidence should be heard in the House of Commons to establish the facts claimed by Wilberforce and his friends and, although he knew this would prolong proceedings, Wilberforce was forced to agree. His house in Old Palace Yard, Westminster, soon became a hotbed of activity for the abolitionist campaigners and people with first-hand experience who were sympathetic to their cause were asked to speak to the House. Henry Hew Dalrymple, newly-home from the West Indies, was one of those who wholeheartedly involved himself in the cause.

How much he was part of the 'Clapham Sect', the name by which the inner circle of Wilberforce and his friends are remembered, is debateable. Certainly he dined with Wilberforce, was known to members of the sect and shared their views on abolition; although never listed as one of the main players, he was at least on the periphery. On 21 September 1790 one of those main players, Granville Sharp, wrote to the secretary of the Sunday School

Society warmly recommending Henry Hew as a person who was against slavery. The letter, which referred to Henry Hew as Captain Dalrymple, gave details of an imminent journey to Paris that he planned to undertake, perhaps to visit his sister Grace.

It was through these connections that in 1791 Henry Hew Dalrymple was appointed by the Sierra Leone Company as governor of the settlement they proposed to create there, providing employment for free blacks and former slaves, a philanthropic scheme that would still allow the creation of wealth for the European settlers of the proposed colony. However, Henry Hew quickly fell out with the directors of the company and was, at the last minute, dismissed from his position. The final straw had been his desire to run the colony as a military regime.

Several of his friends, notably Lieutenant Philip Beaver of the Royal Navy, had also planned to travel to Sierra Leone, before the scheme was abruptly terminated by Henry Hew's dismissal. Philip Beaver, without a ship and eager for adventure, was disappointed by the curtailment of his plans and, during a conversation between the two men, Henry Hew recalled hearing about a fertile and uninhabited island, ripe for colonization, at the mouth of the Rio Grande, not far from Sierra Leone, named Bulam (now Bolama). From Beaver's own account he, on hearing this, exclaimed to Henry Hew, 'Let us then colonize it ourselves.' 'With all my heart,' was the response.

On 2 November 1791 at Old Slaughter's Coffee House in St Martins Lane, Henry Hew, Philip Beaver and four other men formed a committee, the Bulam Association, with the intent of colonizing the island. That they rushed hastily into this is irrefutable and they were certainly more well-intentioned than well-informed, but Henry Hew Dalrymple was a man who acted first and thought later. In some respects, one can see the similarity between this aspect of his character and that of his sister Grace who rushed headlong into marriage and then into divorce.

The aims of this proposed settlement were twofold. For Henry Hew and his fellow trustees, the cultivation of the island was prime as it was an opportunity to prove that the African people could work as hard and industriously as Europeans when they were free to do so and not enslaved (something Henry Hew with his first-hand knowledge was sure of, but which was doubted by others). The second aim was to make money for the men who subscribed to the project by buying land in Bulam.

So the Bulam expedition was something of an experiment as well as a money-making exercise, one which, if successful, would help to end the practice of slavery and one which, if it failed, would play into the hands of those who wished to keep the practice alive. If it worked, the intention was to then introduce 'letters, Religion and civilization, into the very heart of Africa' and they thought to 'promise happiness to myriads of living, and millions of unborn people'.[264]

Henry Hew travelled to Manchester in late December to raise subscriptions from interested inhabitants there and, having acquired almost £9,000 in subscription money, two ships were chartered, the *Calypso* and the *Hankey*, together with a sloop named the *Beggar's Benison*. All three were supplied with food, stores and provisions, tools for cultivating the plantations, building supplies, arms and ammunition. Henry Hew was elected as the governor of Bulam with a man named John Young as his deputy, and a surgeon and surveyor were appointed to the expedition which, by now, included not only the subscribers who wished to travel but also a number of labourers who had been hired together with their families and numbered almost 300 people.

The expedition mustered on 26 March 1792 at Gravesend in Kent and almost at once the problems began. After a delayed start, a case of smallpox was discovered on the *Hankey*: the wife of one of the labourers, not knowing what else to do, had brought her infant child on to the ship, knowing the child had become infected. The three ships became parted from one another, food ran short and smallpox broke out among the passengers on the *Calypso*, commanded by Henry Hew, denying them the opportunity to dock for supplies at Tenerife.

Henry Hew, with a starving ship and still separated from the *Hankey*, took the decision to bypass the next agreed rendezvous point of Santiago on the Cape Verde and make instead for a place he knew well and which was closer, his old army station of Gorée. There he was persuaded not to enlist the help of an interpreter, an act that proved a fatal mistake for the whole expedition. So, after replenishing their stock, they headed for Bulam, arriving there well ahead of the *Hankey*.

Bulam was uninhabited and used only for hunting by the natives of the neighbouring island of Canabac (now Canhabaque), who saw the British occupation of the island as an act of war, not realizing that they had every intention of purchasing it from them. However, the money to do so was on the *Hankey* which was still some distance away, and with no interpreter on board they had so far not approached Canabac.

War canoes started to appear off the coast of Bulam, unsettling the occupants of the *Calypso* who had begun to take possession of the island. Eventually on Sunday, 3 June the natives struck. The British settlers on shore had split up, making shooting and exploration parties into the interior of the island, leaving fourteen men and five women at the beach under the protection of a naval officer. When Henry Hew heard the distant sound of musket fire he assumed it was just the shooting party. The musket fire was followed by the sound of the guns on board the *Calypso* being fired. This was a predetermined signal that would herald the arrival of the *Hankey* and, thinking their comrades had arrived, Henry Hew and his party turned around to make for the beach but got lost along the way and finally arrived at their destination two hours later.

They arrived at a scene of devastation: the Canabac natives had attacked and the beach was littered with the dead and dying. Some of the women and children had been taken prisoner (one of these was later killed as she was elderly and too much of a burden).[265] The guns fired from the decks of the *Calypso* had not heralded the arrival of the *Hankey*; they had been fired to secure the retreat of the survivors of the attack. The ship was, understandably, in chaos and uproar, families having been ripped apart.

The next day they weighed anchor and set sail for the Bissao Channel where they finally found the *Hankey*, to the despair of Philip Beaver. He had left his ship to go ashore with everyone on board healthy and in good spirits and the ship clean and orderly. He returned two days later after the arrival of the *Calypso* and discovered his own ship to now be noisy, dirty and disorderly. Moreover, the *Calypso* had the fever on board and no attempt had been made to quarantine those infected.

Well-intentioned Henry Hew Dalrymple may have been, but he also appears to have been rash, weak when he should have been strong, and stubborn in persisting with his own bad judgement when he should have listened to the advice of others. Philip Beaver accused him of losing control of the settlers under his command. In Beaver's own words: 'Dalrymple was a good man, but he had not firmness enough to check, and keep in awe the unruly and turbulent of the colonists; nor had he zeal and activity enough to lead and direct their restlessness to some useful end.'

When the inhabitants of Canabac heard that the British settlers had come in peace and wished to purchase Bulam, they expressed their remorse at the action they had taken. Negotiations were opened with the two kings, Jalorem and Bellchore, both of whom claimed disputed ownership of Bulam; the hostages were freed but Henry Hew Dalrymple had contracted an illness at Bissao and he played no part in the discussions.

With the rainy season in full force, it was agreed (against Philip Beaver's wishes) that the *Hankey* and the *Beggar's Benison* should remain at Bulam with as many of those who wanted to remain on board as could fit, while the *Calypso* returned to England with those who were ill or had now had quite enough of the expedition and the African coastline. So on 9 July the *Calypso* sailed away from Bulam, heading for Sierra Leone where some of the gentlemen settlers were planning to see out the rainy season, leaving Philip Beaver in charge of Bulam and the project in almost total disarray.

Henry Hew Dalrymple, broken and unwell, remained at Sierra Leone when the *Calypso* sailed for England, recovering from his illness and enjoying the hospitality of Governor John Clarkson who had taken over from Henry Hew after his dismissal from the Sierra Leone project. By the end of the year, Henry Hew was back in England. Philip Beaver gives us a little more insight into his character:

> Dalrymple was a perfect gentleman, and a sensible, amiable, and well-informed man, yet in everything relating to colonization, he was but a mere 'dreamer of dreams'; he felt the difficulties which he had got into, was disgusted with most of the colonists, and had determined to return to Europe: any proposition, therefore, to measure back our steps, whether by Sierra Leone, or direct to England, was sure to meet with his hearty concurrence.

The settlers left on Bulam were struck with fever, one or two a day succumbing to their illness, and the small graveyard on the island was steadily filling with British bones despite the plants cultivated by the settlers perversely flourishing and thriving. Philip Beaver and the remaining colonists reluctantly abandoned Bulam.

With his hopes dashed, Henry Hew Dalrymple returned to England only to find that his sister was in an ever-increasing predicament in revolutionary France. Totally helpless, he had failed in the Bulam project; now he could do nothing to help his sister in her troubles. He made one further attempt to gain a position in an official capacity, writing on 21 March 1794 from 77 Norton Street in Marylebone, and in his elegant copperplate hand, to Home Secretary Henry Dundas asking for 'employment under government' for himself, referring back to the time when he was secretary for the commission for making a commercial treaty at Paris ten years earlier and omitting his involvement in the recent failure at Bulam.[266] His request does not seem to have been complied with.

Henry Hew was prematurely aged by his experiences, by the repeated attacks of illness and fever he had suffered in Africa, and by the weight of guilt that pressed on his mind over the failed expedition, the loss of life involved and the destruction of his hopes for the future. He was not to set eyes on his youngest sister again for he died, aged only 45, at Eltham in Kent on 8 September 1795 and was buried there six days later. If he had any estate to leave, his sister Jacintha was the beneficiary.

Almost a year later, Grace was still living in mainland Europe and in some penury. In June 1796 one newspaper crowed that '"Dolly the Tall", alias Miss DALRYMPLE, and the favourite of the bloody ORLEANS, lives now in obscurity at Basle. Sometimes vice has its own reward', while another had her living on the banks of the river Loire on 1,000 livres a year which they equated to £48.[267]

She was back in Paris later in the year though, renewing her friendship with James Harris, Baron (and later Earl) Malmesbury. Malmesbury was a diplomat and a friend of the Prince of Wales who knew Grace of old. In 1796 he was in Paris trying to negotiate with the French, arriving on 22 October, and he wrote in his diary a few days later on Monday, 7 November of a meeting with Grace; he had 'not seen her since Twickenham'. He also visited and was visited by Dr Gem, and Grace relayed to Malmesbury her tale of their shared experiences while in prison.

Malmesbury and Grace shared many visits while he was there, on one occasion walking together to 'Mousson' (possibly Meudon) while she regaled him with anecdotes of the Duc d'Orléans, the Duc de Biron, Louis d'Arenberg and Queen Marie Antoinette. Malmesbury also dined with 'Mademoiselle' Laurent, the Duc de Biron's former mistress.

Granville Leveson Gower was also there, a young man just 26 years of age, attached to Malmesbury's diplomatic mission and a man who would, in time, be well-known to Grace's daughter (he thought Grace *tres naïve*). He too dined with Grace; even though she was twenty years older than he, she still had her charms. Another guest at Grace's table was Henry Swinburne, in Paris to negotiate the exchange of prisoners with France.

The next year, Grace briefly returned to England for a visit to her family and friends there and to try to raise some cash (Cholmondeley would have been her first port of call), arriving around the middle of September 1797. Lord Malmesbury was in London and she visited him at his house. Two months later, Grace left London for Yarmouth to catch a boat to Cuxhaven on the German coast, en route to France, although an anonymous newspaper correspondent expressed his regret at her returning there as 'every comfort awaited her in her native country'. The elderly Prince of Rohan and his unmarried brother were her fellow travellers.[268]

Criss-crossing the English Channel in search of her annuity, Grace was again to be found in London in February 1798, renting rooms at 3 Portland Street, a house owned by a woman named Anne Pearce. From this address she wrote to the Prince of Wales's private secretary, Admiral Payne.[269] Grace had approached Lord Melbourne, that old friend of her former husband, for help in claiming an annuity she had been promised from the prince, the last quarterly payment of which was still outstanding; Melbourne had waited on Admiral Payne and been assured it would be paid into Grace's bank account early in January. It had not, and now Grace approached the admiral directly in writing, asking if she could have five minutes' conversation with him to find out who to apply to for the payment before she once more left for France.

Grace was successful, if the newspapers are to be believed:

> Mrs Elliott, di-devant Miss Dalrymple, who lately returned to England from France with a certain diplomatic Agent, is said to have received a settlement of four or five hundred a year from a young Gentleman of high rank, on the express condition that she shall for the future reside out of the kingdom. This establishment has taken place in consequence of an amorous attachment that formerly subsisted between them, and which the Gentleman, being now married, is desirous of concealing from his amiable spouse.
>
> A daughter by the above connection, who is a young Lady of great beauty and considerable accomplishments, is expected to be shortly present at Court, under the name of Miss Seymour.[270]

The Prince of Wales had actually been married three years earlier and formally separated from his hated spouse, Caroline of Brunswick, for two of those three years (the separation occurring immediately after the birth of the prince's one legitimate child, Princess Charlotte). However, the prince was short of money and was trying to raise a loan from his estranged wife's relation, the Landgrave of Hesse, and was trying to persuade everyone that he was considering a reconciliation. With money to be gained, the last thing he wanted was Grace raking up the past.

After having gained the loan, the prince dropped the idea of making a go of his marriage and henceforth concentrated on wooing back his long-term mistress and supposed true first wife – albeit one unrecognized by English law – Maria Fitzherbert. A child adopted by Mrs Fitzherbert in December 1798, a girl who was rumoured to have the prince as her father, was also a Miss Seymour.

Mary Georgina Emma (known as Minnie) Seymour, born in November 1798, was ostensibly, and possibly truly, the daughter of Lord Hugh Seymour, a high-ranking naval officer, and his wife Lady Anne Horatia Waldegrave. Both were close confidantes of the prince and Mrs Fitzherbert and, so the official tale goes, when Lady Seymour had to travel abroad for her health just weeks after her daughter had been born, her friend Mrs Fitzherbert took charge of the babe and brought her up as her own. It's an interesting parallel that Grace's daughter Georgiana had adopted the same surname and both reputed daughters of the prince were known as Miss Seymour.[271]

Who was the 'certain diplomatic agent' with whom Grace had crossed the Channel? There is every likelihood that it was Henry Swinburne, returning from his mission regarding the exchange of prisoners; he arrived home in the middle of December 1797, so Grace may have spent Christmas and the New Year in England.[272]

Grace, upon alighting from her boat at Calais, was arrested and conducted, so it was reported, under an armed military guard to St Omer. The papers made light of her predicament, writing that 'Dally the tall complains much of her arrest at Calais. Why force into the service a Lady always willing to serve as a volunteer!' but it was not long before she was freed.[273]

Once the news of her annuity from the prince was reported in the papers (and it was actually £350, paid quarterly), Grace's creditors emerged. They had perhaps given up all hope of recovering the debts she had run up more than thirteen years ago, but now saw their chance. The newspapers had said that Grace had been granted her annuity upon a promise to leave England but this may have been just supposition and, if Grace ever did want to return to England to live, then she needed to clear these debts or she would face the ignominy of the debtor's prison and she had seen quite enough of prisons in France to last her a lifetime:

> The Creditors of Mrs. Grace Elliott, the widow and relict of the late Sir John Elliott, doctor of Physic, and who resided in New Norfolk Street near Hyde Park, and previous to her leaving England about the year 1785, are desired forthwith to send the particulars of their respective demands, in writing to George Stubbs Esq, in Parliament Street, Westminster.[274]

Grace received the annuity (and one hopes settled her debts) up until the spring of 1800. The payment expected in March of that year didn't turn up in Grace's bank account and neither did the one due in June. Grace's banker in Paris, knowing this was an annuity from the prince which he therefore thought assured, paid Grace the money at his own risk, believing he could claim it back in arrears, but when the September payment was also absent things became critical. Grace turned to the one person upon whom she could depend, the Earl of Cholmondeley. It was possibly through his good offices that she had received her annuity at all, for it had been paid quarterly while Cholmondeley was serving in the prince's household and had stopped when he resigned his position. He wrote, on Grace's behalf, to his friend the prince on 5 September 1800 from his Piccadilly mansion, enclosing a letter from the Paris banker. However, Cholmondeley's pleas seem to have fallen on deaf ears and the annuity lapsed.[275]

Chapter Eighteen

Jacintha's Later Life

Grace's world in the latter two decades of the eighteenth century could not have been more different to that inhabited by her widowed sister Jacintha, who lived quietly and unobtrusively in Lancashire with her children after the death of Thomas Hesketh. A huge gulf had opened between the two sisters which could not be breached nor time repair. Jacintha remained a widow for three years before remarrying in July 1785 to another Lancashire gentleman, Thomas Winckley Esquire, at the church of St John in Preston, Lancashire.

Two daughters followed the marriage in swift succession: Margaret (sadly not strong enough to survive and who was buried aged just twelve weeks), and Frances, born just over a year later on 16 June 1787. Frances grew to be a keen diarist, and left behind her an extensive amount of documentation which was later published, a boon to the historian.

Thomas Winckley was a younger son of John Winckley of Brockholes and some seventeen years older than Jacintha.[276] The Winckley family were staunch Jacobites; one John Winckley was executed for treason following the 1715 Jacobite uprising, and a miniature portrait of King Charles I was passed down through the generations as a family heirloom. Frances, daughter of Thomas Winckley and Jacintha, inherited this piece and remembered wearing it attached to a bracelet as a child on some Jacobite anniversary around the year 1790 and, despite her mother having so many relatives and ancestors who had fought for the British army, she remembered Jacintha singing Jacobite songs to her.

Of the five Hesketh sisters – Jacintha's daughters from her first marriage – only the eldest, Harriet, lived with her mother, and Jacintha's son Thomas Dalrymple Hesketh was at a private tutor's in Kent; as Thomas Winckley had taken a dislike to the Heskeths, they rarely met.

Jacintha's second marriage was not as successful as her first and Frances' statement 'I fancy that my mother's home was not a happy one' is sad to read. Jacintha's later life seems to parallel the one led by her mother. Both women led relatively provincial lives, Grissel in Edinburgh and Jacintha in the Lancashire town of Preston and the surrounding area, both shunning the more glamorous lives their sisters had chosen for themselves and both suffering misfortunes in their personal lives. Thomas Winckley, as a younger son, had been destined for the law and had led a bachelor's life in London prior to his marriage. Much more at home with his gentlemen friends than with his wife, Winckley was described as having 'the charms of conversation and wit' by his friends and, once drunk, was capable of playing mad pranks. His daughter Frances remembered, at the age of about 4, being taken from her bed in the middle of the night and carried by her father in his coach to the seaside town of Blackpool, leaving Jacintha behind and terrified for her safety. A friend in Blackpool, recognizing the little girl, rescued her and returned her to her mother. At about this time Thomas Winckley became disgusted by the presence of a number of new factories and cotton mills springing up near his Preston home, '"proud Preston" as it was formerly called, because it was the winter residence of the nobility and the county families', and removed with his family to a rented villa named Larkhill about 4 miles outside Liverpool.[277]

Jacintha's eldest Hesketh daughter, anxious to escape her stepfather, married in March 1793 at Preston. Her husband had known her since her birth for he was none other than John Despard, her father's old army comrade. Now raised to lieutenant colonel in the 7th Foot or Royal Fusiliers, he was some twenty-seven years older than his bride but an honourable and worthy man.

Shortly after the family had moved to Larkhill in 1794, Thomas Winckley died, leaving Jacintha a widow for the second time. His will, written in 1788 with two codicils added later, revealed that, before marrying Jacintha, he had fathered two illegitimate sons, both of whom were registered at their baptism with the surname of Wilson but had been called Winckley for several years.[278] With his illegitimate offspring well provided for, Jacintha was left his house and furniture and the residue of his estate was inherited by his 6-year-old daughter Frances. Should Frances not survive, the estate would descend to his sister Margaret, the wife of Edmund Hornby.

After the death of Thomas Winckley, Jacintha and her daughter Frances moved to London where they lodged in the house of the Earl of Stair in New Street, Spring Gardens. Did Jacintha believe the familial relationship between herself and the Earl of Stair, through her Dalrymple father, was nearer than it actually was? Certainly Frances, writing many years later, seemed to view him as a close relative. Mrs and Miss Winckley were welcomed to London by Jacintha's cousins on her maternal and paternal side, Charles Henry Mordaunt, Earl of Peterborough, and Dr David Pitcairn both welcoming them.

Jacintha stayed in London for some months before placing Frances in a school at Twickenham and taking for herself a house in Bath, where she brought her Hesketh daughters to live with her. Frances remained at Twickenham until she was 10, when she too was brought to live in Bath under the care of her mother and a governess. The governess, a Miss Rundall, was sister-in-law to the Bath actor Robert Elliston, Jane Austen's favourite actor. The year before Frances moved to Bath, Elliston had married Elizabeth Rundall, a dancing teacher, having first eloped with her. Frances, an impressionable child, was as entranced with the theatre as she was with her older half-sisters; they were beautiful and full of secrets of romance and beaux.

A move to Clifton near Bristol followed due to Frances' ill health (Frances said she was inclined to be consumptive at this time), where she was treated by Dr Beddoes at his Hotwells clinic. Dr Beddoes recommended fresh air and exercise for Frances, so she was given the freedom to roam outdoors in the countryside as much as possible. Her friends at the time were the slightly older daughters of Lady Morris Gore; the Gore family were on the best of terms with Robert Elliston and his wife and this friendship was encouraged by Frances' governess.

Frances Winckley next made the acquaintance of the dowager Lady Hesketh who, although no blood relation to Frances, was great-aunt to her Hesketh siblings. Lady Hesketh was the cousin and friend of the poet Cowper, he who had been so aghast at the prospect of a visit in his locale from Robinaiana, Countess of Peterborough. Robinaiana's great-niece was, however, much more socially acceptable and at Lady Hesketh's house Frances listened to her reading Cowper's works aloud and met the famous bluestocking Mrs Hannah More.

Robert Juxon, formerly Hesketh, the father of Captain Thomas Hesketh, had died in December 1796 and on his death the title of Baron Hesketh passed to Jacintha's son, Thomas Dalrymple Hesketh, still a year shy of his majority. The widowed Mrs Jacintha Winckley, once her daughter's health had recovered, moved back to Bath and led a genteel life there, hosting gatherings and card evenings. It was thus that she made the acquaintance of an Irish career soldier, one Major James Barrington.

James Barrington had joined the 56th Regiment of Foot (nicknamed 'the Pompadours') as an ensign in November 1769. The following year the regiment was sent to Gibraltar where they remained on garrison duty for many years, including during the Siege of Gibraltar, before returning to Britain with a posting to Scotland in 1784. Promotion was slow for Barrington: he was raised to the rank of lieutenant in 1773 but had to wait fifteen years before he was made up to captain, shortly before the regiment left for Ireland and another five years of garrison duty. He then saw action in the West Indies when the 56th was sent there under the command of Sir Charles Grey and was finally promoted to the rank of major in September 1795.

We have two conflicting accounts of his personality, one from Frances and another from a man who had known him in armed service. Frances did not like him; although he was of a good family she found him vulgar, mentioning his *ton de garnison* or garrison slang, and she disliked his strong Irish brogue. Joseph Budworth, however, a fellow soldier, knew him as one who was 'as brave and good a hearted man as ever lived', remarking that he doubted there was anyone alive in the army who 'hath been more exposed to cannonades, or has had so many shot and shells gone over his head'.

Loved by his comrades, despised by a society Miss, Major James Barrington had spent the vast majority of his life in garrison mess rooms rather than polite drawing rooms, so perhaps it's no wonder that he spoke like a soldier first and foremost rather than like a gentleman. Perhaps he reminded Jacintha of her past life with her first husband, for she had, after all, travelled with Hesketh's regiment in America.

Frances, in her account, implies that Barrington inveigled his way into Jacintha's affections and proposed marriage. She paints her mother as having no one to turn to and ask for advice, claiming all her Hesketh sisters were absent, including the eldest, Harriet, now Mrs Despard, and saying of Jacintha's decision to marry:

I had no power to revoke her fatal determination. I have an impression that the marriage was strictly private, and that I did not know it had taken place until I was formally introduced to my step-father. This revolted me and I absolutely refused to acknowledge him as a relation. I never felt more deeply humiliated; and nothing, beyond bare civility, could Major Barrington ever obtain from my high and wounded spirit.

The marriage took place at Bath on 1 September 1799. The *Bath Chronicle* of 5 September simply reported the marriage of 'Major Barrington of 56th Regiment to Mrs Winckley of Great Pulteney St, Bath on Sunday'.

Far from being alone when the marriage took place, Jacintha had at least one Hesketh daughter by her side for two of the witnesses to the marriage were Harriet and the recently-promoted Major General John Despard. Harriet, married to a soldier – one who, like Barrington, had been in armed service for most of his life – seemed to approve of her mother's choice.[279]

The Barrington household moved to London where Jacintha became seriously ill. Frances represents Major Barrington as a brute who beat Jacintha and gambled away her money, returning home from the gaming tables drunk and discourteous. Around 1801 (Frances says 1804 but this cannot be), she was taken away from her mother's house by her guardian and cousin, the Reverend Geoffrey Hornby, appointed thus in her father's will, because of concerns over Barrington.

However, Geoffrey Hornby had no great love for Frances; if she died before she came of age then Thomas Winckley's fortune passed to Hornby's son. He would therefore have little incentive to remove her from the care of Major and Mrs Barrington other than a wish to control Frances and her fortune himself. Indeed, we have evidence that Barrington was on better terms with the daughters of Jacintha's first marriage; maybe they were more used to a soldier's way of conducting himself. When the youngest Hesketh daughter, Lucy, was married, one of the witnesses to the wedding was James Barrington, along with Frances Winckley and a Dorothea Lauzun.[280]

Frances' account of her life, *The Diary of Frances, Lady Shelley*, does contain inaccuracies. Notably, she credits Thomas Hesketh with being a major when he was actually a captain, and even mistakes the number of her siblings, mentioning that she had six Hesketh sisters when there were only five, notwithstanding saying that Harriet Despard was absent when Jacintha married when she actually was present at the wedding as a witness. While we can rely on it for being the best first-hand account of Jacintha's life left to us, it must be treated with a little caution, and perhaps Frances had a slightly biased view of Barrington. He did not conform to her ideal of a perfect gentleman but was rather a slightly rough and ready, gruff old battle-hardened Irish soldier, not given to social niceties or flattering young ladies.

Chapter Nineteen

The Dawn of a New Century

At the dawn of the nineteenth century Grace found herself in Paris and a little short of ready money. If a condition of her annuity from the Prince of Wales had been to stay abroad then, as he had ceased to pay it, she was no longer under any obligation to remain away from London, especially if she thought that she could be better provided for in England. So in October 1801, shortly after the signing of the preliminary treaty of peace at Amiens, Grace travelled secretly back to England under the protection of Lord Malmesbury, using the alias Madame St Maur, interestingly a French variant of Seymour and the surname by which her daughter Georgiana was now known.

On her return to England she found herself reliant on her aunt, Janet Edmondes, the one relative on whom she could still depend, and upon her boon friend Lady Worsley who was living at her family residence of Brompton Park in Kensington. Janet was once more a widow (if Colonel Edmondes had married hoping that Janet would predecease him and leave him a wealthy widower, then he had grossly miscalculated; he died, aged 51, in 1793). Grace had not seen her sister for a quarter of a century, both her brothers were dead and her other remaining relatives wanted little to do with her. Initially she lived for a time with the ailing Janet Edmondes in Twickenham, and it was there that she wrote down her account of her experiences in France during the Reign of Terror. Information in the preface to Grace's journal stated that it was written at the request of Dr David Dundas for him to take, instalment by instalment, to another patient, no less a personage than King George III himself. The veracity of this claim remains unproven, but Janet Edmondes was suffering from acute ill health at this time and there could be some truth in the statement, although it remains open to doubt as to whether the intended recipient was the king himself.

Also living at Twickenham while Grace was penning her journal were the three exiled sons of the Duc d'Orléans who resided at Highshot House. The younger sons had managed to escape the fate of their father and had rejoined their older brother.

For one short, bittersweet visit, Grace was given the chance to see her long-estranged older sister, and her niece Frances Winckley, at Jacintha's sickbed. Jacintha was indeed ill; in fact, her sickbed soon became her death-bed for she died at her London town house on 11 January 1802.[281]

Grace, having heard that her sister was so dangerously ill and wanting to see her for one last time, applied for admittance to Jacintha's house. The two sisters had been apart since the early 1770s and so much had happened to both of them in the intervening thirty years. Frances knew little, if anything at all, of the history of her aunt. She recalled coming back unexpectedly to her mother's sick-room and saw, sitting at Jacintha's bedside

> the most beautiful woman I had ever beheld. She was dressed in the indecent style of the French republican period. Tears were rolling down her cheeks; this heightened her beauty without defacing the rouge which had been artistically applied. Her sleeves were of the finest embroidered muslin, and transparent drapery lay over a bust of ivory.

Grace, when Frances entered the room, rushed towards her, as Frances recalled, 'crying out impulsively, "Do let me kiss my darling niece"'. As Grace embraced Frances her perfume of musk enveloped the pair.

This was the only occasion upon which Grace and Frances were to meet and the last occasion on which the two sisters would be in each other's presence. Jacintha regretted the encounter afterwards and shed tears once her sister had left, the visit awakening too many painful memories. While Frances never met her aunt Grace again, she did meet her cousin, Grace's daughter Georgiana, for Georgiana was one of her companions during the short time Frances spent in London at the dawn of the nineteenth century.

Georgiana lived mainly at the Earl of Cholmondeley's mansion in London's Piccadilly (next door to that of Old Q, the Duke of Queensberry) with Lord Cholmondeley's brood of children, including his illegitimate daughter Harriet Saint-Albin who was around three years younger than Frances.[282] Frances described Georgiana and Harriet as 'the bright stars in [the] firmament' of the Cholmondeley household at their town house in London and at their Norfolk estate, Houghton Hall, which Lord Cholmondeley had indeed inherited from his uncle Horace Walpole (his other seat, Cholmondeley Castle at Malpas in Cheshire, was being rebuilt at this time), brought up as Lord and Lady Cholmondeley's own children. Priscilla Susan Bertie adored little Harriet (her opinion of Georgiana has, sadly, not survived), declaring that she had a magic influence on everything around her and her soul-searching eyes bright-ened every object upon which they shone.[283] Beau Brummell, dandy and fashion icon, was a frequent visitor to Houghton and a confidante to the beautiful Georgiana Seymour whom he adored and who was every bit as attractive as her mother had been before her. Georgiana was five years older than her young Winckley cousin; if Georgiana knew of their true relationship, Frances remained largely ignorant but hero-worshipped the older girl. Frances also met Mr Brummell:

> It was there [Houghton] that I first met Beau Brummell. He was supposed to be painting a miniature of George IV, after Cosway; but he made so little progress that we declared he never touched it. He then began to make an album which contained many vers de société, and led to much banter and fun, so the days passed very agreeably. The gentlemen of the party apparently submitted to old Cholmondeley's atrocious wines in order to enjoy the agréments of Houghton.

The Barrington household lived close to Piccadilly and Frances therefore saw plenty of her new friend, who she recalled often wished to have her as a companion. At Houghton Hall, Frances would also come to know another of the Cholmondeley adopted daughters. Priscilla Susan Bertie was the illegitimate daughter of Robert Bertie and a widow named Rebecca Krudener, whom he met while briefly back in England from armed service in North America during the War of Independence to visit his ailing father, the 3rd Duke of Ancaster and Kesteven.[284]

Shortly after Priscilla Susan's birth in 1778, Robert Bertie became the 4th Duke of Ancaster and Kesteven on the death of his father, but caught scarlet fever the following year and prematurely followed his father to the grave. His illegitimate daughter was his only child and his will (in which he said he wished her to use his surname) left her well provided for. When Rebecca Krudener married in 1782, little Priscilla Susan came under the care of her father's relatives and, as Lady Cholmondeley was Priscilla Susan's aunt and Lord Cholmondeley had been a friend to her father while he lived, it was natural enough for her be taken into their household after their marriage.[285] It is a shining testament to Lady Cholmondeley's character that she welcomed these three girls into her family – Georgiana, Harriet and Priscilla Susan – and treated them as her own children, regardless of their parentage and with no jealousy on her own part. When Frances knew Georgiana Seymour and Harriet Saint-Albin, Priscilla Susan was already a married woman; in 1798 she had wed Major General Banastre Tarleton, a man two years older than her father and who had, for some fifteen years, been the lover of the actress Mary Robinson, Grace's rival for the Prince of Wales.

However, upon her removal from London this bright society life came to a temporary halt for Frances. After a brief sojourn with the Hornbys, Frances went to live with her half-brother Thomas Dalrymple Hesketh and his new wife at Rufford Hall. Jacintha died in January 1802 at her London home and was buried on the 11th of that month at St Mary's on Paddington Green.

Grace's cousin Jessy Bebb and her husband John had remained in India for several years after their marriage, returning home aboard the *Earl Howe* in August 1800.[286] Susannah Robiniana and her young son also returned to forge a new life away from India. On the way to England, the Bebbs made a stop in Cape Town, South Africa, where they were introduced to Lady Anne Barnard, a Scotswoman and wife of the colonial secretary there. Lady Anne had also formerly been a confidante of Maria Fitzherbert and had assisted in the secret marriage Maria undertook with the Prince of Wales in 1785; she was also reputedly herself once a lover of the prince. Lady Anne Barnard kept a diary and from this we have a description of Jessy and her husband:

> [1 and 2 May 1800] ... the richest person who for many years has come from Bengal was presented to me – Mrs Bebb with her husband Mr Bebb – she has a sett of teeth so white & placed so staringly in her mouth as to be rather an *imperfection* if that can be possible.
>
> [11 and 12 May 1800] ... The curicle being at the door to carry us back to the country, Mr B[arnard] & I went first to call on the Bebbs to ask them & some others to dine here ... Mrs Bebb seems rather a frank open mannered woman, her husband a true lean bilious East Indian, more prudent that she, as it the husbands business, you know, always ... I find Mr Bebb has a very singular complaint incidental to the climate of Bengal, a spasm in one of the seven nerves, as Mrs Bebb told me, which is under the eye, which nerve somehow is half broken or separated from the rest, so that the only cure for the intense pain it produces is for the person to undergo the operation of having it cut, which Mr Bebb did & is now almost intirely recover'd – next day arriv'd these good folks to dinner with as many more as made 18 people.

Anticipating his permanent return home, John Bebb had purchased the picturesque estate of Donnington Grove in Berkshire in 1795, the former home of the Brummell family. The house had been built between 1763 and 1772 in a style known as 'Strawberry Hill Gothic' that mimicked Horace Walpole's house in Twickenham, and George (Beau) Brummell's father, William, had bought the house in 1783 and was responsible for improving and extending the estate.

Young Beau Brummell was 5 years old when his family moved into Donnington Grove, where he spent most of his childhood days when not away at Eton. William Brummell died in 1794 and his will directed that Donnington be sold and the proceeds divided among his children, and a year later John

Bebb agreed the sale. The estate was to remain in the hands of the Bebbs for over fifty years and they treated it as their country residence.

While still in India, and probably upon the occasion of their marriage, John Bebb and his wife Jessy commissioned a splendid Chinese Qianlong porcelain dinner service with their joined arms painted in enamel on each item. The arms on the service are those of Bebb impaling Brown of Blackburn; it is the custom in heraldry for the arms of a non-heiress of a noble family to be impaled, or joined, with those of her husband, the husband's arms being on the 'dexter' or right-hand side of the viewer and those of the wife on the 'sinister' or left-hand side as you view it.[287]

If George Cornwallis Brown had inherited Blackburn, then Jessy, as the eldest daughter, would have been the heir, and this would seem to indicate that she felt the loss keenly and was clinging to her noble Scottish heritage. Additionally, both John and Jessy obviously believed that the ancestry of the Browns of Blackburn was one that enhanced their social status. John Bebb also adopted Janet's family motto as his own, added to their conjoined arms 'Præmium virtutis honos'.

Upon arriving in London, the widowed Susannah Robiniana slipped into respectable anonymity, while her sister Jessy, as befitted the wife of a wealthy and influential East India Company official, was fêted by high society. The contrast now between Jessy's lifestyle and that of her cousin Grace could not have been more stark. Grace, who had much the more promising start to her adult life with her marriage to a wealthy society doctor compared to Jessy who had been reduced to husband-hunting in India, had ended up the loser, reduced to a life of dependency and shunned by good society. Jessy now launched herself onto the London scene in a glittering show of wealth.

Boodle's, the exclusive London gentlemen's club, gave a dress ball at Ranelagh Gardens in June 1802, attended by their Royal Highnesses the Prince of Wales and his brother the Duke of Cumberland. Mrs Jessy Bebb was also there, one of the 2,000 people of fashion and quality present to enjoy the ball in a covered area of the garden before entering the rotunda for a cold supper in company with Captain and Mrs Rowley, her half-sister Elizabeth, née King.[288] In April 1803 she was presented to Queen Charlotte, wife of King George III, and to the Princesses Elizabeth and Amelia in the queen's drawing room at St James's Palace by Lady Down. The *Morning Post* mentioned that she was 'admirably well dressed in white and silver, her chains of pearls'.[289]

Eager to be accepted into the inner circle of the *ton*, Jessy now hosted a grand ball. Elizabeth Fremantle (née Wynne), wife of Captain (later Vice Admiral) Thomas Francis Fremantle (a man who was to be knighted and was a close associate of Horatio Nelson), recorded in her diary that she called on her friend, the wife of Sir Henry Bankes of Kingston Hall in Dorset, and received an invitation:

[Tuesday, 8 May 1804] ... I called on Mrs. Bankes who gave me a card for Mrs. Bebb's Ball. Mrs. Bebb is a distant relation of hers, who is introducing herself in Society by giving this Ball – for the sake of this Ball everyone is eager to become acquainted with her.

The 'Fashionable World' column of the *Morning Post* newspaper documented the evening:[290]

MRS BEBB'S BALL. On Monday evening, the above Lady had one of the most splendid Balls, at her house in Stratford-place that has been given this season. The ball room, which is very spacious, was adorned with a variety of appropriate ornaments; the chandeliers and lustres reflecting their brilliancy by the aid of several magnificent mirrors, added a beauty to the scene scarcely to be surpassed.

The guest list included the Cholmondeleys, Lord Charles Bentinck who was to marry Grace's daughter four years hence, and a Miss Seymour. Given the fact of her guardians the Earl and Countess of Cholmondeley being present, Miss Seymour is certainly Grace's daughter Georgiana, attending the ball held by her first cousin once removed. Jessy Bebb and Georgiana met at various events over the years including the Prince Regent's Ball held in 1813 where both Mr and Mrs Bebb and Lord and Lady C. Bentinck were recorded among the guests. One can only imagine how envious Grace herself must have been of her cousin's standing in society.

A faded courtesan, now over half a century old, was not a fit guest at a ball held by a wealthy and respectable wife of an East India Company director, even if the two women were first cousins, but Georgiana, with the protection afforded by the Cholmondeleys, was accepted. For the sake of her daughter's future marriage prospects, Grace duly kept in the shadows and did not court attention, scandal or gossip. It would be nice, however, to think that Jessy Bebb did take an especial interest in Miss Georgiana Seymour for her cousin's sake.

In the late summer of 1802 Georgiana, together with her guardians Lord and Lady Cholmondeley, their family and attendants, making up in total a party of twenty people, embarked in some style for the Continent. In doing so they were following the example of many other British visitors who had taken advantage of the temporary end to hostilities with France brought about by the signing of the Treaty of Amiens in March 1802. With four new post-coaches, each with six horses and outriders bedecked in scarlet and gold, their uniform trimmed with gold lace an inch deep, and the couriers in blue and gold, the Cholmondeley retinue made an impressive sight.[291]

So while Grace had returned to London, Georgiana and the Cholmondeleys were in Paris and were still there in the spring of the following year. Just approaching her 21st birthday, young and beautiful, Georgiana fell head-over-heels in love with a dashing diplomat resident in Paris, a man some eleven years her senior, the Honourable Arthur Paget, third son of the Earl of Uxbridge. Business came first, however, and Paget, Envoy Extraordinary and Minister Plenipotentiary to the Court of Austria, was forced to leave Paris and his lover behind. Days later he received a letter from his friend and fellow diplomat James Talbot, the future 3rd Baron Malahide, who was still resident in the city:

> [Paris, 12 March 1803] ... I am charged by a young lady, Miss Seymour, who is here with Lord & Lady Cholmondeley, to convey to you the avowal of her most ardent love. I told her that I should certainly obey her Commands, and literally in those words. She finds, however, some, but it is her only, consolation for your absence in the presence of a Gentleman not from Tripoli, but from Tunis, one of our colleagues at Paris. She thinks him your very image, and perhaps he might be something like you were he shaved of a very fine black beard which I presume it would be no easy matter to prevail on him to part with, certainly if he were aware how much that operation would tend to identify him with you in Miss Seymour's affections we should see him smack smooth to-morrow; but fortunately for you it does not as yet seem to have occurred to him, and I shall beware of suggesting it to him until I hear from you on this subject.

Nothing came of Georgiana's adoration and, with the renewal of war between England and France just a couple of months later, the Cholmondeleys beat a hasty retreat from the latter. Pretty but perhaps spoilt, Georgiana was acquainted with but not a favourite of Lady Harriet Cavendish, daughter of the Duke and Duchess of Devonshire (and known as Haryo), who wrote to her sister Lady Georgiana Morpeth (known as Little G) in December 1803 saying that 'the only flaw in [Priscilla Susan Tarleton's] character is her great admiration of Miss Seymour, but that I am doomed to meet with her.' However, Sarah Harriet Burney, writing in 1806, thought Miss Seymour 'a celebrated beauty, and a very amiable creature'.

In the first decade of the 1800s Grace divided her time between her aunt, Janet Edmondes, who had residences at Twickenham and Upper Brook Street, and an elderly widow named Mrs Sarah Naylor, just possibly the Mrs Meyler from her life in revolutionary Paris, who had a house on Prospect

Row in Brompton. Grace lived with both these ladies but it was at Janet's house where Grace first became acquainted with Sophia Seneschall, a girl from very humble origins but one who Grace would come to count alongside Lady Worsley as one of her closest friends in her later years. Sophia, who lived until 1870, was the friend of Grace's mentioned in the preface to her *Journal of My Life during the French Revolution* and who provided some of the information used in it. It is likely that it is Sophia we have to thank for the incorrect biographical information on Grace in the journal.

Sophia was born in 1779 to unmarried Huguenot parents – Joseph Seneschall, a weaver, and Agnatha Boixleaux (they married in London a few months after her birth) – and so was a quarter of a century younger than Grace and only three years older than Grace's daughter. Sophia had entered Janet's house as a lowly scullery maid but, when Janet's lady's maid Miss Flowers left to marry, Sophia managed to get herself promoted to the position. Coming from a Huguenot background, Sophia was fluent in French and she and Grace were able to converse in this language together in front of Janet, who, to her increasing annoyance, was totally unable to understand any part of their private conversation.[292]

Janet Edmondes, now in her late seventies, had become increasingly feeble and confused. While once pretty, she had now grown fat but still fancied herself a catch. As she had no children of her own her nieces and nephew hovered around her, eager to be declared her favourite and inherit her fortune. Specifically, the two who most contested the position of favourite were Charles Henry, the 5th Earl of Peterborough, and Grace herself, ably assisted by her partner in crime, Sophia. Janet quickly found herself in a tug-of-war between her niece and nephew. In early 1803 she gave Charles Henry the substantial sum of £1,000 in ready money; he claimed it was given as a free gift but Grace countered that it was to cover bed and board, for Janet soon after went to reside in the earl's London town house where she was taken seriously ill.

Charles Henry, holding all the cards, was accused by Grace of obstructing access to their aunt. Sophia Seneschall had moved into the earl's house to accompany her mistress and although it is not clear if Grace was also resident in his house she was certainly accused by the earl of turning away family visitors to Janet's bedside, so she had a degree of freedom and control within it. Jessy Bebb did not visit; the mere presence of Grace in the house was enough to keep her away, lest her newly-established place in society should begin to crumble. Former courtesans were not polite company even if they were a relative and besides, Jessy had no need of her aunt's money and could afford not to visit. John Bebb did attend, chaperoning Susannah Robiniana

Farmer to Janet's bedside on the few occasions they could get past Grace, Sophia and Lord Peterborough, who worried about Susannah's incessant chattering tiring the patient out.

Before being taken ill, on 4 February 1803 Janet had written her will, leaving the bulk of her fortune to her niece Grace who was most in need of financial assistance and who had spent most time in Janet's company. Indeed, we may be doing Grace a disservice for suggesting that her attendance on her aunt was for mercenary reasons alone; perhaps she truly was very fond of the elderly lady. While under the earl's roof, two months later Janet made a codicil to her will, one witnessed by Joseph Bouchier Smith, that trusty old companion ever ready to help out his friend Lord Peterborough. This codicil altered the terms of the will and proved much more favourable to the earl but, alas for him, Janet recovered enough to leave his house and she set out for a stay at Broadstairs on the Kent coast, accompanied by the ever-present Sophia and also by Grace. The trio stayed at the seaside until late autumn, returning to Janet's Upper Brook Street house in October, ready for the London season.

Janet had not attended any places of public amusement for some time before her illness but now, whether through her own desire or the whim of Grace and her accomplice, she began to nightly frequent the playhouses, although she was so corpulent that she had to be lifted up and squeezed in and out of her carriage for every journey. The mental image conjured of a middle-aged Grace Dalrymple, all rouge and lace, squeezing her oversized aunt into a carriage ready for a night at the theatre is a wonderfully comedic one and far removed from the traditional elegant image of her represented in the Gains-borough portraits, but also a vividly realistic snapshot of her life as it truly was in the early nineteenth century. These visits to the theatre continued for some months from late 1803 into early 1804, Janet always accompanied by Grace or Sophia and usually sitting either in the Earl of Peterborough's box at the Covent Garden Theatre or one known as the 'Prince's Box' at Drury Lane, arriving before the candles were lit and staying until everyone else had departed.

Grace attended unnoticed by the gossips of the day, the newspapers remaining silent regarding her presence. Was the subterfuge in taking their seats in the darkness and sneaking out at the end one of propriety and decorum, and a measure that limited any gossip at a time when her daughter was launched upon the *ton*, or did she just not want to be seen squashing her portly aunt back into their carriage and the world to know she was only at the theatre in the position of a dependant, a glorified lady's companion, a neat contrast to her formerly exalted position on the arm of an earl, a prince and a duke? Whatever the reason, Grace was still clinging on to the coat-tails of London high society, not living in anonymity in France or reduced to penury and the debtor's prison, the fate of so many other courtesans. She was living in the shadows, but those shadows existed within the confines of grand London houses and the boxes of noblemen at the theatre.

Janet Edmondes, whether on her own initiative or at the urging of her niece, rewrote her will on 13 November 1803 in terms once more favourable to Grace and witnessed by Abraham Dallimore, Janet's coachman. The Earl of Peterborough denounced this will when he discovered its existence, believing that Janet had lacked the mental intellect to know her own mind. He declared her simple and childish, claiming that Sophia often gave her mistress children's toys in the morning to keep her quiet and amused, and further suggested Janet often had a fancy for seeing her menservants dressed in the maidservants' clothes and the maidservants in the men's, a fancy that was ordered into actuality by Grace and Sophia who pandered to her every whim.

The earl also accused the pair of keeping Janet drunk and running her house as they wished, pretending authority from Janet. As an example of this he recalled a visit from Thomas Harris, manager of the Covent Garden Theatre, whom Grace and Sophia had summoned to ask about taking a box but when he called he was brought to Janet instead who knew nothing of the project. Janet, the earl claimed, fancied herself in love with both the Prince of Wales and Old Q, the Duke of Queensberry, driving daily past the prince's London residence of Carlton House in the hope of seeing him and instructing Grace to leave her card at Old Q's house (Grace merely left a blank card, explaining to Queensberry's servant that she was simply indulging her aunt in her fantasies). With the Earl of Cholmondeley living in the house next to Old Q's, Grace must have also glimpsed her daughter on some of these visits and rides, even if she hesitated to visit. Whether there was any truth in the rumours spread by Lord Peterborough is open to conjecture; it was in the earl's interest to prove that Janet had lost her mental faculties as he wanted the codicil to the previous will, written under his roof and with the assistance of Bouchier Smith, to stand uncontested. Equally, it was in Grace's interest to prove that her aunt was still *compos mentis*. However, the Earl of Peterborough wasn't totally incorrect in his assertions as to his aunt's romantic inclinations. Janet did still have one admirer and one more chance of marriage.

Janet Edmondes had by now made three marriages and been widowed three times. Louisa Maria Edmondes, the niece of her last husband Colonel Thomas Edmondes, supplied the information on the last proposal Janet was to receive:

Mrs Col. Edmondes was going to be married to Lord Dormer who would have been her 4th Husband when she died. He was so old and stiff that when he proposed to her, he fell on his knees and she was obliged to ring for the footman to help him up.[293]

Lord Charles Dormer, 8th Baron Dormer of Wyng, was approaching his 78th year and had been married twice. His second wife had been the widow of Lieutenant Colonel John Mordaunt, nephew of the 3rd Earl of Peterborough and, with further ties to the Mordaunt family, in 1788 he had moved into Robinaiana, Dowager Countess of Peterborough's former home on Dean Street in Soho when she vacated it.[294]

A marriage licence was procured by Charles Dormer, dated 14 January 1803 and naming Janet as the intended bride, so the prospective groom was serious about his proposal.[295] This was shortly before Janet moved into her nephew's house where she was taken ill and, as no marriage took place, it is very tempting to think that Charles Henry might have quickly taken his ailing aunt under his control to prevent a union which might, very easily, have left her wealth to the Dormer family instead of to him.

Does the following snippet from the *Morning Post* newspaper, written after Janet's recovery and return from Broadstairs, refer to Janet and one of her many prospective suitors? 'An antiquated Lady, celebrated for her numerous amours in fashionable life, now makes a daily dash at the West end of the town, with a noble chere ami whose attention the fair object has lately attracted.'[296]

Lord Charles Dormer died on 30 March 1804, putting an end to any suggestions of Janet becoming, in her dotage, Lady Dormer. As the nightly jaunts to the theatre also ended around this time, they were then perhaps at Janet's instigation and an attempt to woo back her titled suitor; the Earl of Peterborough's suggestion that it was Old Q and the Prince of Wales she was setting her cap at were false only because he did not know the full story.

Just over a month after Lord Dormer had died, Janet drew up yet another will and testament. Describing herself as 'Jenet Edmondes of Upper Brook Street ... widow', she quite rightly bequeathed her London town house and all the furniture inside to her first husband's nephew, Sir William A'Court of Heytesbury.[297]

When she was left the Upper Brook Street house by Peirce Ashe A'Court it was expected that it would revert to his family on Janet's death, but it was this bequest that had been reversed under the codicil initiated by Joseph Bouchier Smith and the 5th Earl of Peterborough. Charles Henry was now denied his aunt's town house. Lady Mary Mordaunt, her nephew's half-sister, and Major Barrington both received bequests. To her 'niece Grace Dalrymple formerly the wife of the late Sir John Elliot Baronet and Doctor in Medicine deceased' Janet left her jewels, her musical clock and the prints and pictures in her home, together with a substantial legacy of £4,000. Grace's daughter was not mentioned.

Sophia Seneschall, described as Janet's maid servant, bagged herself £500 and all the wearing apparel belonging to her mistress, as long as she was still in her service. A watch and chain was left to Susannah Robiniana Farmer and the rest of Janet's estate was to be shared equally between

> my nephew Charles Earl of Peterborough and Monmouth, my said niece Grace Dalrymple formerly the wife of the said Sir John Elliot, my said niece Susanna Farmer of Gloucester-place in the parish of St. Mary le bone aforesaid widow and to my niece Janet Lawrence Bebb wife of John Bebb of Stratford place in the parish of St. Mary le bone aforesaid Esq.

Grace and John Bebb were nominated as executrix and executor of the will and it was witnessed by a doctor attending to Janet, Samuel Holland MD, her solicitor William Seymour of Margaret Street, Cavendish Square and Janet's footman, Richard Potter. In poor health, Janet then spent the autumn at Broadstairs with Grace to keep her company and Sophia to attend on her, and her remaining days she saw out at Twickenham where Grace was living when she put pen to paper to record her experiences in France during the Reign of Terror.

August 1805 recorded two noteworthy deaths that impacted on Grace's life. On the 8th of the month Sir Richard Worsley died, freeing his estranged wife from his stranglehold on her fortune. Lady Worsley wasted no time in reverting back to her maiden surname and marrying the man she had long been living with, John Louis Hummell, otherwise Cuchet, becoming known as Lady Fleming. Her much younger husband also adopted Fleming as his surname.

With Lady Worsley, or Lady Fleming as we must now call her, back in control of her estate she had the means to help her friend Grace. Janet Edmondes was the second death, passing away at the reported age of 80 at Twickenham on 19 August and buried at St George's in Hanover Square five days later, the last of Colonel Robert Brown's children to die. Sad as Grace must have been to lose her aunt, the one dependable rock in her life, the prospect of an inheritance of £4,000 plus a quarter share in the remaining estate would see her able to end her days comfortably and put an end to the existence whereby she relied on the charity of her friends and the unreliable payments of her annuity from the prince.

Did Charles Henry, 5th Earl of Peterborough, know of the subsequent wills made by Janet? He perhaps, when his aunt died, expected the former will with the codicil written in his house and at his instigation to come into force and was infuriated to discover a newer one had been made that superseded it. He immediately challenged it, asserting that Janet had not had enough control of her own mind to have been able to write it, putting into action a long-drawn-out legal challenge. Grace was supported in this challenge by her cousins Mrs Farmer and Jessy Bebb and by John Bebb, executor, like Grace, of the will. With no other evidence to show how her family felt about Grace, it's heartening to know that George Cornwallis Brown's two daughters pulled together with their errant cousin and backed her version of events in the tit-for-tat legal battle that ensued and in which Grace and her titled cousin threw accusations at each other, each one insisting the other had wielded undue power over their aunt. It is even more so as Mrs Farmer and Jessy Bebb grew up in the same household as the Earl of Peterborough, with his mother acting as their guardian; that they took Grace's part in this dispute highlights their faith in her. Grace eventually won the day, but it took almost six years for the verdict to be decided, six years in which she still remained reliant on others for her income. Finally, on 10 June 1811, Grace was able to prove the will and take possession of the money left to her.

Luckily Grace had her friendship with Lady Fleming to fall back on while the will was being contested, and by the end of 1810 she had moved just a short distance from Mrs Naylor's Prospect Row house to live in another Brompton house, one owned by Lady Fleming. It had started life as one large house but had been divided into three properties with John Lewis and Lady Fleming living at one side, Charles Greenwood, a partner of Thomas Hammersley, Lady Fleming's banker, at the other and Grace living in the middle property, with Sophia Seneschall as her companion.

Both Grace and Lady Fleming used the house of Ransome, Morland and Hammersley as their bank so having Charles Greenwood as a neighbour would have proved convenient. Moreover, Greenwood and Hammersley were 'playmates' of the Prince of Wales and his circle, Greenwood eventually dying in the arms of the Duke of Clarence after an over-stimulating game of cards.[298]

Around this period Grace and Lady Fleming dined with Lord Byron, and what a dinner table that must have been! Henry Angelo, Byron's friend and an intimate of the Dalrymple family from some three or four decades earlier, was also supposed to be one of the party but was unable to attend:

I was invited by my friend Byron (called by his acquaintance the gallant Lothario) to dine with him, and meet Lady Worsley [sic], and Dally the tall, the name Mrs. Elliott had long gone by. Illness only prevented me from seeing my old inamorato with a new face, which, after such a lapse of time, mine must have kept hers in countenance; however, her notoriety excited the gaze of every one.

Angelo had obviously not seen Grace for some years, and it is such a pity he did not attend the dinner and leave us his recollections of the evening! Lord George Gordon Byron, not born until 1788, was a mere stripling compared to his dinner guests, still in his early twenties, and he must have spent the evening listening to tales from the heyday of these two by now middle-aged ladies, their highs, lows and gossip. Byron's mother, Catherine Gordon, had been the heiress to an estate in Aberdeenshire and Byron spent his early childhood there, so he had his Scottish ancestry in common with Grace. Like Grace's parents Hugh and Grissel Dalrymple, Byron's parents had also separated (his father John 'Mad Jack' Byron proving to be a dissolute wastrel) and, like Grace, after the separation he initially lived in Scotland with his mother.

Byron had inherited his baronetcy when he was only 10 years of age, along with the family seat of Newstead Abbey in Nottinghamshire, but precious little money to go with it. Incredibly handsome but born with a deformed foot that left him lame and for which he blamed his mother, he was already becoming known, with varying degrees of praise in those early days, for his poetic works. For just a short time in the spring of 1808 Byron was a near neighbour of Grace and Lady Fleming, lodging at Brompton while conducting an amour with a pretty young woman named Miss Caroline Cameron, reputedly a 16-year-old Cockney prostitute who he used to dress in boy's clothing and introduce as his 'brother'. From the summer of 1809 Byron was travelling abroad on the Grand Tour, forced to sidestep most of Europe due to the Napoleonic Wars but taking in the Mediterranean countries instead, returning to England in July of 1811. The publication of the first two cantos of *Childe Harold's Pilgrimage* the following year propelled him into celebrity status.

Sir John Shelley, 6th Baronet, was another who was sometimes in Grace Dalrymple Elliott's society, although he professed himself too *volage* or changeable to fall captive to her charms. Did Grace then make a habit of frequenting the dinner tables of men like Byron? Shelley married Grace's niece, Frances Winckley, and he had witnessed the equal devotion of both the Prince of Wales and the Earl of Cholmondeley to Georgiana Seymour, saying 'all the men of the *ton*, and many women, received, and courted ... Grace Dalrymple Eliot, thereby hoping to obtain access to the Prince's favour.' Interesting to note then, that while Grace might not find herself on the invitation list for balls and routs at the best houses, self-serving parents and prospective suitors were not above currying her favour to try to gain the interest of the prince through his reputed daughter, Georgiana. Far from being as much of an outcast as was previously thought, Grace remained on the periphery of the *ton* and took such society as was offered to her.

By 1807 Georgiana Seymour was once more in love, this time with a Mr Peter Robert Burrell, eldest son of Peter Burrell, 1st Baron Gwydyr, and nephew to Lady Cholmondeley. Lord Granville Leveson Gower wrote to a correspondent detailing the tangled amours of Georgiana and her circle. Miss Sarah Clementina Drummond, only child and heiress of the 11th Earl of Perth, 'rich, clever, cross and dirty', was going to be married to Mr William Horace Beckford, Georgiana was in love with Mr Burrell, a foolish man and nephew to Lady Exeter as well as to Lady Cholmondeley.[299]

After Mr Beckford wrote an 'avantageux, impertinent letter' to Miss Drummond, she flew into a passion and Lady Exeter, who was by her side, proposed her nephew as a future husband. Miss Drummond, half in a pique and half persuaded by Lady Exeter's arguments, accepted on the spot. Mr Beckford consoled himself with a Miss Frances Rigby, daughter of Lieutenant Colonel Francis Hale Rigby, who was neither clever nor dirty but was rich and cross and Mr Burrell stated he could not 'refuse such good fortune when it is thrown at my head'. Leveson Gower's description of the amorous muddle ended: 'Poor G. Seymour, Mr Burrell, and Mr Beckford, are all three beauties – and well it is for them they are, or I fear there is little else to be put before the zero emblematick of each.' Mr Burrell and Miss Drummond were married in October 1807, Mr Beckford and Miss Rigby in February 1808; Miss Seymour, despite her beauty, remained a spinster.

The problem can't have been Grace (Georgiana was, after all, thought to be a progeny of the Prince of Wales and royal bastards generally had no shortage of suitors for their hand). She had the additional aplomb of being considered part of the Cholmondeley family, was considered a beauty and, by most, a gracious companion. Was it then lack of a fortune that was holding her back? Cholmondeley, ever careful with his money, would not be ready to offer Georgiana a fortune if one might be forthcoming from the prince, and the prince, ever short of funds, would be hoping Cholmondeley would step forth and provide. Grace, everyone assumed, had only the expectation of her share of her aunt's fortune and that was still being decided by the courts. Georgiana remained caught in the middle, watching her youth slip away.

Towards the end of April 1808 the Marquess and Marchioness of Abercorn hosted a party at their country villa, Bentley Priory at Stanmore, a fine house designed in 1775 by Sir John Soane where all the great and the good of the day assembled. At these particular festivities in April 1808, the Princess of Wales, Caroline of Brunswick, estranged wife of the Prince of Wales, was the most honoured guest. Caroline arrived at Bentley Priory at six o'clock on the evening of Friday, 22 April in a post-chaise drawn by six horses and attended by four outriders. Sitting inside the carriage with the princess, and described politely in the newspapers as a niece of the Earl and Countess of Cholmondeley, was Grace's daughter Georgiana.[300]

The occasion for the festivities was the baptism of the infant daughter of the Earl and Countess of Aberdeen, the countess being the daughter of Lord Abercorn by his first wife. The Princess of Wales was to stand as godmother for the little girl who was named Charlotte Catherine Hamilton-Gordon, also known as Caroline in honour of her godparent. Emma, Lady Hamilton and mistress of Horatio Nelson until his death three years previously, was also present and entertained the guests with her fine singing voice. Lady Cholmondeley had formerly been an attendant to the Princess of Wales and Georgiana must then have come to the attention of the maternal Caroline who, having had to give up her own daughter, was known for adopting several of the poor children who lived near her and fostering them out, all but one boy who she kept with her. It seems she had also taken her husband's illegitimate daughter under her wing.

A curious letter from Georgiana Seymour survives, written to her friend Beau Brummell. Undated, we can only guess when it was written and to whom she was referring in her letter; was it written after she returned to England from France in 1803 or after her passion for Mr Burrell in 1807? Perhaps it was written in 1808 upon her return to London from Bentley Priory and refers to the latest man she had set her sights on, Lord Charles Bentinck?

> Wednesday morning
> I am more obliged to you than I can express for your note: be assured that your approbation of my conduct has given me very sincere pleasure: this is the only means I have of telling you so; for I am in such disgrace, that I do not know if I shall be taken to the play; – in any case, I shall be watched; therefore accept my most cordial thanks, and believe that I shall remember your good nature to me on this occasion with gratitude to the end of my life.
>
> ____ does not know how unkindly I have been treated, but is more affectionate than ever, because he sees I am unhappy. We did not arrive in town till seven last night, therefore no play; to-morrow they go to Coventgarden: – perhaps I may be allowed to be of the party.
>
> Pray don't neglect my drawing; you would make me very happy by lending me the yellow book again; the other I don't dare ask for, much as

I wish for it. Adieu! I shall be steady in my opinion of you, and always remain,

Yours, very sincerely,

Georgiana A.F. Seymour

Whatever Georgiana had done to deserve the Cholmondeleys' censure, Beau Brummell remained a true friend to her. A mark of this comes in the form of an anguished inscription written by him some years later on the end of this letter which says 'This beautiful creature is dead!' and he treasured the letter as a memento of their friendship until four years before his own death. He then parted with it but only to a very intimate friend of his who wished to own it for the autograph. Possibly this intimate friend was Lord Granville Leveson Gower or his wife Haryo, despite her dislike for Georgiana? Leveson Gower was Ambassador to Paris in the early summer of 1835 and raised a subscription to help Brummell who was in desperate need of assistance, penniless, almost friendless and suffering from syphilis, a far cry from the elegant man-about-town he had once been. Leveson Gower, who had been part of the same set as Georgiana in her youth, may well have induced Brummell to part with her letter in gratitude for his help.

If not Leveson Gower, then maybe it was Sir George Warrender or, as Sir Joseph Copley pronounced him, Sir Gorge Provender, a famous bon-vivant? Sir George was another man who appears to have been in Georgiana's sights during June 1808. At Lady Warburton's masquerade ball in Grosvenor Place, Georgiana, dressed as a gypsy, led off the evening's dancing with Captain Warrender. A few days later she was at another masquerade, this time one given by Mrs Coxe at her magnificent house in Hanover Square, where Georgiana and Lady Cholmondeley, dressed as nuns of the Order of St Catherine, 'arrested' Sir George Warrender who was dressed as a pilgrim on his way to Mecca.[301]

With the interest excited by her parentage and bearing in mind that she had many suitors, remarkably Georgiana Seymour remained unmarried until she was 26 years of age, an old maid for the times, but an interesting parallel to the similarly beautiful but also illegitimate Harriat Mordaunt who did not marry Maurice George Bisset until she was aged 34.

When Georgiana eventually married she chose as her husband Lord Charles Bentinck, younger son of the 3rd Duke of Portland, an officer in the Grenadier Guards, Member of Parliament for Ashburton in Devon and an equerry to her reputed father, the Prince of Wales. Lord Charles, actually Lieutenant Colonel Lord William Charles Augustus Cavendish Bentinck (all the sons were given William as a first name but only the eldest used it as such), was just two years Georgiana's senior and, when not on military service, was a permanent fixture in all the best ballrooms, particularly noted for his dancing abilities. As equerry to the prince he was among the inner circle surrounding him and it is probable that the prince and Georgiana's guardian Lord Cholmondeley did not fully approve of the match (his charms failing to make up for a lack of independent wealth). The couple applied for a marriage licence at the Faculty Office in London on 17 September 1808 to allow them to marry in the Cheshire town of Malpas where the newly-built Cholmondeley Castle was situated.[302] Three days later they applied to the Bishop of Chester for another licence, this time to marry in Chester itself. Did Cholmondeley therefore object to or veto the marriage? The prince certainly drew the line at allowing the couple to use the royal arms:

> To Miss Seymour his [Cholmondeley's] claims of paternity were more disputed; George Selwyn was on the list, but George Prince of Wales always privately seemed to take the honour to himself, and showed great interest in her welfare; she married Lord Charles Bentinck; but when, in consequence of this royal protection, an attempt was made on the marriage to quarter the royal arms with the bar of bastardy, a royal veto was immediately issued to prevent it.[303]

Although Lord Charles, being a younger son, had no great hopes of any inheritance, marrying a daughter of royalty, even an illegitimate daughter, opened the door to future prospects for an ambitious man and he was ever rash and impulsive, following his heart first and foremost rather than his head. If he was ambitious, Lord Charles was also, unfortunately for Georgiana, something of a wastrel and of a character that disposed him to be easily led. In company with his younger brother Frederick, he had frequented the houses of the demireps and courtesans, paying court to the younger versions of his mother-in-law Grace and in particular to the famous Harriette Wilson. Both Bentinck boys warranted a mention in her memoirs written in 1825 in which her clients were invited, before publication, to pay a sum of money to keep their names from her book (Arthur Wellesley, the Duke of Wellington, and another of Harriette's customers reputedly said 'publish, and be damned!' when approached). Lords Charles and Frederick Bentinck took a similar approach, or perhaps just didn't have the money to hand to extricate themselves from her pages, although they escaped Harriette's treatment fairly lightly as Frederick in particular seemed to have been a particular favourite.

Georgiana and Lord Charles were married at Chester on 21 September 1808, the two witnesses to the wedding named as James Jackson, a local man who witnessed other marriages at the church, and Fanny Orby Hunter.

Fanny, whose brother-in-law Albemarle Bertie RN was an illegitimate son of Lady Cholmondeley's uncle (a very tenuous family connection), was twenty years Georgiana's senior. While no record has survived to say whether or not Grace was in attendance at her beloved daughter's wedding, it looks likely that it took place without either the Cholmondeley or Bentinck families, or with their blessing, as otherwise surely a family member would have added their name to the marriage register as a witness. Additionally, no marriage settlement was drawn up before the wedding and Lord Cholmondeley was not the kind of man who would have neglected attending to such an important consideration.

In a parallel, just over three years later, Lord Cholmondeley also vetoed the marriage of his daughter Harriet by Madame Saint-Albin, who had fallen in love with the young John George Lambton, the future 1st Earl of Durham. Lambton, whose mother was a daughter of the 4th Earl of Jersey, was just 19 years old when he took matters into his own hands and eloped, in the depths of winter, to Gretna Green in Scotland with Harriet, who was just about of age. The young couple went through a marriage ceremony there on 11 January 1812, and after their parents realized that there was little they could do retrospectively, a more formal marriage ceremony was hastily conducted at the Cholmondeley family church at Malpas. Sadly, after three children in quick succession, Harriet succumbed to tuberculosis and died in the summer of 1815 while still aged only 24.

Within days of his wedding to Georgiana, Lord Charles received military call-up papers directing him to join his regiment at Yarmouth on the Norfolk coast, from where they were due to sail to Spain. The regiment sailed, the new Lady Charles Bentinck was left bereft and she fell ill.[304]

On mainland Europe the Peninsular War was raging. Following the 1807 invasion of Portugal by combined French and Spanish forces, Britain had entered the conflict when France turned upon Spain. Lord Charles Bentinck was one of many thousands of reinforcements sent over under the command of General Sir David Baird to bolster the British forces already there with Lieutenant General Sir John Moore, landing at Corunna in north-western Spain on 13 October, less than a month after his marriage. At the beginning of December 1808 he was stationed, under Moore, a little further inland at Ponferrada but was not happy with his situation. On 3 December he wrote to William Dacres Adams, secretary to his father, the Duke of Portland:

> On my opinion we ought to have been sent to the southmost part of Spain ... as we might have gained possession of one of the passes of the Pyrennes [sic]. The army in general have many sick. Most of the Regts

being second Battalions & composed of Boys who cannot stand the fatigue at the same time not receiving their due allowance of Rations at the time they ought.[305]

The French force, under the command of Napoléon Bonaparte himself and Marshal Soult, swiftly defeated the Spanish army standing against them and set off in pursuit of the British. Vastly outnumbered and in a mountainous area, beset by blizzards and freezing weather and with a withdrawal to Portugal impossible, Moore ordered a wholesale retreat to the port of Corunna. The British were closely followed by the French troops with skirmishes and battles along the way, but the main body of the army made Corunna on 11 January 1809, only to be disappointed to find that most of the expected transport ships had been delayed by bad weather and had not yet arrived to take them back to England and safety.

The Battle of Corunna took place on 16 January, the British now having the upper hand in terms of numbers of troops and the benefit of a few days' rest. The transports had arrived in the harbour and while the embarkation began, Moore was given the news of a French attack. During the afternoon and into the evening the British held off the French, Sir John Moore losing his life in the battle and Sir David Baird an arm, and by nightfall the troops manning the piquet lines began to slip away to the ships. By the next morning most of the British army was aboard the transports and the rear guard embarked a day later.

The British had lost just under 1,000 men in the battle and had destroyed six times as many horses belonging to the cavalry, the artillery and the baggage train, unable to take them aboard the transports. Furthermore, upon their return to England, 6,000 men were listed as sick or injured.

Lord Charles Bentinck had managed to get aboard the transports but sparked temporary consternation regarding his safety. Travelling home to his new wife, a transport he was thought to be aboard, the *Dispatch*, foundered and sank at Black Head off the coast of Cornwall in the early hours of 22 January in a gale. Only six men out of the near 100 on board survived the wreck and at around the same time and just a short distance away, HMS *Primrose*, sailing in the opposite direction, ran aground on the Manacles, a treacherous rocky outcrop, with a similarly devastating loss of life. However, Lord Charles had been aboard a different ship and landed safely. Back in London, he wrote to William Dacres Adams from Welbeck Street, referring to his pension prospects and clearly not intending to return to action for some time.[306]

Lady Charles' old protagonist, Haryo, penned a letter to her brother the Marquess of Hartington mourning the loss of their cousin, George

Cavendish, only 25 years of age, who had been on the *Dispatch* with his regiment the 7th Hussars:

> Dearest Hartington,
>
> Since I wrote we have received the melancholy intelligence of poor George Cavendish's loss. After behaving with the greatest bravery, the transport on which he was returning was sunk ... It is impossible to say how much I feel for his family. It is dreadful for them, having first received the news of the embarkation and supposing him safe.

Haryo had written to her brother days earlier too, commenting on the heroic role played by Lord Charles' elder brother, Lord William Bentinck, and saying of Lady William that 'I think it must have driven her wild, first the anxiety, then the joy. How do people keep their senses in such cases?' before remarking tartly to him: 'Lady Charles Bentinck probably does, from having had originally so few that they could not muster into insanity. I hear nothing of husband.'

After his safe return Lord Charles and Georgiana resided for some weeks at Bulstrode Park in Buckinghamshire, a mansion owned by the Duke of Portland. From Bulstrode, Lord Charles excused himself for not attending the House of Commons, pleading illness and writing to say that his throat had not improved.[307]

The Duke of Portland settled a sum of £5,000 in the form of a bond on his son and Georgiana belatedly brought a fortune of the same amount as documented in a marriage settlement drawn up on 15 July 1809, some months after the wedding. Yet where did this fortune come from? It was actually provided by Grace.

This £5,000 was the value in sterling of capital held by Grace: £841 8s 2d 5 per cent bank annuities dating from 1797, bank stock and money in the navy 5 per cents. Grace was to receive the dividends of these for her lifetime but they were to be held by the Duke of Portland for the future benefit of his son and new daughter-in-law.[308] Far from being destitute, Grace had in fact been sitting on a reasonable fortune. She also had new expectations of inheriting a considerable sum of money.

On 7 January 1809 Old Q, the now aged Duke of Queensberry, made a long codicil to his will, handing out bequests of up to £10,000 to a long list of people. Grace's old paramour Richard FitzPatrick was the recipient of a £10,000 bequest; Emma, Lady Hamilton, received £1,000 and an annuity of £1,000 a year for life; and the cross-dressing Chevalier D'Éon received an annuity of 100 guineas a year. Grace, described as 'Mrs Elliot sometime wife of the late Sir John Elliot', was to receive £5,000. A myriad of possibilities opens up as to why Old Q should name Grace as a benefactor in his will. Grace's Dalrymple ancestors had acted as stewards to his Scottish estate and old family loyalties may have bound him to help Grace when she needed it. Janet Edmondes had professed herself in love with him and Grace had called at Old Q's house and colluded with his servants in working a kindly deception on the old lady, so possibly Grace was in the habit of calling on him.

In another positive move for Grace she also, in January 1809, once more began to receive her annuity from the Prince of Wales; a regular quarterly annuity of £75 and one that would continue to be paid until her death.[309]

Now she was married, Georgiana was finally presented at court. She was in attendance there at the celebration in June for King George III's birthday and cut a splendid and elegant figure. Her dress was described in the newspapers and no doubt Grace radiated with pride at her daughter who had managed to attain both the title and place in society that she had been denied.

> [Lady Charles Bentinck] wore a white crape petticoat, embroidered in waves with concave spangles; draperies of crape, elegantly embroidered with spangles, and a handsome border of wheat-ears, with cockle-shells intermixed, the draperies tastefully drawn up with rich silver tassels and ropes of bullion; body and train of crape in silver to correspond, trimmed with point lace. [The *Morning Post*, 6 June 1809.]

Lord Charles Bentinck, fully recovered, was once more called up to his regiment, embarking sometime after 18 July for The Netherlands and the Walcheren campaign in General Hope's Division.[310] The Walcheren campaign saw some 40,000 soldiers cross to The Netherlands, commanded by John Pitt, 2nd Earl of Chatham, their first and foremost target being the destruction of the French fleet that was thought to be nearby. Unfortunately, the swampy conditions of the island of Walcheren, which the British troops seized together with South Beveland Island, were an effective breeding ground for malaria. Walcheren Fever, thought to be a combination of malaria and typhus, swept through both the British and the combined French and Dutch troops and nearly half the British succumbed to the disease with over 4,000 dying (there was little action and they only lost just over 100 men in combat). Lord Charles found himself stationed on South Beveland Island where Chatham established his headquarters and, as Lord Charles wrote home to William Dacres Adams, 'the Army is beginning to [be] very sickly.'[311]

Almost nine months to the day after Lord Charles' return from Spain, on 8 November 1809 Lady Charles Bentinck gave birth to a son who died an hour after his birth.[312] Lord Charles was still overseas and the knowledge of the numbers dying from disease at his station must have taken a toll on

Georgiana and perhaps contributed to what was possibly a premature birth. However, this was not the only tragedy being played out in the Bentinck family. On the same day that Georgiana suffered the birth and death of her firstborn child, the burial of her father-in-law, the 3rd Duke of Portland, was taking place. The duke had resigned from his position as First Lord of the Treasury just months earlier due to ill health and on 30 October had undergone an operation to remove a kidney stone. Initially the operation appeared to have been a success but a few hours later he suffered an epileptic fit and died.

The surviving soldiers of the regiment taking part in the Walcheren campaign withdrew a month later, many returning home to recuperate. Lord Charles Bentinck made his way back to his wife's side, both of them having suffered greatly during the previous months.

The new Duke of Portland, William Henry Cavendish Bentinck, Lord Charles' elder brother, acted upon a promise his father had made and settled a considerable sum of money, by a rent charge on his estate, on his brothers, sisters and near relations. The finances of his brother and sister-in-law, Lord and Lady Charles Bentinck, which were generally in need of a little assistance, were thereby eased a little.

A couple of months before her lying-in, Georgiana had departed London for Middleton Hall near Bicester in Oxfordshire.[313] This hall was the seat of the Jersey family, the name synonymous with the Prince of Wales as the dowager Lady Jersey had at one time been the foremost mistress of the prince despite being a grandmother and the wrong side of 40, displacing Maria Fitzherbert in his affections. She then supported the prince's ill-fated marriage to Caroline of Brunswick, probably just to further annoy Mrs Fitzherbert.

In 1809 there were two Lady Jerseys: the notorious dowager, formerly Frances Twysden, and the new incumbent of the title, the former Lady Sarah Sophia Fane, daughter of the Earl of Westmoreland. It was the younger Lady Jersey who was Georgiana's particular friend, Sally Villiers, known as 'Silence' because she never stopped talking. A society darling, and later a hostess of Almack's, she followed to a degree in her mother-in-law's footsteps (her husband once laconically suggested that if he had to fight a duel to preserve his wife's reputation, he would have to fight every man in London).

This friendship with Sally Villiers continued until August 1810 when Sally, talking too fast as usual, launched into a diatribe against the late Administration and declared to Lord Charles Bentinck that everybody knew his late father was 'the greatest fool that ever liv'd'. Georgiana, who was present with her husband and fond of a quarrel, took up her pen to defend her late father-in-law. Lady Jersey regretted saying those words but stood by the truth of her statement; Georgiana refused to associate with her and both sides wrote long letters to each other daily, keeping the argument flowing.[314]

On 23 December 1810 the 4th Duke of Queensberry died. Alas, for all those expectantly waiting for their promised bequests in his will, the whole estate was placed in Chancery and, as was the case with Janet Edmondes' will, there would be a wait of some years before payment was received. The legal arguments over Janet's will were, however, coming to a close. The case was heard the following year in the Prerogative Court of Doctors' Commons, where it was decided that the alleged insanity of Mrs Edmondes was by no means proved, and the will that was so much more beneficial to Grace was allowed to stand. Grace could now take control of the money left to her by Janet and had the expectation of more once Old Q's will was finally executed.

Just days before Old Q died Parliament had voted on the Regency Question. King George III had once more descended into madness, this particular bout thought to have been brought on by the recent death of his daughter, the Princess Amelia. Lord Charles Bentinck voted in favour of this bill, prompted, many thought, by the influence of his wife. The Prince of Wales was officially declared regent on 5 February 1811, and Lord Charles retired from the army two months later, retaining the rank of captain and lieutenant colonel.

After many years of living under a waning star, life once again seemed to offer prospects for Grace. She had some independent wealth of her own, besides the annuities on which she had relied for so long, she had the friendship and patronage of Lady Seymour Fleming, a fine home in Brompton, her daughter was happily married and the man who supposed himself the father was now regent of the kingdom. Grace no longer wished to thrust herself into the spotlight, but her position in society had improved even if her past could never be forgotten. The diarist Henry Greville, born in 1801 and nephew to Lord Charles Bentinck, in later life recalled being taken by Lady Charles Bentinck when he was a young boy to visit Grace, describing her as a 'tall, handsome, much-rouged old lady, dressed in white muslin draperies'. One more positive in Grace's life came to light during the year; Georgiana was once again pregnant. The Prince Regent would soon have a prospective grandchild, a situation that could only confer further benefits on Grace and her daughter.

The child proved to be a girl, born on 11 August 1811 and, just in case anyone doubted the likelihood of blue blood flowing through her veins, she was named for the Prince Regent as her mother had been named for him before her, Georgiana Augusta Frederica Henrietta Cavendish Bentinck. The Bentincks then took a lease on Ragmore House in Heckfield Heath,

Hampshire and it was at the parish church in Heckfield where the babe was baptized when she was a year old.[315] A near contemporary description of the house appeared in the *Morning Post* five years earlier when the freehold estate was available:

> Valuable and highly eligible FREEHOLD ESTATE, in the parish of Heck-field, about four miles from Hertford Bridge and the Southampton Road, seven from Reading, and thirty-eight from London, in a healthy and pleas-ant situation; consisting of Ragmore House, with proper offices, kitchen garden, plantations and pleasure grounds, seated on a dry, healthy soil, approached by excellent roads, and surrounded by about Eighty Acres of Land. The Premises are in perfect and substantial repair, and a most com-fortable and convenient Residence for a genteel Family. The Land is in good condition. May be entered on immediately, and the purchaser may have the Furniture, &c. at a fair valuation.[316]

By the end of 1811, after the culmination of the legal battle over Janet Edmondes' will, Lord Peterborough, now just over 50 years of age, was an invalid and perhaps had been so for some years. His friend the Reverend George Illingworth, rector of South Tidworth, wrote to another acquain-tance, Sir Arthur Paget (coincidentally the man whom Georgiana Seymour had fancied herself in love with at Paris), mentioning the earl:

> DANTSEY, Decr 3, 1811
> Dear Paget, ... I passed three days of the last week and I am doing the same this week with my poor friend Ld P. – he is very, very unwell and labours under a complication of maladies; still there seems to be such a strength of stamina that I shall not be surprized at his lingering on for many years, his clearness of understanding and natural cheerfulness and good spirits con-tinue in spite of his illness. I return home on Saturday, but probably shall come to him again in the course of next week for a day or two. With regard to his wine I can only say that it is the very best I ever drank, he has had all the Claret near ten years in his cellar, the Madeira was all of his own importing and never in a Wine Merchant's hands, the Hermitage and Cote Rotie bought by himself 25 years ago in France – in short, I don't suppose ever such a batch of wine was before offered for sale – that the whole might be preserved entire for sale, he did not permit himself to take any out of his cellar when he quitted the house; and the Auctioneer even has not been in possession of the keys.

Peterborough's friend, Joseph Bouchier Smith, had abandoned his wife Frances and was living with a woman by the name of Emelie. While they claimed to be married, Smith was certainly not free to make a second marriage with a wife already living.[317] The couple were to have at least one child together, a daughter named Constance (or Constantia) Louisa, born around 1793.

In August 1812, when Charles Henry wrote his will, Joseph Bouchier Smith was living with him; he left an annuity of £500 a year to his old friend and a similar one of £250 a year to Constantia Smith, Joseph's daughter.

He made a codicil to the will two years later in which he left two additional bequests, one of £1,000 to his friend the Reverend G. Illingworth and a larger one of £2,000 to Constantia who was residing in his house at Dauntsey.[318] Constantia was by now a young woman and, while it is a possibility that she was the earl's mistress, it is more reasonable to suppose her inheritance was her reward for nursing an ailing, aged nobleman who had little family to rely on other than his sister Harriat Bisset.

Shortly after adding the codicil, the 5th Earl of Peterborough and Monmouth died at his house in Dauntsey, in all likelihood with the Smiths by his bedside, and with him ended the Peterborough earldom. The barony of Mordaunt of Turvey devolved on his only living relative who had been legitimately born, his unmarried half-sister Lady Mary Anastasia Mordaunt.

Charles Henry, 5th Earl of Peterborough, is chiefly remembered to history, if he is remembered at all, for the lavish and extravagant funeral provided for him. Joseph Bouchier Smith, together with one of the named executors of Lord Peterborough's will, Mr Antrobus of Coutts Bank, was present at Dauntsey for three days before the grand ceremony and they were among the chief mourners on the day. It is doubtful whether Grace would have attended.

Bouchier Smith made free and easy with the money of others in organizing his friend's last ceremony, which the undertaker said was on the largest and most expensive scale he had witnessed during his twelve years in the funeral business. An argument then waged over the expense and it took four years for the undertaker's bill to be settled.[319]

However, as well as being remembered for his sumptuous funeral, Lord Peterborough should really be remembered for two more mundane but much more beneficial benevolences: firstly, for his involvement with the Berkshire and Wiltshire Canal; and secondly for his assistance with an agricultural project in his manor of Dauntsey. Some seven years after his death, the following article appeared in the newspapers:

MANAGEMENT OF THE POOR ... A few years back, the farmers of Dauntsey, Wilts, let to the poor labourers of their parish, who had large families, three acres of land at two pounds per acre; and soon afterwards the late Earl of Peterborough built a barn for them, where they could thrash their corn; the consequence was, that the names of these men disappeared from the parish book; they brought up families in credit and now pay rates themselves. The parish declares that it has saved hundreds by this system.[320]

This model was held up as an example to other parishes to follow and it is heartening to know that, whatever the follies of his youth, the 5th and last Earl of Peterborough was capable of performing charitable acts for the benefit of his parishioners.

Maurice George Bisset died during 1821 and Joseph Bouchier Smith lasted little longer, dying during the last days of the following year. He suffered spasms in his chest while spending Christmas at Croome, the house of his friend Viscount Deerhurst (since 1809 the Earl of Coventry), 'which in a few moments terminated his existence'.[321] His daughter, Constantia Louisa, some years later married Count Roehenstart, otherwise Charles Edward Stuart, the Jacobite claimant to the British throne and the grandson of the 'Young Pretender'.

The Earl of Coventry outlived his three friends, dying in 1831.

Chapter Twenty

Grace in Regency England

In 1812 the new Prince Regent shuffled his household and made some new appointments. Lord Cholmondeley became his lord steward (described at his appointment as 'our right trusty and right well-beloved cousin and counseller') and Lord Charles Bentinck, as befitted a former equerry and, moreover, husband to the girl the prince believed to be his daughter, was made treasurer of the household.[322]

The royal favour only went so far though; while Charles retained his household position (although even that seemed to hang in the balance for a while), he was thwarted in his determination to obtain a seat in Parliament when the prince persuaded Cholmondeley to bring in someone other than Lord Charles for the borough of Castle Rising in Norfolk. Cholmondeley urged Charles to go to Ashburton where he had already considered backing him financially in the contest but it was already too late for the seat there. His determination to enter Parliament had put his household post under threat; had Lord and Lady Charles Bentinck presumed too much on the prince, made too many demands on him and made free with their royal connection, leading to his favour being withdrawn? Charles, in desperation, wrote to the Prince Regent's secretary, Colonel McMahon, from his London address, 24 Grosvenor Place:

October 7th 1812
It is impossible for me to express the distress I am in at finding that Lord Cholmondeley's borough of Castle Rising is to be given to Mr Cavendish Bradshaw. I have had many difficulties to struggle through for some years but now from the Prince Regents goodness to me I hoped to go on a little better, & eager to retain my place went to a considerable expense to be re-elected for Ashburton. Lord Cholmondeley had talked of contesting that place for the Parliament but having altered his intention I lost my seat there but was made quite comfortable from receiving a letter from him offering to bring me in for Castle Rising.

My brother does not take any part in politicks & will not bring any body in. On an income of eighteen hundred a year it is impossible I can either buy a borough or contest an election. I must therefore lose my place unless

His Royal Highness will be graciously pleased to allow me to come in for Castle Rising.

The expense of my last election which was upwards of six hundred pounds has so involved me that added to other expenses I have incurred counting on my salary I must be ABSOLUTELY RUINED if I lose my situation in His Royal Highness's family.

I understand from Arbuthnot that I am supposed to have made a promise of bringing myself into parliament; this never was the case – and had this promise been proposed to me as the alternative I must have given up all hope of the place from the first, knowing I could have no chance of keeping such a promise. For God sake lose no time in laying my case before His Royal Highness & forgive the trouble I am giving you but I really am so extremely distressed I hardly know what I am writing.[323]

The Prince Regent did not help in the matter of politics but, perhaps seeing how desperate the young couple's situation might otherwise be, Charles continued as treasurer of the household. The following year Georgiana was once more pregnant and the Bentincks were living comfortably, totally besotted by their young daughter, now a 2-year-old toddler. Quite possibly Grace visited them to dote on the little girl too, for if the Bentincks were making free and easy with their royal connections then they can hardly have looked askance at the woman who had instigated them, and Georgiana was known to have a deep regard for her mother.

Lady Charlotte Campbell (later Lady Charlotte Bury), lady-in-waiting to Caroline, Princess of Wales, and an intimate of Georgiana for some twenty years, remembered Georgiana as being 'so happy and young … a lovely creature … and without calling her a great friend, we were always upon the best terms at all times, and I liked her conversation and society whenever I was in it; though perhaps we were not congenial souls.'[324]

Georgiana's young age, only 31, made it all the more tragic when disaster struck. Heavily pregnant, it was universally believed that she fell, injuring her spine.[325] Death soon followed on 10 December 1813, shocking to all who heard of it and devastating to her mother, husband and infant daughter, and likewise to the two father-figures in her life, Lord Cholmondeley and the prince. The babe she was carrying died with her.[326]

A miniature by Mrs Joseph Mee now held in the Royal Collection was painted for the Prince of Wales in 1813 as part of his Galleries of Beauties collection; it was to become a treasured memento of a lost daughter.

Much as Grace might have wanted to look after her motherless 2-year-old granddaughter, the Cholmondeleys stepped in and, as they had looked after

Georgiana Seymour as a daughter, now looked after Georgiana Bentinck. Lord Charles seems to have raised no objection to this; the double shock of losing his beloved wife and unborn child was no doubt compounded with a fear of also losing the patronage of his two probable fathers-in-law, the prince and Lord Cholmondeley. With Cholmondeley being so close to the prince, everyone would be kept happy by little Georgiana being taken into their household. Everyone except Grace, that is. Her wishes on the subject are unknown but one would hope the Cholmondeleys allowed her to see her granddaughter, as they had allowed her to receive visits from her own daughter. Life continued quietly, if sadly, for the next year and a half until scandal once more revisited itself upon Grace's story, this time in the form of her son-in-law's indiscretions.

Lord Charles Bentinck sought solace for his bereavement in the arms of the wife of an acquaintance, Lady Anne Abdy, the wife of Sir William Abdy of Felix Hall in Essex. Lady Anne, pretty but described as 'proud, disdainful and stupid', had herself been born to scandal, one of the five illegitimate children of Richard, Marquess of Wellesley, and his French opera dancing mistress, Hyacinthe Gabrielle Rolland. Although Richard and Hyacinthe had eventually married, it was not till long after the births of their children, a belated attempt to legitimize them.

Anne had married in 1806 and her union had proved relatively happy, if childless (Abdy was rumoured to be impotent). It was something of a shock then when she eloped with Lord Charles Bentinck on 5 September 1815, more so as London was still in the midst of celebrations over the decisive victory of the allied forces commanded by Lady Anne's uncle, Sir Arthur Wellesley, Duke of Wellington, over Napoléon Bonaparte at Waterloo just weeks earlier. Although Grace would be something of a hypocrite to pass judgement on the couple, having trod a similar path to Lady Anne with Viscount Valentia all those years ago, she probably did do so, having her little granddaughter now in mind as her first priority.

The Cholmondeleys must also have been exasperated. As the reprobate couple set up house together, the cuckolded husband commenced divorce proceedings. The case was heard in the House of Lords in June 1816 where a full divorce was granted. A marriage hastily followed, only just in time as the new Lady Charles Bentinck was delivered of a daughter on 1 September 1816.

The situation in France had changed. The House of Bourbon had been restored to the monarchy in 1814, the old king's second brother taking the throne as Louis XVIII. Subsequently Grace's old paramour, the Comte d'Artois, took the French throne as Charles X, abdicating some years later in favour of the Duc d'Orléans' eldest son.

Lady Seymour Fleming and her husband took advantage of the freedom to travel once more afforded to the British now peace had descended on Europe following the victory at Waterloo. They moved to a villa at Passy just outside Paris but kept their Brompton house, travelling back and forth. If Grace felt the absence of her friend it was more than made up for as Lord Charles Bentinck settled his new family at Brompton, leasing a house known as The Hermitage that had formerly been the residence of the Italian opera diva Madame Angelica Catalini. More importantly for Grace, little Georgiana had returned to live with her father but a tug-of-war soon developed over the child, a battle in which everybody but Grace seemed to have a say. The little girl had expectations of a great fortune, the money settled on her parents being ultimately for her benefit and not for any children of her father's second marriage.

No doubt this fortune had a great deal to do with the new Lady Charles wanting to keep her step-daughter under her own control. Lord and Lady Cholmondeley, since 1815 titled the Marquess and Marchioness of Chol-mondeley, wanted her back; Lady Cholmondeley in particular, with her own children now grown, had doted on the little girl and missed her terribly when she was returned to her father. Lord Charles used her as leverage, probably at the instigation of his new wife, for the financial benefit of his new daughter and his future children. He agreed to let Georgiana return to the Chol-mondeleys but only if a sum of money was settled on the children of his second marriage. While everybody else argued and the poor child seemed to be passed around like a piece of baggage, Grace was possibly happy with the situation as it was. She had little Georgiana living close by in the same neigh-bourhood and Anne could hardly have turned up her nose at Grace as a visitor; after all, nobody else would willingly associate with her in the imme-diate aftermath of her divorce. Grace demonstrated a marked fondness and attachment for her granddaughter in later life, so hopefully she did enjoy the role of doting grandmother while it was available to her.

All too soon Georgiana was returned to the care of the Cholmondeley family and on 6 November 1817 a settlement of £4,000 was made on the younger children of Lord Charles by his elder brother, the 4th Duke of Port-land. At the same time, two sums of £5,000 were settled upon Georgiana; one by the Marquess of Cholmondeley and the other the money that Grace had originally put forward for her daughter's settlement but, since her daughter's death, instead vested with the young Marquess of Titchfield (the Duke of Portland's eldest son) and Peter Burrell, Lord Gwydyr (Lady Cholmondeley's brother-in-law).[327] As before, Grace was still to receive the dividends on her stock while she lived. Lady Cholmondeley was appointed as the young girl's guardian, with her sister, Lord Gwydr's wife, or her daughter Lady Charlotte Cholmondeley, to take over in the event of Lady Cholmondeley's death before Georgiana came of age. On the same day upon which this settlement was signed, Lord Charles Bentinck became a father once more, a son who was to be named Charles being born at the villa in Brompton.

With Georgiana in the care of the Cholmondeley family, the need for contact with Lord Charles Bentinck decreased for Grace. Her good friend Lady Fleming died at her villa in Passy on 9 September 1818, and the following year, on 15 June 1819, her friend Sophia Seneschall, whom Grace possibly viewed almost as a daughter, made a good marriage to the Reverend Joshua Greville at the church of St Mary Abbott's in Kensington. Joshua Greville, a widower, was the curate of St George's in Hanover Square and also vicar of Duston in Northamptonshire and it was an exceptional marriage for a girl who had started out as a scullery maid.

Almost a year later the Grevilles' son was born at their South Audley Street home. The baptism took place privately, immediately after he was born, and was recorded in the register of St George's, Hanover Square; Sophia asked her friend Grace to be the boy's godmother, a sure sign of Grace's presence at the birth if the baptism was carried out so hastily.[328] He was named Peniston Grosvenor Greville, his forename being given in honour of his father's patron Peniston Lamb, Lord Melbourne, that old friend of Sir John Eliot's. Grace's past was never too far behind her.

With Lady Fleming dead, control and ownership of her estate had fallen to her husband and Grace now moved out of the house she had lived in for so many years. She didn't go far though, remaining in Brompton and taking up residence in St Michael's Place. The Prince of Wales had become king on the death of his father on 29 January 1820, but Grace had traded off their relationship for so long now that there was little else to be gained. The Bentinck family was still at The Hermitage (their daughter Emily was born there), but little Georgiana was not.

With her friend Sophia now occupied in caring for her husband and newborn son, Grace decided it was time to leave. She had cashed in some stock she owned in India Bonds in 1818, raising a significant amount of money, but now, once again short of funds and having no one else to turn to, she borrowed £1,000 from Sophia and her husband and used this money to obtain a property at Ville d'Avray near Paris.[329] There, in September 1822, ill and alone apart from a servant, she made out her last will and testament.

She still hoped to 'receive money by the settling of the Queensberry cause' (as the dispute over Old Q's will had come to be known) and if the money was ever paid, which would now amount to substantially more than the original bequest when fourteen years of interest due on it was taken into account, she wished her debt to Sophia Greville to be settled. She also willed a bequest of £100 to her godson Peniston Greville together with her gold watch as a token of remembrance. Peniston did indeed remember his godmother with affection, naming a daughter Georgiana Grace Bentinck Greville in later years. Although she began her will in September 1822, she did not complete it until six months later. Everything else Grace died possessed of, she wished her granddaughter to have, although she held out few hopes as to the value of this:

> I fear when my lawful debts are paid little will remain for my dearest Granddaughter but I in my last moments pray for her happiness and for that of her kind and respectable protectors and if my blessing is all I can leave her may she ever be good and grateful and may God Almighty ever protect her and all the Cholmondeley family and may we all meet in heaven if our blessed Lord forgives my sins and disobedience to his commandments these shall be my last prayers.[330]

Grace signed the will as G. Dalrymple, omitting her married name, and it was witnessed by a Mary Curtis, probably Grace's servant.

In the original will someone has noted, above the reference to the money due from the Queensberry Cause, 'no chance'. In the opinion of Mr Allen, an English attorney at Paris who was hired by the Marquess of Cholmondeley to sort out Grace's affairs after her death, the hand that wrote those words was the same one that had written the will; in other words, probably Grace herself. In a letter to Lord Cholmondeley, he theorized that Grace had heard she would get nothing by the Queensberry Cause, writing her disgust in the comment found on the will, and had then written the later part. Possibly Grace had ripped up a second page of her original will (maybe leaving her belongings in France to her adopted daughter, Miss Staunton?) and replaced it with a heartfelt plea that her granddaughter should inherit all, however little.

Death was not far away for Grace now. She died on 15 May 1823 at six o'clock in the evening in the house of Monsieur Dupuis, the mayor of Ville d'Avray. Her death was registered the following day when she was recorded as *Dame Georgette née D'alrymple en Ecosse, veuve Elliotte* (Georgette Dalrymple born in Scotland, widow Elliotte). Was Georgette a mistake or yet another variation upon her name? The two men who registered her death were Messieurs Augustin Baudemont, a whitener who bleached Grace's linen, and Jean Philippe Sellier, a teacher. She was buried in the Père Lachaise Cemetery on the outskirts of Paris.

The Marquess of Cholmondeley advanced £100 to Paris to cover Grace's funeral, writing tartly that he expected to be reimbursed and hoping Grace had died possessed of money in the funds. Mr Allen was despatched post-haste in search of Grace's will but found, when he questioned the mayor and servants, that it had been sent to a notary at Sèvres, a man who was a stickler for the rules and cared little for the customs of law relative to England. Mr Allen was forced to cajole and wheedle between this notary and the President of Council at Versailles to try to get the will sent back to England; the Consular Secretary at Paris was also involved. A probable cause of the problem was Miss Staunton, by now married and in 'indigent circumstances' with several children, who had indeed laid claim to Grace's property. Mr Allen advised Lord Cholmondeley to let Miss Staunton have what remained of Grace's possessions in France; the cost of contesting this would amount to more than could be gained in return. Nothing of Grace's property in France was recovered to England but instead was used to settle her debts there. It is not known if her adopted daughter received anything at all.

Among all the to-ing and fro-ing between Versailles and Sèvres in the immediate aftermath of Grace's death, a woman, described by Mr Allen as Grace's sister, took a carriage to Sèvres with the intention of certifying to Grace's handwriting. He must have been mistaken in his assumption regarding the relationship but who could she have been? The one lady who had both an interest in Grace's will and a genuine affection for her was Sophia Greville; could this have been Sophia trying to sort out her friend's affairs?

Mr Allen finally succeeded in getting Grace's will sent to London where it could be probated and the Marchioness of Cholmondeley, as the guardian of young Georgiana Cavendish Bentinck, ended up with the responsibility of administering the will (Grace had named no executor). In England, Grace had left little. Her bank held the sum of £163 3s 3d and the little plate, ornaments and clothing she had left stored did not, in Lady Cholmondeley's opinion, exceed £200 in value.[331]

In the aftermath of settling Grace's affairs, one letter from a creditor of hers sheds a little light on the relationship between grandmother and grand-daughter. A shopkeeper named Hobby, formerly Madame Daniel, had known Grace for many years and undertook commissions for her to bring articles from London to Paris, everything from Windsor soap to fancy dresses and silk stockings. There seems to have been a friendly and trusting bond between the two women up to Grace's death and, when Hobby eventually resorted to writing to Lady Cholmondeley to try to recover an outstanding debt, she declared that she was 'sure Miss Bentinck [would] recollect her'. Young Georgiana did indeed recollect Hobby; Lord Cholmondeley confirmed this in a letter he wrote enclosing Hobby's and, as Hobby was unknown to the Cholmondeleys, Georgiana must have spent some time at Grace's side.

Chapter Twenty-One

Jessy Bebb, Society Hostess, or How Grace's Life Could Have Been

Between 1805 and 1809 the Bebbs had moved to a house on Gloucester Place, near Regents Park, in London. Their appearances in the 'Fashionable World' column of the *Morning Post* newspaper are too numerous to list; Jessy and her husband in almost constant movement, retiring to their elegant house in the country, Donnington Grove, and returning to their London town house to hold balls, routs and concerts, and in between visiting all the fashionable spas and watering-places.

However, one particular ball in 1821 deserves note, not only as it gives us a glimpse into Mrs Bebb's London town house but also as it was attended by royalty. It took place while Grace, with the wheel of fortune once more turning, was reduced to borrowing money from a woman who had once been her aunt's scullery maid in order to eke out a lonely existence in France. The parallels between her situation and that of her cousin could not be more striking:

> MRS. BEBB'S BALL. This Lady's mansion, in Gloucester-place, presented a scene of great splendour on Friday evening, when the long-promised Ball and Supper were given in a style of infinite magnificence and taste.
>
> The drawing-rooms and the apartments on the ground floor were illuminated; the great hall and the staircase were decorated with flowering shrubs; the balconies were ornamented in a similar manner. Dancing commenced in the Saloon at eleven o'clock; a Supper, replete with every delicacy, was set out in the Banqueting-room at two o'clock. The spirit of the scene was kept up till half-past four o'clock. There were present about three hundred Fashionables.[332]

Among the guests present were His Royal Highness the Duke of Gloucester, the Duchesses of Richmond and Marlborough, Captain Fitzclarence (the illegitimate son of King William IV and his mistress Dorothea Jordan) and Janet's half-brother, Admiral Sir Richard King.[333] Life for Jessy continued in a whirl of social engagements for some years, interrupted only by the death of her husband at their London town house on 27 September 1830. He had possibly been ailing for some time as in February 1829 the directors of the East India Company tried to persuade him to resign as he had 'lost both sight and hearing'. John, however, had hearing enough to understand what they were suggesting and 'indignantly opposed the Court's verdict because "he hoped to be restored to useful vision and his hearing is liable to variation, being sometimes worse, sometimes better"' and he eventually retired in April 1830.[334] John Bebb's will left both Donnington Grove and the London house at 13 Gloucester Place to his wife for the term of her life and, as a wealthy widow, she was able to retain her position in high society, her continual appearances in the 'Fashionable World' newspaper column testimony to this fact.

Jessy's older sister, Susannah Robiniana, was also living in London. As the widow of a major in the East India Company's service she was a shareholder and entitled to a vote in their General Courts. She appeared in a list of such members in 1815, her address given as Orchard Street, just around the corner from her sister Jessy's Gloucester Place house and adjoining Oxford Street. By October 1824 Susannah had moved to Park Place, Regent's Park, where she wrote her last will and testament. To her sister she left her topaz ornaments and to the daughter of her half-brother, Sir Richard King, a set of emerald and pearl jewellery.

There were bequests to her servants, after which she devised everything else she owned to pass to her only child, her son John Charles Farmer. She appointed as her executors Sir Richard King and her brother-in-law John Bebb. Susannah Robiniana Farmer died ten years after writing her will in 1834, and in those intervening ten years John Charles Farmer, Sir Richard King and John Bebb had all died and so, as the only surviving blood relative, Jessy Lawrence Bebb was granted administration of the will and inherited all her sister's estate.[335]

Little is known of Susannah's son; he studied at the East India College School from 1807, instructed in classical and commercial learning. His uncle, John Bebb, then used his influence with the East India Company to recommend his nephew for further study with the aim of becoming a writer with the company.

His headmaster at the East India College gave him a good reference, saying that his conduct had been regular and proper. Regardless of the interest of his uncle, John Charles Farmer joined the regular army as an ensign in 1815, rising to be a captain of the 7th Regiment of Dragoon Guards, and he died early in 1827 at Fort Clarence in Chatham, Kent which, as the threat of invasion from France had subsided, was being used as a military hospital and lunatic asylum. He was buried at St Margaret's in Rochester, Kent, aged just 32; coincidentally the same church in which Jacintha Dalrymple had married Thomas Hesketh all those years earlier.[336]

In the *Morning Chronicle* of 30 June 1835 there was an announcement that 'The Landgravine of Hesse Homberg honoured Mrs Bebb with her company at dinner last evening, at her residence in Gloucester-place.' The Land-gravine of Hesse-Homburg was no less a personage than Princess Elizabeth, daughter of King George III, who had married a German prince, Frederick of Hesse-Homburg, in 1814 and had since then lived mainly in Germany. Widowed six years earlier, she was on a family visit home to England when she dined with Jessy. The two women were of a comparable age and the princess again dined at Jessy's Gloucester Place house a year later during May 1836.[337] The royal connections do not stop there, for just three weeks after the Landgravine of Hesse-Homburg, Jessy dined with her brother: 'The Duke of Cumberland honoured Mrs Bebb with his company at dinner on Sunday evening in Gloucester-place.'[338]

The Duke of Cumberland was Prince Ernest Augustus, the fifth son of King George III. A colonel in the dragoons, he had received a sabre wound that resulted in a disfiguring scar to the left side of his face (causing the loss of sight in his left eye) and a cannonball injury to his left arm. The duke was involved in many slanderous allegations over the years, implicated in two suicides which, without substantiation, were suggested to have actually been murder.

After marrying his cousin, the Duke of Cumberland had also lived mainly in Germany, returning to England in the late 1820s. To complete a royal hat trick the Duke of Cumberland and Princess Elizabeth's younger brother, Prince Adolphus, Duke of Cambridge, dined at Gloucester Place, honouring the 74-year-old Jessy Bebb with his company in 1841.[339]

Jessy wrote her own will on 17 May 1849. She didn't mention her resi-dences as they had already been disposed of by her husband in his will and would pass, after Jessy's death, to his nephew Horatio Lawrell who assumed the surname of Bebb, but instead left many monetary bequests to her servants, friends and members of the King family and disposed of her extensive jewel-lery collection. The topaz ornaments (which Jessy described as consisting of necklace, earrings, head ornament, waist buckle, brooch and bracelets) that she had inherited from her sister Susannah Robiniana she bequeathed to her niece Maria Philadelphia Louisa King, daughter of her half-brother Richard King.[340]

To Sir David Kinloch of Gilmerton, the 9th Baronet and nephew of her first husband John Kinloch, Jessy left the full-length portrait of her first husband by Devis that hung in her dressing room at 13 Gloucester Place and

the full-length portrait of herself by Hickey that was on the wall of her drawing room, both of which she said belonged to Sir David, he presumably having
allowed her the use of them during her lifetime. The two portraits still hang at
Gilmerton House in Scotland, the Kinloch family home.[341] A sapphire ring
and a cameo brooch set with amethysts were left to her goddaughter, Jessey
Swinton, the daughter of Samuel Swinton Esquire of Swinton in Berwickshire, and a fine collection of pearls, most of them bought when 'just out of
the sea' and never worn by anyone but Jessy herself, to the use of the family of
her friend Elizabeth, Duchess of Saint Albans. Perhaps these were the same
pearls with which Jessy was adorned when she was presented to Queen
Charlotte in 1803?

However, there was one bequest which, over and above all the others in
her will, is the most relevant to her own family line:

> I give and bequeath unto the heir ... at my decease of the late Earl of
> Peterborough my two bracelet pictures set with diamonds and the settings
> thereof and the bracelets attached thereto because these pictures are
> family pictures, the one being the picture of the late Earl of Peterborough
> when a child and the other of his uncle Captain Brown, my father, and
> also my tortoise shell snuff box with my Grandmothers (Mrs Brown)
> picture in it. Also the miniature picture in a case of a lady with powdered
> hair, it being the portrait of Mrs Bisset whose maiden name was Harriet
> Mordaunt.

Perhaps Jessy had been given these mementos to remember her family by
before she sailed to India, or maybe she received them upon the death of her
aunt and guardian, the Countess of Peterborough? However she came by
them, the bracelet picture of her cousin Charles Henry, the future 5th Earl of
Peterborough, seems to be a companion piece to one of her own father,
George Cornwallis Brown. This little collection of trinkets associated with
the father she never knew, her grandmother and cousins must have been
treasured by Jessy throughout her life.

After more than half a century of lavish entertainments and a life spent
in perpetual motion between town and country residences, Jessy Lawrence
Bebb, née Brown, died at her London house on 7 April 1850, aged 83 and
having outlived all her cousins but leaving no descendants. She was buried in
the same vault as her husband at St Mary and St Marylebone on 13 April, the
same church in which Grace's daughter Georgiana had been baptized all
those years before.[342]

By virtue of a good marriage she had managed to attain a lifestyle that
eluded her better-known cousin Grace Dalrymple; had Grace been content

to live with her husband, Dr John Eliot, it is very likely that her life in her middle and old age would have been extremely similar to Jessy's. In 1775 the *Matrimonial Magazine* had called Grace a 'velvet wanton' and pitied her for destroying her marriage so quickly when a life of lengthened pleasure might have belonged to her. However, there was happiness in her later life when she had the love, if not the hand in marriage, of well-born and wealthy men, and on the whole she chose them well. Cholmondeley and d'Orléans protected her and provided for her as long as they were able and showed her friendship and consideration.

Whether or not Grace, on looking back at her life when it was ending, would have exchanged it for one of respectability and good social standing is not known; hopefully, at the end of a life well and adventurously lived, full of experiences denied to most, she had no regrets.

Twenty-six years after Grace's death her friend Sophia Greville, née Seneschall, elderly and almost blind, wrote to Richard Bentley, the publisher of Grace's journal.[343] It was Sophia who owned the miniature of Grace as a young woman; a treasured memento of a much-loved friend, gone but very much not forgotten.

Notes

Chapter 1: Scottish Roots

1. No record of the marriage between Hugh Dalrymple and Grissel Brown has yet been discovered.
2. Henry Hew's is, so far, the only baptism record found of the four children born to Hugh Dalrymple and his wife Grissel.
3. OPR Births 685/003 0080 0409 Canongate. Collington is now known as Colinton.
4. Dr John Hyndman was a Moderator of the General Assembly of the Church of Scotland, described as 'a clever fellow, a good preacher, and a ready debater' (*Fasti ecclesiæ scoticanæ*; the succession of ministers in the Church of Scotland from the reformation, Edinburgh 1915).
5. Adam de Dalrymple, who died in 1300, had a son, Gilchrist de Dalrymple, who was a contemporary of Robert the Bruce and was the father of Malcolm de Dalrymple.
6. Letter from Sophia Greville to Richard Bentley, 1859. Richard Bentley records, 1806–1915, Rare Book & Manuscript Library, University of Illinois at Urbana-Champaign. The Dalrymple arms have nine diamond lozenges on them, hence the name the 'nine of diamonds'; the nine of diamonds playing card is often referred to as the 'Curse of Scotland' and may be an association with Sir John Dalrymple, 1st Earl of Stair, who ordered the Glencoe Massacre in 1692.
7. On her marriage licence, dated 19 October 1771, Grace was stated to be upwards of 17 but under the age of 21, putting her date of birth between 20 October 1750 and 19 October 1754 but more likely towards the latter end of this timescale.
8. Register of Marriages of the City of Edinburgh 1751–1800 by the Scottish Record Society, edited by Francis J. Grant, WS, Edinburgh, 1922. Although Grace's baptism record has not been discovered, finding Hugh resident in Edinburgh at this date would strongly suggest that this was the location of Grace's birth.
9. *Some Old Families*, Society of Genealogists, London, and also *My Lady Scandalous*, Jo Manning.
10. William Murray's mother was Elizabeth Dalrymple (not to be confused with Hugh's sister of the same name who married John Pitcairn).
11. National Archives of Scotland (hereafter NAS), GD219/289/2.
12. Records of the Court of Justiciary, as reported in *Letters of George Dempster*. A bailie was a civic official in Scottish local government.

Chapter 2: The Browns of Blackburn House

13. CC8/8/97 Edinburgh Commissary Court, NAS. A testament dative was the document drawn up by the Commissary Court after the death to appoint and confirm executor(s) to administer the deceased's estate. It often includes an inventory of the possessions of the deceased and debts due. It does not include a copy will and does not indicate how the deceased wished to dispose of their possessions.
14. George Brown, Andrew's father, had four children: Robert, William, Andrew and Helen.

15. Arms are sable a dagger in bend proper and in chief a boar's head erased argent or a helmet befitting his degree with a mantle gules doubled argent and wreathed of his colours and for a crest a vine tree proper. *Public Register of All Arms and Bearings in Scotland*, Volume 1, Folio 254. In the Lyon's Office, Scotland, the name of this family is recorded with an additional 'e' at the end, as is Blackburn, i.e. Browne of Blackburne.

16. The pistols featured an automatic priming magazine, a reloadable metal cartridge and a hinged, drop-down barrel. Highly valuable, one is now in the possession of the Victoria & Albert Museum in London and the other is in a private collection.

17. *Publications of the Scottish History Society*, Volume XV, Miscellany (First Volume), *The Diary of George Turnbull, Minister of Alloa and Tyninghame 1657–1704*, December 1893. It is interesting to note that George Turnbull also dined with the Kinlochs of Gilmerton in 1702, a family connected with the later history of the Browns of Blackburn.

18. The book *Memorials of the Haliburtons* by Sir Walter Scott, 1824, contains the following information: 'Thomas Davidson, surgeon in Kelso, who married ___ Scott, daughter to John Scott of Belford. Thomas Davidson succeeded to the estate of Kirkraw, which he sold to the Duke of Roxburgh; died in the year 17__, leaving issue a daughter, Mrs Brown, relict of Col. Brown of Blackburn'; however, Sir Walter seems to have muddled the generations somewhat so the surname of Robert Brown's wife Janet cannot be corroborated.

19. There is a baptism record for a Grissel Brown, daughter of Robert and Janet Brown, at Duns, Berwickshire born on 5 May and baptized on 22 May 1726, which, without further proof, may be the baptism of Grace's mother.

20. The whereabouts of the baptisms of all the children remain a mystery, as does the record of Captain Robert Brown's marriage to his wife Janet. If his family had travelled with him then these records could be scattered among the various places where his regiment was quartered, and if in Ireland then they could have been lost in the 1922 Dublin Public Record Office fire in which more than half the parish registers for the country were destroyed.

21. The Act was to be read in every parish church throughout Scotland on the first Sunday in the month for a whole year. Captain John Porteous, captain of the City Guard of Edinburgh, had been killed by a mob on 7 September 1736. A riot following the hanging of a convicted smuggler had led to Captain Porteous giving orders to his men to fire into the mob and six people lost their lives. Porteous was subsequently found guilty of murder and sentenced to death himself but a mob, worried that he would be reprieved, dragged him from his cell and killed him. Those guilty of his murder were not found and the Act was designed to appeal for information.

22. *Report on the manuscripts of Lord Polwarth, preserved at Mertoun House, Berwickshire*, volume V, Historical Manuscripts Commission, 1961.

23. This document, written in September 1737, specifically mentions the two sons of Captain Robert Brown, putting the death of the younger of the two after this date.

24. John Blaw was imprisoned after the 1745 uprisings but eventually released. He was hung at Stirling in 1767 after murdering a local farmer during a fracas.

25. The *London Evening Post*, 22 September 1739; Graham Smith Esquire of Salisbury, an ensign in the 34th, was the bondsman to the wedding.

26. Cartagena de Indias is now a city in Colombia. The objective had been to take the four main ports held by Spain in the Caribbean basin, enabling the British to control the routes in and out of South America.

27. WO 25/20, Commission books (series I), 1740–1744, The National Archives (hereafter TNA).

28. The *London Evening Post*, 19–21 October 1742.
29. The *Daily Advertiser*, 17 October 1743.
30. NAS: The Petition of George Cornwallis Brown, 25 June 1745, Answers for Lieutenant Charles Dundas, 4 July 1745, RH 18/3 157.
31. Stephen Cornwallis became colonel of the 34th in 1732, which suggests the timescale for George's birth may possibly be narrowed down still further to 1732–1735 unless Robert Brown knew Cornwallis before this. His birthdate of 1725–1735 is derived from George being classed as a minor in 1745 and the information that in 1737 he had a brother who was younger than him.
32. Letter to Hugh Dalrymple from John Murray, 31 December 1754, NAS, GD219/289/2. George Cornwallis Brown is referred to simply as Mr Brown.
33. Adjutant is essentially a personal assistant to the commander of the regiment.
34. The *Public Advertiser*, 17 February 1759.
35. George Ridpath was born c.1716 at Ladykirk in Berwickshire; he died in 1772 at Stichill.
36. *Diary of George Ridpath, minister of Stitchel* [original spelling], *1755–1761*, Scottish History Society. The editor of the book speculates that the two ladies referred to are related to Margaret Crow, the second wife of John Mow, but as she did not marry him until 1763 this is false and has possibly given rise to the repeated allusions to the mother of Grace Dalrymple having the maiden name of Craw or Crow.
37. 01/04/1753 Mow, John [OPR Marriages 730/00 0020 0176 Chirnside] and 29/12/1754 Brown, Jean [OPR Deaths 730/00 0020 0178 Chirnside].
38. Richard Cooper the Elder (1701–1764).
39. NAS RS27/152, ff. 264v–268r Sasine dated 5 October 1758, referring to a disposition dated 28/29 September 1758. The two men trusted by Robert Dalrymple who witnessed the sale were Robert Henderson and James Hay senior, both Writers to the Signet.
40. OPR Deaths 685/01 0950 0093 Edinburgh.
41. *Diary of George Ridpath, minister of Stitchel* [original spelling], *1755–1761*, Scottish History Society; *Douglas* had been rejected by the London theatre manager David Garrick but had been shown in Edinburgh on 14 December 1756.

Chapter 3: The Pen of Hugh Dalrymple

42. Hugh is recorded in the Middle Temple register as the 'eldest son of Robert Dalrymple of the City of Edinburgh, North Britain Esq'. In the preface to Grace's journal, Hugh is noted as one of the lawyers in the famous 'Douglas Cause' that was heard between 1761 and 1767. This is incorrect; instead it was Sir Hew Dalrymple of North Berwick who was concerned in the case. Richard Bentley was responsible for perpetrating this error as he wrote to Grace's friend, Sophia Greville, née Seneschall, asking for information on this, about which she knew nothing. The confusion has probably arisen via Grace's involvement in the 'Queensberry Cause'. Richard Bentley records, 1806–1915, Rare Book & Manuscript Library, University of Illinois at Urbana-Champaign.
43. Robert Walpole (1676–1745) was the first head of government to be known by the unofficial title of prime minister, although this term was not used officially until 1905.
44. CC8/8/130 Edinburgh Commissary Court.

Chapter 4: The Military Uncle

45. *Lloyd's Evening Post*, 25 June 1759, and *Whitehall Evening Post*, 6 November 1759.
46. An Inventory of the Historical Monuments in Dorset by the Royal Commission on Historical Monuments. The estate was bought in 1745 by the Honourable John Spencer (an

ancestor of Diana, Princess of Wales), who demolished the house and rebuilt a smaller one in its stead.

47. PROB 11/907, TNA.

48. The name Robinaiana is, unsurprisingly, spelled in a variety of ways across different sources but Robinaiana favoured hers with an extra 'a', while her niece's middle name was generally recorded as Robiniana. We have therefore used the spellings that they seemed to prefer for themselves.

Chapter 5: Robinaiana and Janet Brown: Mistress and Wife

49. Charles Mordaunt, the future 4th Earl of Peterborough, was born in York where his father was stationed with his regiment. His baptism took place on 19 October 1708 at St Mary Bishophill Senior. That of his younger brother, John, was at the same church on 16 December 1709. The family was residing at Middlethorpe Hall at the time, a country house 2 miles from York city centre built in 1699 for Thomas Barlow, a master cutler from Sheffield.

50. *Post Boy*, 6–8 April 1710, and administration of John, Viscount Mordaunt, dated 28 September 1711. Prerogative & Exchequer Courts of York, Borthwick Institute for Archives, University of York.

51. A cicisbeo was a married woman's male companion or lover.

52. PROB 11/674, TNA.

53. John Mordaunt married the widowed Mary, Countess of Pembroke, on 9 October 1735.

54. Several sources incorrectly put Frances' birth in April 1736, possibly confusing her with her sister Caroline. See *Read's Weekly Journal*, 17 April 1736, *London Daily Post*, 31 May 1736, and *Daily Journal*, 23 July 1736 for announcements of Caroline's birth, baptism and death respectively.

55. The article in the October 1777 edition of the *Town and Country Magazine* dates the amour between the Earl of Peterborough and Miss Falkner to when she was singing at 'Marylebone Gardens' but before she married and became Mrs Donaldson. Anna Maria Falkner (Faulkner) sang at Marylebone Gardens every summer from 1747 to 1752, as confirmed in the *Oxford Dictionary of National Biography*. From the same source, her marriage to William George Donaldson took place on 19 May 1748, thereby placing this anecdote relating to the Earl of Peterborough during the summer months of 1747.

56. London Land Tax Records, 1692–1932, London Metropolitan Archives.

57. Birthdate based on the fact that he joined the EIC in 1772 and could not have been born later than 5 December 1755 or he would have been legitimate.

58. *Survey of London*, vols 31 & 32: St James Westminster, Part 2 by F.H.W. Sheppard (General Editor) 1963. Robinaiana was the occupier in 1755. New Burlington Street was built c.1735 to 1739, the last of the streets to be built on the Burlington Estate, and was intended, as were the other houses on this estate, for residential occupation by people of substance.

59. In 1749 William Ashe had married Catherine Powlett, daughter of the future 4th Duke of Bolton and therefore cousin to Charles, 4th Earl of Peterborough.

60. The *London Evening Post*, 9–12 October 1731.

61. The *Gentleman's Magazine*, March 1732.

62. *The House of Commons, 1754–1790*, Sir Lewis Namier and John Brooke, vol. I, 1964.

63. PROB 11/945/442, TNA; no record of the marriage, either in parish register records or the newspapers, has been found to date.

64. www.historyofparliamentonline.org.
65. Burgage tenements or property, the owner of which was entitled to vote (www.historyof parliamentonline.org).

Chapter 6: The Doctor's Wife

66. OPR Deaths 685/010004/Edinburgh. Grissel's burial plot is described as being near the Foulis tomb.
67. Alexander Orr was the son of Agnes Dalrymple and the Reverend Alexander Orr, Agnes being the daughter of John Dalrymple and one of the heirs to Waterside. He was therefore second cousin to Grace.
68. *Gazetteer and New Daily Advertiser*, 25 September 1769.
69. Domenico Angelo (born Angelo Domenico Malevolti Tremamondo; Malevolti was the maiden name of his mother, which he used as his surname when he married) (1716–1820), Italian by birth, riding and fencing master, came to England in company with the actress Peg Woffington and opened Angelo's School of Arms in Soho, London, enjoying many noble, wealthy and royal patrons.
70. *Angelo's Pic Nic, Or, Table Talk*, Henry Angelo, London, 1834; the *Gentleman's Magazine* reported Mrs Skerrett's death in 1824 at a relative's house in London, 'at the advanced age of 88, Mrs. Bridget Skerrett, formerly and during 40 years, member of a religious community in the convent of Ursulines, at Lisle'.
71. *Middlesex Journal*, 17 October 1769; *Gazetteer and New Daily Advertiser*, 19 October 1769.
72. In 1792 Robert Hesketh changed his surname to Juxon, for himself only, according to the terms of the will of his maternal great-uncle Sir William Juxon of Little Compton; *London Gazette*, 29 May – 2 June 1792.
73. Northumberland Archives, ZCE/F/1/1/15/81, Letter from Reverend Edmund Lodge to Ralph Carr, 23 January 1772.
74. Jacintha signed her name on the marriage register as Janet Dalrymple.
75. *The Diary of Frances, Lady Shelley*, vol. I, London, 1913.
76. The timber-framed Rufford Old Hall, as it is known, is now in the possession of the National Trust. A smaller two-storey new hall was built c.1763 and later enlarged.
77. Governor Melville's Commission Book, to 1771, ends with the 'Appointment of Sir Hugh Dalrymple to be Solicitor General dated 20 Ap. 1771', signed by 'Hillsborough', *Catalogus librorum manuscriptorum in bibliotheca* (note Hugh has erroneously been titled 'Sir'; Governor Melville was Robert Melville (1723–1809), a Scotsman who was acting governor of Grenada 1764 and 1770–1771. He returned home in 1771. Hillsborough was Wills Hill, 1st Marquess of Downshire, Earl of Hillsborough, who, between 1768 and 1772, served as Secretary of State for the Colonies).
78. If Sir Walter Scott, in *Memorials of the Haliburtons*, was correct and Janet Brown's maiden name was Davidson, then she may have been related to John Eliot's mother who was also a Davidson, strengthening the possibility that Grace was encouraged into the marriage by her maternal relatives.
79. Guildhall Ms 10.091/125; Marriage Licence Allegation, London Metropolitan Archives, Ms 10091/125 and London Metropolitan Archives, DL/A/D/24/MS10091E/84. The marriage bond made them jointly liable for the sum of £200 if any of the information given by them should prove to be false and so invalidate the marriage.
80. By law all church weddings had to be conducted between the hours of 8am and 12 noon.
81. *Irish Times* review, 7 January 1984, by Dr Dennis Kennedy on Macartney of Lisanoure.

82. The *Morning Post and Daily Advertiser*, 5 December 1786.
83. *Historians of Essex VII – Elizabeth Ogborne* by Edward A. Fitch, No. 31, July 1899.
84. The *Public Advertiser*, 26 September 1772, and the St Clement Danes parish baptism register.
85. Sophia Baddeley (1745–1786), actress, singer and courtesan.
86. Robert Douglas was from a family that was a branch of the Clan Douglas and who owned land at Mains in Kilpatrick, Dunbartonshire, Scotland. Robert Douglas was to become the 15th Laird of Mains in due course but at the time Henry Hew wrote his will, Douglas and his partner Robert Lambert owned a successful tailoring business in St Martin's Lane (*Archibald Monteath: Igbo, Jamaican, Moravian* by Maureen Warner-Lewis, 2007).
87. PROB 11/1267, TNA.
88. The *Public Advertiser*, 8 May 1773.
89. *Abridgement of the Minutes of the Evidence taken before a Committee of the Whole House to whom it was referred to consider of the Slave-Trade*, 1789.
90. Grenada Deeds E2/1772, ff.490–93, ff.508–14; War Office: Printed Annual Army Lists, 1772 and 1775, TNA.

Chapter 7: Viscount Valentia and a Trip to a Bagnio
91. A mantua-maker was a dressmaker.
92. Berkeley Row was also known as Berkeley Street; the two names are interchangeable at this period.

Chapter 8: Divorce from the Cucumber Physician
93. *General Evening Post*, 2–4 September 1773.
94. The *Military and Naval Magazine of the United States*, vol. v, 1835.
95. The Colonial Records Project, Road to Revolution (1763–1775), from the *Pennsylvania Gazette*, 17 November 1773.
96. *The House of Commons, 1754–1790*, Sir Lewis Namier and John Brooke, Volume 1, 1964.
97. *Collections of the New York Historical Society for the year 1903*, New York.
98. The *Public Advertiser*, 13 August 1774.
99. Letter from the Reverend Edmund Lodge to Ralph Carr dated 23 January 1773, Northumberland Archives, ZCE/F/1/1/15/81.
100. The son, named Thomas for his father, was baptized on 15 March 1773 at the church of St Andrew's in Plymouth.
101. In the eighteenth century the cucumber (or cowcumber) was thought by some to be poisonous; see Dr Samuel Johnson's dictionary.
102. *Middlesex Journal and Evening Advertiser*, 21 June 1774.
103. *Middlesex Journal and Evening Advertiser*, 24 January 1775.
104. The *Morning Post*, 24 February 1776.
105. Sir John Soane's Museum Drawings (http://jeromeonline.co.uk).
106. The baptism took place on 11 May 1783.
107. *Historians of Essex VII – Elizabeth Ogborne* by Edward A. Fitch, No. 31, July 1899.
108. Captain Noble's forename is given in the *London Gazette*, 1–4 September 1781.
109. *A New and General Biographical Dictionary*, 1798, vol. 5.
110. *London Chronicle*, 29 April 1786, and *Gazetteer and New Daily Advertiser*, 9 May 1786.
111. NAS, Papers of the Gillanders family of Highfield, GD427/221; the letter was dated 27 July 1786.

112. *Travels in the Western Hebrides*, Reverend John Lane Buchanan, 1793.
113. Mary Davidson Eliot died on 13 July 1804. At the time of her death she was living on Brompton Terrace in Kensington with a Mrs English. PROB 11/1411/213, TNA.
114. Richmond Makepeace Thackeray's son, born in India, grew up to become the author William Makepeace Thackeray.

Chapter 9: A Celebrated Courtesan

115. William Bird Esquire was named in the 1778 Crim. Con. case between Baron and Baroness Percy. Baron Percy, Duke of Northumberland, had married Lady Anne Stuart, daughter of the Earl of Bute, in 1764. Thomas Morris, footman to Lady Percy, described William Bird as 'a young gentleman, about three-and-twenty years of age' whose 'estate lay at Coventry'.
116. *The Complete Peerage of England, Scotland, Ireland, Great Britain and the United Kingdom*, 1913.
117. 'The Whimsical Lover and Miss D__le', *Town and Country Magazine* 1778, refers to the pretended Marquis del Bruce; the events relating to this man took place in 1749, the year George James Cholmondeley the 4th Earl was born, although the article seems to suggest it relates to him and not to his father. It is an ill-written piece and the accuracy of the individuals referred to cannot be fully established, whether relating to the son, father or possibly even grandfather.
118. *A Portion of the Journal kept by Thomas Raikes Esq from 1831 to 1847*, vol. 3, 1857.
119. *Ladies Fair and Frail*, Horace Bleackley.
120. The *Morning Post*, 22 February 1776.
121. The *Morning Post*, 11 March 1776.
122. *Old and New London*, vol. 4, 1878.
123. The *Morning Post*, 19 June 1776.
124. *The diary of John Baker, barrister of the Middle Temple, solicitor general of the Leeward Islands*; his daughter Martha had attended the same convent school as Grace but some years earlier, and his son Thomas succeeded Hugh Dalrymple as attorney general of Grenada.
125. The *Morning Post*, 9 September 1776.
126. *Daily Advertiser*, 13 August 1774.
127. Dorothea Hesketh was born on 23 August 1774.
128. The wedding of Charles Cochrane to Catharina Pitcairn took place in June 1772.
129. The father of Captain Thomas and Ensign Robert Hesketh, Sir Robert Juxon (Hesketh) had a third (illegitimate) son by his 'housekeeper' Miss Ann Townsend, to whom he also gave the forename Robert as recorded by the following memorial in Folkestone Church, Kent: 'Lieut. Robert Hesketh RN, son of Sir Robert Juxon of Rufford, Lancs. Age 36, died 15th April 1796.' An illegitimate daughter Charlotte was born to the same woman.
130. *St James's Chronicle*, 28 November 1775.
131. In various Hesketh family pedigrees, Jacinthia-Catherine's birthplace is given as Montreal.
132. American Archives: Documents of the American Revolutionary Period, 1774–1776 (http://amarch.lib.niu.edu).
133. American Archives: Documents of the American Revolutionary Period, 1774–1776 (http://amarch.lib.niu.edu). Letter dated 30 November 1776.

134. American Archives: Documents of the American Revolutionary Period, 1774–1776 (http://amarch.lib.niu.edu).
135. Thomas Dalrymple Hesketh was born in New York on 5 January 1777.
136. General Benedict Arnold defected to the British in 1780, after André's arrest.
137. *General Evening Post*, 30 April 1778.
138. John Dean or Deane, c.1754–1798, draughtsman and engraver (mezzotint).
139. *British Paintings in the Metropolitan Museum of Art, 1575–1875*, by Metropolitan Museum of Art (New York), Katharine Baetjer, 2009.
140. The *Morning Post*, 25 November 1777.
141. The *Morning Post*, 5 November 1777.
142. Anne-Charlotte Hesketh was born on 21 March 1778.

Chapter 10: From Maid to Countess
143. The burial took place on 4 October 1756.
144. Charles Mordaunt, 4th Earl of Peterborough, drew up his last will and testament on 23 March 1758. PROB 11/1056/58, TNA.
145. The *London Chronicle*, 18 May 1758.
146. The baptism took place on 10 June 1758.
147. Reports of Cases Argued and Determined in the High Court of Chancery from 1757 to 1766.
148. Dean Street in Soho is not to be confused with Dean Street (now known as Deanery Street) in Mayfair, where Grace had a residence towards the end of the 1770s.
149. *Middlesex Journal*, 4 June 1771: 'Canterbury, June 1. Just passed through the city, Lord Peterborough, Lord Willes, a German Prince, &c. for France.' *Morning Chronicle*, 15 September 1772: 'Canterbury, Sept. 12. Passed through this city since our last … Lady Craven, from France, and Lord Peterborough to London.' The notorious Lady Craven, who had made an unhappy marriage, was known to have had many lovers; the *Morning Chronicle* is perhaps hinting that one of these was the 4th Earl of Peterborough.
150. National Library of Scotland, letter from J. (or G.) Swinton to Sir Walter Scott, ref. no. 14320.
151. *Survey of London*, vols 33 & 34: St Anne Soho.
152. *General Evening Post*, 13 June 1776.
153. *London Chronicle*, 18 March 1777.
154. The *Morning Post*, 14 October 1778.
155. *Morgannwg: transactions of the Glamorgan History Society*, vols 33–37, 1989. A document produced by the Glamorgan History Society claims he was the father of numerous illegitimate children but he names only one, a daughter called Elizabeth Teasdale, in his will.
156. *General Evening Post*, 16 May 1778, and Glamorgan Archives, DED/516.
157. The *Morning Post*, 15 July 1777.
158. The *London Evening Post*, 21 August 1777.
159. The *Morning Chronicle*, 25 August 1777.
160. The *Morning Post*, 27 August 1777.
161. Fanny Burney (1752–1840) published her first novel, *Evelina*, anonymously in 1778, but her identity becoming known she gained notoriety and the friendship of Mrs Hester Thrale, in whose company she spent much time.

162. *The Diary and Letters of Madame D'Arblay*, vol. I, Frances Burney (Madame D'Arblay was Fanny Burney's later married name). Major H___ was John Baker Holroyd, the future 1st Earl of Sheffield and, in 1779, MP for Bristol and major of the Sussex militia. Born in 1735, he was very much older than his languid young house guest.

Chapter 11: Horizons New

163. *Gazetteer and New Daily Advertiser*, 31 July 1778.
164. *General Advertiser and Morning Intelligencer*, 25 June 1778.
165. The *Morning Post and Daily Advertiser*, 27 May 1779.
166. The *Morning Post and Daily Advertiser*, 1 June 1779.
167. *Whitehall Evening Post*, 3 June 1780; the article continues, re. Grace: 'A certain Earl is said to be on the eve of a very advantageous matrimonial union, which may probably occasion the above Lady's temporary secession from her native country' (the earl referred to is Cholmondeley).
168. The *Morning Herald*, 25 June 1781.
169. The *Morning Herald*, 2 July 1781.
170. In Grace's journal the portrait is said to be hanging at Houghton Hall when the prince spied it but Cholmondeley did not inherit Houghton until Horace Walpole died in 1797. In 1781 the painting would have hung in Cholmondeley's Piccadilly mansion.
171. The *Morning Herald*, 16 August 1781.
172. The *Morning Herald*, 25 August 1781. The art historian Oliver Millar (1923–2007), who served in the Royal household for much of his career, believed this portrait to be the one referred to as 'a Head of Mrs. Elliot' in a list of pictures painted by Thomas Gainsborough by order of the Prince of Wales, priced at £31 10s (information via the Frick Collection).
173. *Public Advertiser*, 2 May 1782.
174. *Morning Herald*, 4 October 1781. Cumberland Street, a crescent, is known today as Great Cumberland Place, and Marble Arch now stands close to where the gallows were once situated.
175. Grace often gave her surname as Elliot. We have chosen to use Elliott as this is the name variant on her journal and by which she is best known to history.
176. *Morning Herald*, 19 October 1781.

Chapter 12: Anglo-Indian Relationships

177. *Universal Magazine*, April 1808.
178. William Hickey (1749–1827), lawyer in India and memoirist, formerly a cadet in the EIC's Madras army.
179. Sir George Colebrooke (1729–1809), wealthy banker and chairman of the EIC in 1769, 1770 and 1772. He is described as a 'rather pompous, self-important man who considered himself to be the second most influential politician in England' in the *Oxford Dictionary of National Biography*. Nottingham University Manuscripts Library, Portland Collection, PWF 2990, 8 August 1770.
180. Nottingham University Manuscripts Library, Portland Collection, PWF 6950, 22 September 1770.
181. Nottingham University Manuscripts Library, Portland Collection, PWF 6951, 26 January 1771.
182. The *St James's Chronicle*, 10 February 1781.

183. Dr John Eliot, the by now divorced husband of Grace, had retained their marital home in Cecil Street and was living there in 1780. One wonders if he saw and recognized her cousin visiting on the same street!

184. Lord Peterborough left for the Continent early in June 1780, which helps to date Henry's visit home. *Whitehall Evening Post*, 3 June 1780.

185. Grace Dalrymple had been discovered in her assignations with Lord Valentia at a house of ill repute in Berkeley Row, owned by the 'notorious Mrs Jane Price' some four years earlier. Possibly this was even the same bagnio visited by Grace's cousin Henry to sample the services of 'The Lady Abbess and her Nuns'. Emma, the future Lady Hamilton and mistress of Nelson, was known to have lived at Mrs Kelly's house in Arlington Street around 1779.

186. *Lady Worsley's Whim*, Hallie Rubenhold, 2008.

187. Joseph Bouchier Smith and his wife Frances were to have a daughter, Frances Mary Smith, baptized on 5 March 1782 at St Martin-in-the-Fields in Westminster.

188. Lady Elizabeth Henley married the diplomat Morton Frederick Eden on 7 August 1783. Eden was created the 1st Baron Henley in 1799.

189. The *Morning Herald*, 8 April 1782.

190. Information given some years later to Richard Bentley, to be used in the preface to Grace's journal.

191. *Ladies Fair and Frail*, Horace Bleackley.

Chapter 13: The 5th Earl of Peterborough and Criminal Conversation

192. The *Morning Herald*, 22 April 1782. The 'domino' was the costume most often seen at masquerades, comprising a simple cloak covering the body and a mask, usually black.

193. The *London Chronicle*, 11 May 1782.

194. The *Morning Post*, 22 February 1783.

195. Marie Antoinette, after being criticized for her excesses, was now criticized for her simpler style, people claiming that she was putting French silk-weavers out of business and lowering the status of the French monarchy.

196. *General Evening Post*, 24 April 1783. The *Morning Herald*, 5 May 1783.

197. FitzPatrick's sister Mary had been the wife of C.J. Fox's brother Stephen, 2nd Baron Holland.

198. www.historyofparliamentonline.org.

199. *The Whig Club*, 1794.

200. The *Morning Post*, 10 April 1783.

201. Letter from Colonel FitzPatrick to Mary Benwell, 10 April 1783, printed in the *Westminster Review*, 1825.

202. The *Morning Herald*, 13 May 1783.

203. *Public Advertiser*, 2 June 1783.

204. Letter from Colonel FitzPatrick to Mary Benwell, 16 December 1783, printed in the *Westminster Review*, 1825.

205. *Gazetteer and New Daily Advertiser*, 22 April 1784.

206. *Oracle and Public Advertiser*, 29 March 1798.

207. The *Morning Herald and Daily Advertiser*, 9 August 1784.

208. The *Morning Post*, 14 May 1784.

209. Details revealed by an X-radiograph in 2009; *British Paintings in the Metropolitan Museum of Art, 1575–1875*, by Metropolitan Museum of Art (New York), Katharine Baetjer, 2009.
210. *The Works of William Cowper*, vol. 5; the letter is dated 27 August 1785 but may actually be 27 August 1786 as further evidence shows this to be the date of the visit to Clifton Reynes by Lord Peterborough and Lady Anne Foley; possibly the letter has been misdated.
211. *The Times*, 4 May 1787.
212. The *Morning Herald*, 22 June 1785; 'Lord Peterborough is determined to have *meal* for *malt* and as heavy damages have been awarded to Mr. Foley, his Lordship and Lady Anne, appear resolved to keep the *mill stick going!*'
213. *House of Lords Journal*, vol. 37.
214. *Public Advertiser*, 15 February 1787.
215. The *World and Fashionable Advertiser*, 7 May 1787.
216. The *World and Fashionable Advertiser*, 6 June 1787.
217. The *World and Fashionable Advertiser*, 28 July 1787; 'Lord PETERBOROUGH is now at Margate – and Lady ANN FOLEY at Leostoffe; of course, from the separating distance – *off by consent*.' (Leostoffe is the old spelling of Lowestoft.)

Chapter 14: French Affairs

218. The copy survived and was sold at Sotheby's auction house in New York during 2010.
219. The *Morning Herald*, 6 January 1786.
220. In a list of her bills held at Houghton Hall, she contracted a debt of £52 3s 3d to Louis Bazalgette prior to January 1784. Charles Bazalgette, author of *Prinny's Taylor: The Life and Times of Louis Bazalgette (1750–1830)*, advised that Louis made riding habits during this period for Mrs Fitzherbert, costing a little over £10 each.
221. *General Evening Post*, 30 March 1786.
222. *General Evening Post*, 23 September 1786.
223. The Houghton Library, Harvard University, bMS Hyde 10 (133); the letter is to an unidentified recipient but is marked as being received on 5 March 1787 by a French hand.
224. The *Morning Post*, 5 April 1785.
225. Sir Philip Francis to his wife, writing from Paris on 7 September 1784.
226. *Public Advertiser*, 30 September 1785.
227. The *Morning Post*, 18 August 1789.
228. Marie-Françoise Henriette Laché, Madame Saint-Albin, went on to marry a soldier from Swedish Pomerania, Major (Johann) Wilhelm von Runge, also known as the Chevalier de Runge. She died in 1804.
229. The *World and Fashionable Advertiser*, 1 August 1789.
230. The *Morning Post*, 10 January 1791.

Chapter 15: Cock-fighting in Calcutta

231. *Bengal Past and Present*, vol. 106, Calcutta, 1987.
232. This incident occurred towards the end of 1782. *Letters of Warren Hastings to his Wife*, introduced and annotated by Sydney C. Grier.
233. Calcutta is now known as Kolkata.
234. *Letters of Warren Hastings to his Wife*, introduced and annotated by Sydney C. Grier.
235. John is recorded as a captain in 1785 but by his death in 1790 was being referred to as a lieutenant colonel; the title of the painting, which was not finished until 1788, relates to the title he was to be known by.

236. 'Colonel Mordaunt's Cock Match' is displayed in the Tate Gallery in London and their notes on it state that 'after its acquisition [the painting] was cleaned, revealing new subtleties of colour, detail and meaning. The Nawab's state of sexual arousal, his agitated pose and inclination towards his chief minister and favourite bodyguard Hassan Resa Khan (in the ornate red turban), add an erotic dimension to the nature of the cock fight. The vignette just behind the Nawab shows a bearded Hindu (in turban) fondling a Moslem boy catamite (in the white cap worn by Moslem men), to the outrage of the man in the red turban who must be restrained by a courtier. Lewis Ferdinand Smith recounted that the Nawab "has many adopted children, but none of his own" – despite a harem of 500 beauties – and that towards his wife of sixteen years "he has never fulfilled the duties of a husband"' (quoted in Archer, p.144). This painting was perhaps Hastings' select joke, a memento of his time in India. (See also Mildred Archer, *India and British Portraiture 1770–1825*, London, 1979, pp.130–77.)

237. *Bengal Past and Present*, vol. 106, Calcutta, 1987; the letter was dated 4 February 1785.

238. *Bengal Past and Present*, vol. 106, Calcutta, 1987. The 5th Earl of Peterborough was still trying to recover the money owed by the nawab to his brother several years later (Letter to Henry Dundas, December 1797, NAS, GD 51/18/23).

239. National Library of Scotland, letter from J. (or G.) Swinton to Sir Walter Scott, ref. no. 14320.

240. William Hickey left some notes, dated 1 December 1789, that are reprinted in *Bengal Past and Present*, vol. 49, pt. 2; these record John living at Cheringhee in Calcutta next door to the Honourable Mr Charles Stuart who was one of the signatories to the marriage settlement made between Janet and her second husband in 1793.

241. The Register of Marriages, Births and Deaths at the Presidency of Fort William, in Bengal, for the Year of Our Lord 1788.

242. Arthur William Devis (1762–1822), an English painter known for his portraits and history paintings.

243. Thomas Hickey (1741–1824), an Irish painter who travelled widely in his work.

244. *Bengal Past and Present*, vol. 6, part 2.

245. *Morning Chronicle*, 25 April 1791.

246. PROB 31/815, TNA.

247. PROB 31/820/75, TNA.

248. The *Gentleman's Magazine*, vol. LXIV, 1794. Her husband Admiral Sir Richard King died in 1806.

Chapter 16: Prisoner in France

249. This journal was published by Richard Bentley in 1859 with the permission of Grace's granddaughter; the original manuscript has since been lost and it is not possible to verify whether the falsehoods and inaccuracies contained within it come from Grace's own pen or are embellishments by Bentley to make the book more saleable.

250. Although different dates are given for these noblemen fleeing into exile, the *London Chronicle* of 16 July 1789 prints an extract of a letter from Paris dated 13 July stating 'The Comte de Artois is fled', which does confirm Grace's information.

251. Grace calls the banker Walgains in her journal. In 1791 he bought d'Orléans' collection of paintings. The day Grace dined with d'Orléans upon his return was the first anniversary of the Storming of the Bastille.

252. Grace names him as General Boileau.

253. Grace's Meudon cottage was demolished around 1870. *Mémoires de la Société de l'Histoire de Paris et de l'Ile-de-France*, Tome XX, Paris, 1893.
254. In the journal Rue Saint-Fiacre is mistranscribed as Rue de l'Encre.
255. The Websters were quarrelling and Lady Webster would later embark on an affair with Henry Richard (Vassall) Fox, Charles James Fox's nephew, marrying him once she was divorced from her husband. Sir William Hamilton, husband of the infamous Emma Hamilton, was the British envoy to Naples at the time.
256. *The Times*, 28 January 1859.
257. Grace calls him Milor; his wife was the older sister of the dancer Émilie Bigottini.
258. The *World and Fashionable Advertiser*, 26 September 1793.
259. Grace does not mention any pet dogs in her journal.
260. How long she remained in the Meudon *maison d'arrêt* is unknown but if she was in prison when she heard of the execution of the Duc de Biron, which occurred on 31 December, then it is likely it was Meudon. Dr Gem lived in Meudon and it also has to be a possibility that Meudon was the place of their joint imprisonment and not the Récollets.
261. *My Lady Scandalous*, Jo Manning (however, no source for this information is quoted).
262. The *Observer*, 18 March 1798.

Chapter 17: The Further Adventures of Henry Hew Dalrymple

263. This was probably a different plantation from the one owned by his father; the French had taken and occupied Grenada in 1779 and the island was only ceded back to Britain in 1783.
264. The project received the backing of Paul Le Mesurier, a Guernsey man who was both an MP and a director of the EIC (he would later be Lord Mayor of London), and Carl Bernhard Wadström, a Swedish slavery abolitionist who had recently moved to London.
265. Those killed were Aaron Baker, Stephen Mollineaux (whose wife was taken prisoner), Edward Williamson, William Howard, Constantine Long and Mrs Gardiner; the wounded were Mr H.B. Gardiner, Richard Pool, Dolphin Price and Godfrey Norman. The women taken hostage along with Mrs Mollineaux were Mrs Harley, Mrs Barnwell and Elizabeth Thompson, together with three children surnamed Baker and one belonging to Mrs Harley.
266. NAS, GD51/6/974, Papers of the Dundas Family of Melville. Norton Street is now known as Bolsover Street.
267. *Oracle and Public Daily Advertiser* and the *Telegraph*, both 20 June 1796.
268. *Oracle and Public Daily Advertiser*, 16 November 1797.
269. The letter is dated 14 February but with no year given; however, the paper upon which it is written is watermarked as 1798 (Alison Derrett, Windsor Castle Royal Archives).
270. The *Morning Herald*, 15 March 1798.
271. Documents at Cheshire Archives record her being named as a Seymour by Cholmondeley as early as 1787 (DCH – Cholmondeley of Cholmondeley Estate Records).
272. The *London Chronicle*, 14 December 1797.
273. The *Observer*, 18 March 1798, and the *Morning Post*, 21 March 1798.
274. The *Morning Post and Gazetteer*, 6 April 1798. A list of Grace's bills, split between those contracted before January 1784 and those after, is in the archives at Houghton Hall, suggesting that Lord Cholmondeley had a hand in paying some of them.
275. Windsor Castle Royal Archives.

Chapter 18: Jacintha's Later Life

276. Thomas Winckley was born c.1731.
277. The villa may have been about 4 miles outside Liverpool in 1792 but the city has now encompassed the area. It is possibly the house known as Larkhill Mansion; the area was used for a housing estate built after the First World War and the mansion was subsequently used as a library before being demolished in 1962.
278. PROB 11/1256/9, TNA.
279. Frances claimed that the Despards had sailed for Cape Breton, an island in Nova Scotia off the coast of Canada, before Jacintha's wedding but in fact they did not sail until later in the year. Despard had been appointed the military commander of Cape Breton.
280. Lucy Hesketh married Edward Pearson on 3 March 1801 at St George, Hanover Square, with the consent of her mother as she was under age.

Chapter 19: The Dawn of a New Century

281. Frances, with her usual inaccuracy, records the date of the meeting as 1803 when it must almost certainly have taken place up to two years earlier.
282. Cholmondeley moved some years later to a neighbouring mansion that became known as Cholmondeley House, now Cambridge House.
283. Sneyd Papers, Keele University, 200–203 Tarleton 1817–1819.
284. Rebecca Krudener, widow, is listed as living on Poland Street in Westminster on a 1781 Sun Fire Insurance document. Most sources name Miss Bertie as Susan Priscilla, but she signed herself Priscilla Susan at her wedding and as P.S. Tarleton on later correspondence (Sneyd Papers, Keele University, 200–203 Tarleton 1817–1819).
285. Rebecca Krudener married William Walker of the Middle Temple, son of a Dublin merchant named Matthew Walker, on 30 November 1782 at St James, Westminster. One of the witnesses to the marriage was William Morton Pitt (1754–1836) of Kingston House, Dorset, kinsman of Pitt the Younger.
286. The *London Chronicle*, 28 August 1800.
287. The service has been dated to c.1790 and of the period of the Qianlong Emperor who abdicated on 9 February 1796, so was probably bought via the trade routes between the EIC and the Chinese merchants and then shipped home with them. These arms were incorrectly identified in *Chinese Armorial Porcelain*, D.S. Howard, 1974, as 'Oliphant impaling Browne'. The *Apollo* magazine, in 1938, mentioned the sale of some items from this service, saying it 'must have been a large one, as several portions of it have appeared in the salerooms during the past thirty years'. At least two of the items are now in the V&A Museum in London.
288. *The Times*, 4 June 1802.
289. Lord Down, a title held by the Stewart family, Earls of Moray, and therefore a link to Janet's Scottish ancestry. Reported in the *Morning Post*, 29 April 1803.
290. The *Morning Post*, 16 May 1804.
291. The *Bury and Norwich Post*, 25 August 1802.
292. PROB 37/119, TNA. Dalrymple and others v Earl of Peterborough Testator or intestate: Edmondes, Janet otherwise Jenet of Upper Brook Street, St George, Hanover Sq., Middlesex, widow (1805–1811).
293. Glamorgan Archives, DED/516.
294. *Survey of London*, vols 33 & 34: St Anne Soho.
295. The Faculty Office Archives.

296. The *Morning Post*, 15 September 1803.
297. Janet wrote her new will on 8 May 1804.
298. *Lady Worsley's Whim*, Hallie Rubenhold.
299. The letter was dated 26 September 1807. William Horace Beckford later took the sur-name Pitt-Rivers in order to inherit from his brother-in-law George Pitt, 2nd Baron Rivers.
300. The *Morning Post*, 26 April 1808.
301. The *Morning Post*, 16 and 22 June 1808.
302. *Royal Mistresses and Bastards: Fact and Fiction 1714–1936*, Anthony Camp (published privately, London, 2007).
303. *A Portion of the Journal kept by Thomas Raikes, Esq., from 1831 to 1847*, vol. I, 1858.
304. The *Morning Post*, 8 October 1808.
305. British Library, MS 89036/3/4 ff324.
306. British Library, MS 89036/3/2 ff84-185. The letter was dated 7 February 1809.
307. British Library, MS 89036/3/2 ff84-185.
308. Nottingham University Manuscripts PI F8-8-8-1-1.
309. Information supplied by the Royal Archives Windsor; the name against this annuity is merely 'Mrs Elliott' but the dates of it strongly suggest that Grace is the person referred to.
310. British Library, MS 89036/3/3 ff118 and 120.
311. British Library, MS89036/3/3 ff130.
312. The *Morning Post*, 11 November 1809.
313. The *Morning Post*, 28 August 1809.
314. *Lord Granville Leveson Gower (first Earl Granville), Private Correspondence 1781 to 1821*, edited by Castalia, Countess Granville, vol. II, 1916.
315. Portland Collection, Nottingham University Manuscripts Collection, Pl F8/9/6/1.
316. The *Morning Post*, 18 July 1806.
317. Frances Wilson Smith died at Brompton in Knightsbridge on 19 January 1833.
318. PROB 11/1561, TNA.
319. The *Bury and Norwich Post*, 9 December 1818.
320. *Royal Cornwall Gazette*, 22 December 1821.
321. The *Gentleman's Magazine*, 29 December 1822.

Chapter 20: Grace in Regency England

322. Royal Mews Warrant Books, 1760–1867.
323. Aspinall, Arthur (ed.), *The Correspondence of George, Prince of Wales, 1770–1812* (Oxford University Press, 1971).
324. The Countess of Cholmondeley had been a lady of the bedchamber to Caroline, Princess of Wales, and possibly this is how Lady Charlotte Bury knew Georgiana from her childhood.
325. *The Diary of a Lady-in-Waiting*, Charlotte Bury, vol. 2, 1838.
326. Lady Bentinck died on 10 December 1813 at her Grosvenor Place house, the newspapers saying that her death followed a short but severe illness, and she was laid to rest in the Cavendish Bentinck family vault at the church in St Marylebone. The *Morning Post*, 14 December 1813.
327. Nottingham University Manuscripts PI F8-8-8-1-1.
328. The date of the birth and baptism was 4 June 1820.

329. Information about Grace cashing in her bonds is to be found in the Houghton Hall archives.
330. PROB/11/1693/245, TNA.
331. PROB 31/1214/1157, TNA.

Chapter 21: Jessy Bebb, Society Hostess, or How Grace's Life Could Have Been
332. The *Morning Post*, 16 July 1821.
333. Prince William Frederick, Duke of Gloucester and Edinburgh (1776–1834), was nephew to King George III. He had been encouraged to stay single in order to supply a spouse for Princess Charlotte of Wales, should no other more suitable suitor present his hand. When she married Prince Leopold of Saxe-Coburg in 1816, the Duke of Gloucester married his cousin, Princess Mary, daughter of George III, ten weeks later. Both bride and groom were 40 years old and the marriage proved childless. The duke was known by the nickname 'Silly Billy', giving an insight into his character and personality.
334. 'Minutes, Secret Court of Directors, 4th February 1829', reprinted in *The East India Company, 1784–1834*, Patrick J.N. Tuck, 1998.
335. PROB 11/1840, TNA.
336. Thames & Medway burials.
337. The *Morning Chronicle*, 30 June 1835, and the *Morning Post*, 9 May 1836.
338. The *Morning Post*, 31 May 1836.
339. Prince Ernest Augustus gained the throne of Hanover in 1837 when his elder brother William IV died; Salic law in Germany prevented Victoria from inheriting the Hanoverian throne and she inherited the crown of England only. The *Morning Post*, 26 June 1841.
340. PROB 11/2111, TNA.
341. Gilmerton House, a Grade A listed Georgian mansion, is still a home but also operates as a luxury private retreat.
342. The *Morning Post*, 9 April 1850.
343. Richard Bentley records, 1806–1915, Rare Book & Manuscript Library, University of Illinois at Urbana-Champaign.

Bibliography

Primary sources

Albert, Henri, *Promenade à Bellevue et à Meudon* (Causse et Cie, 1968)

Albin, John, *A new, correct and much improved History of the Isle of Wight* (London, 1795)

Anderson, William, *The Scottish Nation; or, the Surnames, Families, Literature, Honours and Biographical History of the People of Scotland* (Edinburgh, 1878)

Andress, David, *The Terror: Civil War in the French Revolution* (Abacus, 2006)

Angelo, Henry, *Angelo's Pic Nic, Or, Table Talk: including numerous recollections of public characters, who have figured in some part or another of the stage of life for the last fifty years; forming an endless variety of talent, amusement, and interest, calculated to please every person fond of biographical sketches and anecdotes* (London, 1834)

Angot, E., *Un Neveu du Prince de Bénévent, Louis de Talleyrand-Périgord, 1784–1808* (Paris, 1911)

Anonymous, *Characters of the present most celebrated Courtezans, interspersed with a variety of secret anecdotes never before published* (London, 1780)

Anonymous, *The Royal Register, with annotations by another hand*, vol. IV (London, 1780)

Anonymous, *The Torpedo, a poem to the Electrical Eel, addressed to Mr John Hunter, Surgeon: and dedicated to The Right Honourable Lord Cholmondeley* (London, 1777)

Aspinall, Arthur (ed.), *The Correspondence of George, Prince of Wales, 1770–1812: 1799–1804* (Oxford University Press, 1971)

Aspinall, Arthur (ed.), *The Letters of King George IV, 1812–1830*, vol. I (Cambridge University Press, 1938)

Baejter, Katharine, *British Paintings in the Metropolitan Museum of Art, 1575–1875*, Metropolitan Museum of Art (New York) (2009)

Barker, G.F. Russell (comp.), *Records of Old Westminsters* (Chiswick Press, 1928)

Barrett, Charlotte (ed.), *The Diary and Letters of Madame D'Arblay (1778–1840)* (Macmillan and Co., 1904)

Bazalgette, Charles, *Prinny's Taylor: The Life and Times of Louis Bazalgette (1750–1830)* (Kindle e-book, 2015)

Bickley, Francis (ed.), *The Diaries of Sylvester Douglas, Baron Glenbervie*, vol. II (London, 1928)

Billard, Dr Max, *Les femmes enceintes devant le tribunal révolutionnaire, d'aprés des documents inédits* (Paris, 1911)

Blanc, Oliver (translated by Alan Sheridan), *Last Letters, Prisons and Prisoners of the French Revolution* (André Deutsch, 1987)

Bleackley, Horace, *Ladies Fair and Frail: Sketches of the demi-monde during the eighteenth century* (John Lane, The Bodley Head, 1909)

Bleackley, Horace, *The Story of a Beautiful Duchess: Being an Account of the Life and Times of Elizabeth Gunning, Duchess of Hamilton and Argyll* (E.P. Dutton and Company, 1907)

Buchanan, the Reverend John Lane, *Travels in the Western Hebrides: from 1782 to 1790* (London, 1793)

Budworth, Joseph, Esq. FSA, A Fortnight's ramble to the lakes in Westmoreland, Lancashire, and Cumberland by A Rambler (J. Nichols, London, 1795)

Bullar, John, A Historical and Picturesque Guide to the Isle of Wight (Southampton, 1820)

Bury, Lady Charlotte, The Diary of a Lady-in-Waiting, vol. II (John Lane, The Bodley Head, 1908)

Camp, Anthony, Royal Mistresses and Bastards: fact and fiction 1714–1936 (published privately, London, 2007)

Campan, Madame, First Lady of the Bedchamber to the Queen, Memoirs of the Court of Marie Antoinette, Queen of France, vol. I (Henry Colburn, 1852)

Carré, Henri, La Noblesse de France et l'opinion publique au XVIIIe siècle (Slatkine Reprints, 1977)

Cecil, David, The Stricken Deer: or, The Life of Cowper (Constable, 1943)

Clark, Lorna J. (ed.), Letters of Sarah Harriet Burney (University of Georgia Press, 1997)

Dalrymple, William, White Mughals (HarperCollins, 2002)

Dodwell and Miles, Messrs (eds), East India Army Agents, Alphabetical List of the Officers of the Bengal Army; with the dates of their respective promotion, retirement, resignation, or death, whether in India or in Europe; from the year 1760, to the year 1834 inclusive, corrected to September 30, 1837 (Longman, Orme, Brown and Co., 1838)

Dolan, Brian, Ladies of the Grand Tour (Flamingo, 2002)

East India Company, A List of the Names of the Members of the United Company of Merchants of England, Trading to the East-Indies, who appear Qualified to Vote and their General Courts (1815)

Elliott, Grace Dalrymple, Journal of My Life during the French Revolution (Richard Bentley, 1859)

Fare, Malcolm, Angelo, Domenico (1717–1802), Oxford Dictionary of National Biography (Oxford University Press, 2004)

Farmar, Hugh, A Regency Elopement (Michael Joseph, 1969)

Ferguson, Sir James (ed.), Letters of George Dempster to Sir Adam Fergusson, 1756–1813: with some account of his life (Macmillan and Co., 1936)

Fife, Graeme, The Terror: the shadow of the guillotine, France 1792–1794 (Portrait, 2004)

Fitch, Edward A., The Essex Review: An Illustrated Quarterly Record of Everything of Permanent Interest in the County, Historians of Essex VII – Elizabeth Ogborne, vol. VIII, no. 31 (Benham & Co., July 1899)

Flexner, James Thomas, The Traitor and the Spy: Benedict Arnold and John André (Harcourt, Brace, 1953)

Foreman, Amanda, Georgiana, Duchess of Devonshire (HarperCollins, 1999)

Foster, Joseph (ed.), Alumni Oxoniensis: the Members of the University of Oxford 1715–1886: their parentage, birthplace and year of birth, with a record of their degrees, later series, A–D (Parker and Co., 1888)

Foster, Joseph (ed.), Alumni Oxonienses: the Members of the University of Oxford 1715–1886: their parentage, birthplace and year of birth, with a record of their degrees, vols I, III and IV (James Parker & Co., 1891)

Francis, Sir Philip, The Francis Letters by Sir Philip Francis and other members of the family, vol. II (Hutchinson and Co., 1901)

Fraser, Flora, The Unruly Queen: The Life of Queen Caroline (Bloomsbury Paperbacks, 2012)

Gibbs, the Hon. Vicary (ed.), The Complete Peerage of England, Scotland, Ireland, Great Britain and the United Kingdom, vol. III (London, 1913)

Gooch, Mrs, *The Life of Mrs Gooch, written by herself*, vol. II (London, 1792)

Goudemetz, H., *Historical Epochs of the French Revolution, with the Judgment and Execution of Louis XVI, King of France; and a List of the Members of the National Convention, who voted for and against his death*, translated by the The Rev Dr Francis Randolph (England, 1796)

Grant, Francis J. (ed.), *Register of Marriages of the City of Edinburgh, 1751–1800 by the Scottish Record Society* (Edinburgh, 1922)

Granville, Countess Castalia (ed.), *Letters of Lord Granville Leveson Gower, private correspondence 1781 to 1821*, edited by his daughter-in-law, vol. II (John Murray, 1916)

Graydon, Alexander, *Memoirs of his own time with reminiscences of the men and events of the revolution*, edited by John Stockton Littell (Philadelphia, 1846)

Grego, Joseph, *History of Parliamentary Elections and Electioneering in the old days* (Chatto and Windus, 1886)

Grier, Sydney C., *The Letters of Warren Hastings to his Wife* (transcribed in full from the originals in the British Museum, London, 1905)

Groves, John Percy; Cannon, Richard; and Waller, G.H., *Historical records of the 7th or Royal Regiment of Fusiliers: now known as the Royal Fusiliers (the City of London Regiment), 1685–1903* (F.B. Guerin, 1903)

Hylton, Lord (ed.), *The Paget Brothers 1790–1840* (John Murray, 1918)

Ilchester, Earl of (ed.), *The Journal of Elizabeth, Lady Holland (1791–1811)*, vol. I (Longmans, Green & Co., 1908)

Jesse, William, *The Life of George Brummell Esq., commonly called Beau Brummell*, vol. I (Scribner & Welford, 1886)

Jewers, Arthur J. (ed.), *The Registers of the Abbey Church of SS. Peter and Paul, Bath*, vol. II (London, 1901)

Kelly, Linda, *Holland House: A History of London's Most Celebrated Salon* (I.B. Tauris, 2013)

Lenta, Margaret and le Cordeur, Basil (eds), *The Cape Diaries of Lady Anne Barnard, 1799–1800*, vol. II, Van Riebeeck Society Second Series, No. 30 (1999)

Leroy, J. (ed.), *Meudon et Bellevue* (Paris, 1907)

Leveson Gower KBE, Sir George (ed.), *Hary-O: The Letters of Lady Harriet Cavendish, 1796–1809* (John Murray, 1940)

Llewellyn-Jones, Rosie (ed.), *A Man of the Enlightenment in Eighteenth-century India: the letters of Claude Martin, 1766–1800* (Orient Blackswan, 2003)

Malmesbury, 3rd Earl of (ed.), *Diaries and Correspondence of James Harris, First Earl of Malmesbury*, vol. III (Richard Bentley, 1844)

Manning, Jo, *My Lady Scandalous: The Amazing Life and Outrageous Times of Grace Dalrymple Elliott* (Simon & Schuster, 2005)

Marchand, Leslie A., *Byron's Letters and Journals: The Complete and Unexpurgated Text of All the Letters Available in Manuscript and the Full Printed Version of All Others*, vol. I (Harvard University Press, 1973)

McConnel Hatch, Robert, *Major John André: a gallant in spy's clothing* (Houghton Miffin Harcourt, 1986)

Moore, Thomas, *Letters and Journals of Lord Byron with Notices of his Life* (John Murray, 1830)

Moore, Thomas, *The Journal of Thomas Moore*, vol. III (University of Delaware Press, 1986)

Namier, Sir Lewis and Brooke, John (eds), *The House of Commons, 1754–1790*, vol. I (London, 1964)

Nisbet, Alexander, *A System of Heraldry, Speculative and Practical: with the True Art of Blazon* (Edinburgh, 1722)

O'Brien, R. Barry (ed.), *Two centuries of Irish history 1691–1870* (London, 1907)

Overy, Caroline, *Oxford Dictionary of National Biography, Dr John Eliot* (Oxford University Press, 2004)

Paget, the Right Hon. Sir Augustus B., GCB (ed.), *The Paget Papers, diplomatic and other correspondence of the Right Hon. Sir Arthur Paget, G.C.B. 1794–1807 (with two appendices 1808 & 1821-1829)*, vol. II (William Heinemann, 1896)

Paul, Sir James Balfour, CVO, LL.D (ed.), *Diary of George Ridpath, minister of Stitchel* [original spelling], *1755–1761* (Scottish History Society, University Press, 1922)

Pigott, Charles, *The Whig Club, Or a Sketch of the Manners of the Age* (London, 1794)

Prinsep, Charles C. (ed.), *Record of Services of the Honourable East India Company's Civil Servants in the Madras Presidency from 1741 to 1858, compiled and edited from Records in the Possession of the Secretary of State for India* (Turner & Co., 1885)

Raikes, Thomas, *A Portion of the Journal kept by Thomas Raikes Esq from 1831 to 1847*, vol. III (Longman, Brown, Green, Longmans & Roberts, 1857)

Rambaud, Jacques (ed.), *Memoirs of the Comte Roger de Damas (1787–1806), translated by Mrs Rodolph Stawell* (Chapman and Hall, 1913)

Robinson, John Robert, *'Old Q': A Memoir of William Douglas Fourth Duke of Queensberry KT* (second edition, London, 1895)

Roscoe, E.S. and Clergue, Helen (ed.), *George Selwyn, his Letters and his Life* (London, 1899)

Rubenhold, Hallie, *Lady Worsley's Whim* (Chatto & Windus, 2008)

Sabran, Delphine de, *Memoirs of Delphine de Sabran, Marquise de Custine, from the French of Gaston Maugras and Le Cte P. de Croze-Lemercier* (Heinemann, 1912)

Scott, Hew, DD, *Fasti ecclesiæ scoticanæ; the succession of ministers in the Church of Scotland from the reformation*, vol. I (Synod of Lothian and Tweeddale, Edinburgh, 1915)

Scott, Sir Walter, *Memorials of the Haliburtons* (Edinburgh, 1820)

Sérignan, Le Comte de Lort de, *Le Duc de Lauzun (Général Biron) 1791–1792 Correspondance Intime* (Paris, 1906)

Shelley, Lady Frances and Edgcumbe, Richard (ed.), *The Diary of Frances, Lady Shelley* (John Murray, 1913)

Sheppard, F.H.W. (General Editor), *Survey of London*, vols 31 and 32: St James Westminster, Part 2 (London County Council, 1963)

Sheppard, F.H.W. (General Editor), *Survey of London*, vols 33 and 34: St Anne Soho (London County Council, 1966)

Smollet, Tobias George, *The Critical Review or, Annals of literature*, vol. 15 (London, 1763)

Société de l'histoire de Paris et de l'Ile-de-France, *Mémoires de la Société de l'histoire de Paris et de l'Ile-de-France*, Tome XX (Paris, 1893)

Southey, Robert, LL.D (ed.), *The Works of William Cowper, comprising his poems, correspondence and translations*, vol. II (H.G. Bohn, 1853)

Southey, Robert, LL.D (ed.), *The Works of William Cowper, comprising his poems, correspondence and translations*, vol. V (Baldwin and Cradock, 1836)

Spencer, Alfred (ed.), *Memoirs of William Hickey*, vol. I (1749–1775) (fourth edition, Hurst & Blackett Ltd, undated)

Spencer, Alfred (ed.), *Memoirs of William Hickey*, vol. II (1775–1782) (fifth edition, Hurst & Blackett Ltd, undated)

Spencer, Alfred (ed.), *Memoirs of William Hickey*, vol. III (1782–1790) and vol. IV (1790–1809) (Hurst & Blackett Ltd, undated)

Stafford, Countess of (ed.), *Leaves from the Diary of Henry Greville*, third series (Smith, Elder & Co., 1904)

Steele, Mrs Elizabeth, *The Memoirs of Mrs Sophia Baddeley, late of Drury Lane Theatre*, vol. I (London, 1787)

Swinburne, Henry, *The Courts of Europe at the close of the last Century*, vol. II (Henry Colburn, 1841)

The Scottish History Society, *The Diary of George Turnbull, Minister of Alloa and Tyninghame 1657–1704* (University Press, 1893)

Thomson, Richard (ed.), *A Faithful Account of the Processions and Ceremonies observed in the Coronation of the Kings and Queen of England: exemplified in that of their late most sacred Majesties King George the Third and Queen Charlotte with all the other interesting proceedings connected with that magnificent festival* (London, 1820)

Tomkins, Stephen, *The Clapham Sect: How Wilberforce's Circle Transformed Britain* (Lion Hudson plc, 2010)

Tooke, William (ed.), *A new and general biographical dictionary*, vol. V (London, 1798)

Toynbee, Mrs Paget (ed.), *The Letters of Horace Walpole, fourth Earl of Orford*, vol. V: 1760–1764 (Clarendon Press, 1904)

Toynbee, Mrs Paget (ed.), *The Letters of Horace Walpole, fourth Earl of Orford*, vol. IX: 1774–1776 (Clarendon Press, 1904)

Tribunal Révolutionnaire, *Liste des victimes du Tribunal révolutionnaire à Paris* (Paris, 1911)

Vickery, Amanda, *The Gentleman's Daughter: Women's Lives in Georgian England* (Yale University Press, 1998)

Walford, Edward, *Old and New London*, vol. IV (London, 1878)

Wilberforce, Robert Isaac, MA and Samuel, MA, *The Life of William Wilberforce, by his sons*, vol. I (second edition, Philadelphia, 1839)

Williams, Helen Maria, *Letters written in the summer 1790 to a friend in England, containing various anecdotes relative to the French Revolution and Memoirs of Mons and Madame du F___* (London, 1794)

Williams, Helen Maria, *Letters containing a Sketch of the Politics of France: From the 31st of May 1793, till the 28th of July 1794: and of the Scenes which have Passed in the Prisons of Paris* (London, 1795)

Wilson, Frances, *The Courtesan's Revenge: Harriette Wilson, the Woman who Blackmailed the King* (Faber & Faber, 2003)

Wright, H.P., MA, Chaplain to the Forces and to HRH The Duke of Cambridge, KG, *The Story of the 'Domus Dei' of Portsmouth commonly called The Royal Garrison Church* (London, 1873)

Wynne Fremantle, Elizabeth; Wynne Campbell, Eugenia; and Jackson Fremantle, Anne, *The Wynne diaries*, vol. III (Oxford University Press, 1935)

Yorke, Philip Chesney (ed.), *The diary of John Baker, barrister of the Middle Temple, solicitor-general of the Leeward Islands: being extracts therefrom* (Hutchinson & Co., 1931)

Internet Sources

http://founders.archives.gov/documents

www.historyofparliamentonline.org

http://demodecouture.com/2011/02/18th-century-riding-habitses

https://books.google.co.uk/books

Magazines and Periodicals

Apollo Magazine, vols 27 and 28, 1938

Bengal Past and Present, vol. 6, pt. 2, Calcutta, 1910

Bengal Past and Present, vol. 49, pt. 2, Calcutta, 1935

Bengal Past and Present, vol. 106, Calcutta, 1987

Kennedy, Dennis, *Irish Times* review, on Macartney of Lisanoure, 7 January 1984

Morgannwg: transactions of the Glamorgan History Society, vols 33–37, 1989

The *Military and Naval Magazine of the United States* from March 1835 to September 1835, vol. V, Washington DC, 1835

The *Rambler's Magazine*, or *The Annals of Gallantry, Glee, Pleasure, and the Bon Ton; calculated for the entertainment of the polite world; and to furnish the man of pleasure with a most delicious banquet of amorous, bacchanalian, whimsical, humorous, theatrical and polite entertainment*, January 1783, July 1784

The *Sporting Magazine*, vol. 32, 1808

The *Town and Country Magazine*, or *Universal Repository of Knowledge, Instruction, and Entertainment*, August 1774, October 1777, July 1778, February 1784, March 1785

The *Universal Magazine*, April 1808

Manuscript Sources

Commission books (series I), 1740–1744, WO 25/20, The National Archives

East India Company records, British Library

Historical Manuscripts Collection, Report on the manuscripts of Lord Polwarth, preserved at Mertoun House, Berwickshire, vol. V, London, 1961

Papers of the Murray Family of Murraythwaite, Dumfriesshire, Letter to Hugh Dalrymple from John Murray, 31 Dec 1754, GD219/289/2, National Archives of Scotland

Public Register of All Arms and Bearings in Scotland, vol. I, folio 254

Reports of Cases Argued and Determined in the High Court of Chancery, from 1757 to 1766. From the original manuscripts of Lord Chancellor Northington, vol. I, Philadelphia, 1839

The history of the trial of Warren Hastings, Esq., late Governor General of Bengal, before the High Court of Parliament in Westminster Hall, London, 1796

The Petition of George Cornwallis Brown, 25 June 1745, Answers for Lieutenant Charles Dundas, 4 July 1745, RH 18/3 157, National Archives for Scotland

The Register of Marriages, Births and Deaths at the Presidency of Fort William in Bengal, for the Year of Our Lord 1788

The Trial with the Whole of the Evidence, between the Right Hon. Sir Richard Worsley, Bart., Comptroller of his Majesty's Household, Governor of the Isle of Wight, Member of Parliament for Newport in that Island, &c. &c. Plaintiff and George Maurice Bissett, Esq. Defendant, for Criminal Conversation with the Plaintiff's wife. Before the Right Hon. William Earl of Mansfield and a Special Jury, in His Majesty's Court of King's Bench, Westminster Hall, on Thursday 21 February, 1782, London

TRIAL *between the Hon.* EDWARD FOLEY, *Plaintiff and the Right Hon. the* EARL *of* PETERBOROUGH, *Defendant, for Criminal Conversation with* LADY ANN FOLEY, London, 1785

Newspapers

As referenced in the text and endnotes.

Index